Ending
Your Day
Right

Ending Your Day Right

DEVOTIONS FOR
EVERY EVENING OF THE YEAR

Joyce Meyer

NEW YORK   BOSTON   NASHVILLE

*Let my prayer be set
before You as incense, the
lifting up of my hands as
the evening sacrifice.*

PSALM 141:2 NKJV

Introduction

God wants you to enjoy everyday life—it is His will for you. As a Christian you can have a quality of life that far exceeds your expectations, but it requires cooperation on your part. Jesus said in John 15:10-11 that if you obey His instructions and abide in His love, your joy and gladness will be full, complete, and overflowing.

Enjoying life to the fullest begins by making a decision to set aside time each day to pray and meditate on God's Word and to learn His will and direction for your life. The people who most enjoy life are those who spend time with God, seeking His direction and then following His leading.

Starting your day right by spending time with God in the morning is an important part of enjoying life. But spending time with God at night before you go to bed is an extra special time—an unhurried time that allows you to relax in the presence of God and reflect on the activities of the day.

It is a great time to acknowledge and thank Him

for His presence with you throughout the day, and to seek His help with any unresolved problems or concerns you may have. Consider His invitation in Matthew 11:28-29:

> *Come to Me, all you who labor and are heavy-laden and overburdened, and I will cause you to rest. [I will ease and relieve and refresh your souls.] Take My yoke upon you and learn of Me, for I am gentle (meek) and humble (lowly) in heart, and you will find rest (relief and ease and refreshment and recreation and blessed quiet) for your souls.*

My purpose in writing this book is to help you focus on God at the end of your busy days. In the quiet solitude of the night He will refresh and re-store you, lead you in paths of righteousness (see Psalm 23:3), and teach you how to enjoy every day of your life.

> *It is vain for you to rise up early, to take rest late, to eat the bread of (anxious) toil—for He gives (blessings) to His beloved in sleep.* PSALM 127:2

Ending Your Day Right

You Can Have a New Beginning

Do not [earnestly] remember the former things;
neither consider the things of old. Behold, I am doing
a new thing!

ISAIAH 43:18-19

God created us to need new beginnings— places where we can release our faith and say, "This is a place of new beginnings for me, a place to have a fresh start." The dawn of a new year is always a good time for a fresh start.

You can experience the abundant life Jesus says you can have, but it requires making a decision to let go of the past. Unless you refuse to go on the way you have been, no change will come. God wants to change things for you, but He is waiting for your total cooperation.

Seldom do your circumstances change without something first changing in you. So if you want to experience God's "new thing" this year, release your faith right now and say, "This is a place of new beginnings for me." Then watch for the results.

Seek to Know God Better

[For my determined purpose is] that I may know Him [that I may progressively become more deeply and intimately acquainted with Him, perceiving and recognizing and understanding the wonders of His Person more strongly and more clearly].

PHILIPPIANS 3:10

This was the cry of the apostle Paul's heart as he sought to have such a deep relationship with Christ that the trials of life would barely be noticeable.

At the beginning of this new year, it is a wise thing for you to seek also. There are plenty of problems in life that can weigh you down and cause you to become discouraged, but God wants to provide the strength and power you need to be victorious in every battle of life. Such a relationship requires that you seek God like never before.

So start this year right by becoming more deeply and intimately acquainted with the One who has all power in heaven and earth.

Trust in the Power of Hope

*Hope deferred makes the heart sick, but when the
desire is fulfilled, it is a tree of life.*

PROVERBS 13:12

I define *hope* as "the happy anticipation of good things." You can hope for something good to happen to you by learning how to celebrate and enjoy life.

Everything in life is a process in motion. Without movement and progression there is no life. As long as you live you are always heading somewhere, and you should enjoy yourself on the way. God created you to be a goal-oriented visionary. Without a vision you become bored and hopeless.

But there's something about hope that makes people lighthearted and happy. Hope is a powerful spiritual force that is activated through your positive attitude. God is positive and He wants positive things to happen to you, but that probably won't happen unless you have hope and faith.

Expect God to bring good out of every circumstance in your life. Whatever happens, trust in the Lord . . . and trust in the power of hope!

Watch Your Words

There are those who speak rashly, like the piercing
of a sword, but the tongue of the wise brings healing.

PROVERBS 12:18

Your life is greatly impacted by the words that have been spoken to you. Likewise, your words impact the lives of those around you—for better or for worse. That's a sobering thought.

Many people have been crippled with insecurity because their parents spoke words of judgment, criticism, and failure to them. These wounded people can be healed by receiving God's unconditional love, but it takes time to overcome the wrong image they have of themselves.

That's why it is important to use your words for blessing, healing, and building up instead of for cursing, wounding, and tearing down.

If you've been wounded by words, be quick to receive God's unconditional love. Let Him heal any unhealthy images you may have of yourself. If you have been fortunate enough to escape such damage, determine that your words will bring blessing and healing to others.

Possess Your Soul

By your steadfastness and patient endurance you
shall win the true life of your souls.

LUKE 21:19

You need to learn not to let your mind and emotions get the best of you, especially when it involves things over which you have no control.

Suppose you are on your way to an important interview and get caught in a traffic jam. How do you react? Is it worth getting all upset and unleashing a wild spirit? Wouldn't it be much better for you and everyone else if you just remained calm, even if you were late for the interview? If you have done your best God will do the rest.

Refuse to get upset when things don't go as you planned. Refuse to allow your mind, will, and emotions to rule your spirit. In your patience you will learn to possess your soul.

Praise Your Way to Victory

Be not afraid or dismayed . . .
for the battle is not yours, but God's.

2 CHRONICLES 20:15

If life sometimes seems to be a battle that causes you to feel upset and fearful, you'll be glad to know you were not meant to fight the battle alone. The Bible says the battle is God's.

God never loses a battle. And when you work with Him according to His plan, you won't either.

During trying times, do you worry or worship? Praise and worship should not be limited to a few minutes in church. If you're not worshipping at home on a regular basis you may feel like the victim instead of the victor.

But God's Word clearly details the Holy Ghost-anointed battle plan to combat every challenge you face. When you begin to substitute praise for petition and worship for worry, God will move on your behalf.

Choose Inner Purity

The inward adorning and beauty of the hidden
person of the heart, with the incorruptible and
unfading charm of a gentle and peaceful
spirit . . . is very precious in the sight of God.

1 PETER 3:4

In light of this Scripture, how would you classify your thoughts, attitudes, imaginations, opinions, and judgments? Are they clean or corrupt? Pure or carnal?

Inner purity is a challenge that requires you to watch over your inner life with determination and diligence. In the beginning you may feel that most of your thoughts, imaginations, and attitudes are corrupt. But as you persist, new habits develop, and with regular maintenance you can enjoy inner purity.

What you do outwardly—the things that people see—determines your reputation with man. But your inner life determines your reputation with God.

Choosing inner purity is something you do unto the Lord to honor Him. No wonder He says a pure heart is precious in His sight!

Choose God's Secret Place

> *He who dwells in the secret place of the Most*
> *High shall remain stable and fixed under the shadow*
> *of the Almighty [Whose power no foe can withstand].*
> *I will say of the Lord, He is my Refuge and my*
> *Fortress, my God; on Him I lean and rely, and in Him*
> *I [confidently] trust!*
>
> PSALM 91:1-2

This Scripture holds the key to overcoming worry, anxiety, discouragement, disappointment, depression, despair, and disease. It is simply trusting God.

Perhaps you want to trust God, but it seems you just don't know how. Trusting God requires knowing Him—knowing His character and having experience with Him. Going through trials with God by your side builds your faith.

So when you face problems, you can choose trust or torment. Choose to trust God and dwell in the "secret place," enjoying divine provision in the midst of attacks and walking through dark times in His presence.

Receive God's Healing and Restoration

The Spirit of the Lord God is upon me . . . to bind up and heal the brokenhearted, to proclaim liberty to the [physical and spiritual] captives and the opening of the prison and of the eyes to those who are bound.

ISAIAH 61:1

If you are struggling with emotional distress or a broken heart, God wants to renew your mind, restore your soul, and give you a fresh start.

I don't know your circumstances, past or present, but you may have hurts that are holding you back and keeping you captive.

I know firsthand how that feels. But I also know what it's like to be healed and restored. As I received the truth of God's Word and began to understand that I didn't have to stay trapped in my past, I experienced emotional healing and deliverance from bondage.

God loves you unconditionally and He wants to do the same for you. So learn how to receive from God . . . and be made whole.

Accept God's Grace

[God] . . . is able to do immeasurably more than
all we ask or imagine, according to his power
that is at work within us.

EPHESIANS 3:20 NIV

Life is hectic—and if you try to do everything yourself you'll stay exhausted. Rushing and struggling to keep up the pace wears you out physically, mentally, emotionally, and spiritually. But you can make some changes.

First, examine all your activities and allow the Holy Spirit to show you the things that drain your energy and don't produce worthwhile fruit. Then be willing to give them up. You may even have to choose between the good and the best.

Second, learn to receive more of God's grace. Grace is power—God getting involved and doing through you what you could never do on your own. His power can help you accomplish more than you could imagine. So accept His help and start enjoying life.

Take Authority over the Devil

Be well balanced, . . . vigilant and cautious at all times; for that enemy of yours, the devil, roams around like a lion roaring [in fierce hunger], seeking someone to seize upon and devour.

1 PETER 5:8

Satan's attacks are fierce in these last days but you don't need to run from his roar. As a child of God you have the authority to defeat him in the name of Jesus.

Satan can attack your mind, will, and emotions. He will attack your body with weariness and all manner of illness. His lies are endless and persistent and he delights in playing on your emotions. But you can learn to discern and aggressively confront every satanic assault, and be victorious over his evil plans.

Exercising authority over the enemy is more than verbal commands . . . your words and actions must go together. Speaking or praying the Word releases faith, but you must also walk in new levels of obedience. So follow God's plan and put the devil on the run.

Let God Restore Your Soul

The Lord is my Shepherd . . . He refreshes and restores my life . . . He leads me in the paths of righteousness . . . not for my earning it . . . but for His name's sake.

PSALM 23:1,3

This psalm is a great comfort and encouragement. Your Shepherd refreshes and restores your life, or as the King James Version says, your soul.

The word *restore* means, "to return to a former condition," to refresh. In this psalm David is telling you God will return you to the state you were in before you erred from following the good plan He had predestined for you before your birth.

God's plan for you is not failure, misery, poverty, sickness, or disease. His plan is for you to have a wonderful life full of health, happiness, and fulfillment.

So don't let the devil steal it away from you. The evening is a great time to quietly wait in the presence of the Lord and allow Him to refresh and restore your soul.

Be Confident in Christ

I have strength for all things in Christ
Who empowers me [I am ready for anything
and equal to anything through Him Who infuses
inner strength into me].

PHILIPPIANS 4:13

You were created by a great God to do great things. But without confidence you will never fulfill your destiny. It is important, however, to remember you are to be confident not in yourself but in Christ who dwells in you.

Satan tries to steal your confidence, but you must resist him at all times. If he has tormented you with fears about your worth and abilities, boldly remind him God is with you and you are equal to anything.

It is encouraging to know God is able even when you are not. He has His eye on you and is waiting for you to show confidence in Him. Faith opens the door for God's greatness to be seen through your life, so trust Him and enjoy the peace and power of a confident life.

Dwell in Peace

Depart from evil and do good; seek, inquire for,
and crave peace and pursue (go after) it!

PSALM 34:14

In our strife-torn world, do you ever long for a few peaceful moments? That is what God wants for you. He instructs you in His Word to live in unity and harmony and to pursue peace.

Why then is it so difficult to get through a day without being invaded by the spirit of strife? Satan works through the weaknesses in your flesh to keep the atmosphere in your life and the attitudes of your heart in continual turmoil. He seeks to draw you away from peace and into strife, which brings devastation and destruction.

But God's power is greater than the devil's, and when you come against strife in the name of Jesus you render it powerless to rob you of the peace and joy that is your divine inheritance. Take a few moments in the quiet of this evening to enjoy the wonderful peace and presence of God, and you will enjoy a good night's sleep.

Let God Be Good to You

*The Lord [earnestly] waits [expecting, looking,
and longing] to be gracious to you; and therefore He
lifts Himself up, that He may have mercy on you and
show loving-kindness to you.*

ISAIAH 30:18

Isn't this a wonderful verse? It tells you God is waiting to be good to you. He's actually looking and longing for an opportunity to show His goodness. He is a God of justice and He desires to make every wrong thing right. But He can only be good to those who are waiting for Him to be good to them—those who believe His promises.

Are you available? Don't fall into Satan's trap of being negative. Don't believe it when he tells you your past is really not past and your future is bleak. Choose to believe God and get ready to receive the wonderful gifts He is waiting to give to you. Go to sleep meditating on this thought: *Something good is going to happen to me!*

Don't Give Up!

Let us not be weary in well doing: for in due
season we shall reap, if we faint not.
GALATIANS 6:9 KJV

Do you ever feel like giving up? Perhaps you're discouraged about your finances or you're facing problems with your health, your marriage, or your children. Sometimes problems seem so overwhelming that the road ahead seems too steep to climb.

We all go through these times. I've wanted to give up and quit many times through the years. But when I realized I had nothing interesting to go back to, I determined to keep pressing on.

Even though continuing to move forward is sometimes painful, it is far better than giving up and sliding backwards. God is doing a good work in you so He can do more for you and through you. So ask Him to fill you with holy determination tonight and keep moving in the right direction.

Learn to Love

*I give you a new commandment: that you should
love one another. Just as I have loved you, so you too
should love one another.*

JOHN 13:34

How much do you know about real
love . . . God's kind of love?

Everybody knows love is always spoken of in
connection with Christianity. There are lots of sermons on love—it's a pretty plain and simple subject. Everybody talks about love.

But where are all the people who love?

God's kind of love is unconditional and always
available. He extends His love toward you and He
wants you to receive it and be blessed. Then He wants
you to give it away to others.

What the world needs now is love—real love. I
have discovered that lonely and hurting people often
don't expect you to meet their needs . . . they simply want to be loved and understood.

If you're in need of real love, receive it from
God right now. Then let it flow through you to bless
others.

God Has Not Forgotten You

God is faithful; he will not let you be tempted
beyond what you can bear. But when you are
tempted, he will also provide a way out so that you
can stand up under it.

1 CORINTHIANS 10:13 NIV

The world is full of people struggling with trials and temptations and looking for a way out. If you have ever felt pressed on every side and couldn't find an escape, or confused and didn't know what to do, you know what a desperate and lonely feeling that can be.

The Word tells you God is faithful and He will provide a way for you, but He doesn't always show us the way immediately. That is when you must wait . . . and trust.

Waiting on God purifies your faith and builds character in you. You may not like waiting, but God's way is perfect! So be assured God has not forgotten you. Trust Him, and in His time He will reveal His perfect plan for you. While you're waiting, don't forget to enjoy your life.

Expect the Blessings of God

*Wait and hope for and expect the Lord; be brave
and of good courage and let your heart be
stout and enduring.*

PSALM 27:14

Sometimes you may feel discouraged, miserable, and depressed. In those times you need to take a close look at what's been going on in your mind. Isaiah 26:3 tells you when you keep your mind on the Lord you will have "perfect and constant peace."

By focusing on the goodness of God and waiting, hoping, and expecting Him to encourage you and fill you with His peace and joy, you can overcome negative thoughts that drag you down.

Think and speak positively. Begin believing right now that you are about to see God's goodness in your life. Wait, hope, and expect His blessings to be abundant in your life.

Say Yes to God

No one's ever seen or heard anything like this,
Never so much as imagined anything quite like it—
what God has arranged for those who love him.

1 CORINTHIANS 2:9 THE MESSAGE

God prearranged and paid for you to have and enjoy a good life before you ever showed up on planet Earth. Then He sent the Holy Spirit to guide you into all truth and the blessings He wants you to have. The key to receiving is simply obedience.

When you don't obey God's promptings you get off track and fail to enjoy all the good things He has in mind for you. Don't let the devil trick you into losing out on God's superabundance because of disobedience.

Begin sowing seeds of prompt obedience and divine blessing will overtake you. Radical, outrageous obedience will bring radical, outrageous blessings. Obeying God during the day helps us sleep good at night.

Overcome Fear with Faith

God has not given us a spirit of fear, but of power
and of love and of a sound mind.

2 TIMOTHY 1:7 NKJV

Have you ever thought how great it would be if you could live without ever having to deal with fear?

Of course, there are healthy fears that alert you to danger in time to avoid it—and these are good because they protect you. But there are many other fears Satan tries to put on you that should not be legitimate concerns. They are **F**alse **E**vidence **A**ppearing **R**eal, and they are intended to keep you from having the power, love, and sound mind God wants you to have.

Fear is a spirit that must be confronted head on—it will not just go away. But God has given you the power to boldly confront your fear and break its hold on your life.

So when fear knocks on your door, send faith to answer!

Let God Be God

*For who has known or understood the mind (the
counsels and purposes) of the Lord so as to guide and
instruct Him and give Him knowledge?*

I CORINTHIANS 2:16

It is not your job to give God guidance, counsel, or direction. It is your job to listen to God and let Him tell you what is going on and what you are to do about it—leaving the rest to Him to work out according to His knowledge and will, not yours.

God is God—and you are not. You need to recognize that truth and simply trust yourself to Him, because He is greater than you are in every way. You are created in His image, but He is still above and beyond you. His thoughts and ways are higher than yours. So listen to God tonight, be obedient to Him, and He will teach you His ways. Cast off your care, releasing the weight of all your burdens and sleep peacefully.

Allow God to Change You

And while He was in Bethany . . . a woman came
with an alabaster jar of ointment (perfume) of pure
nard, very costly and precious; and she broke the jar
and poured [the perfume] over His head.

MARK 14:3

So often people are afraid of brokenness.
But if your outer man is broken, the powerful things inside you can pour forth. The perfume of the Holy Spirit is within you, but the alabaster box, which represents the flesh, has to be broken for that sweet fragrance to be released. The flesh is naturally prideful and stubborn.

To fully release the power of the Holy Spirit within you, you must allow God to do with you as He wills, knowing that everything in life changes.

If you are to have stability in your life you must remember life is a continual process in which everything—including you—is constantly changing. You must hope in God, the only one who "is the same yesterday, today, and forever" (Hebrews 13:8 NKJV).

Stay in Balance

I have learned how to be content (satisfied to the point where I am not disturbed or disquieted) in whatever state I am.

PHILIPPIANS 4:11

Stability is maturity. To grow up in God is to come to the place where you can be content no matter what your situation or circumstances may be because you are rooted and grounded, not in things, but in the Lord.

Paul was emotionally and spiritually mature because he knew whatever state he was in would pass. He had learned the secret of facing every situation of life, whether good or bad.

God wants to bless you and use you as a vessel through which His Holy Spirit can work. But in order for that to happen you must learn how to handle both the good times and the bad. That's why it is so important to remember that whatever comes your way, "This too shall pass." The good times and the bad never last forever, but *through Christ* we can handle either with joy and stability.

You're Just Passing Through

*Yes, though I walk through the [deep, sunless]
valley of the shadow of death, I will fear or dread no
evil, for You are with me; Your rod [to protect] and
Your staff [to guide], they comfort me.*

PSALM 23:4

The psalmist David said he walked through the valley of the shadow of death. That's what you must do in all the situations and circumstances of this life. You must remember you are just passing through.

When you feel as if you're stuck in a situation that will never change, you must allow God to guide you through it. When the devil says, "You're trapped," boldly say to him, "Wrong! I'm just passing through!"

Shadrach, Meshach, and Abednego were cast into the fiery furnace, but God brought them safely through the fire (see Daniel 3).

God's Word says He will provide that same protection and deliverance to all who put their faith and trust in Him. So believe it as you walk through the valley of your own situation.

We Shall All Be Changed!

*We shall not all fall asleep [in death], but we
shall all be changed (transformed) in a moment, in
the twinkling of an eye, at the [sound of the]
last trumpet call.*

I CORINTHIANS 15:51-52

We all like "suddenlies," and God promises
that whatever remains to be accomplished
in us will be done "suddenly" when Jesus returns to
the earth. Until then, we can confidently trust He is
working in us through His word and Spirit on a regular basis. If you are spending time in God's word and
believing He is doing work in you, then you are changing from one degree of glory to another.

You don't have to be discouraged about your
spiritual growth or in your walk with God, because
no matter what remains to be done in the transformation of your old man into your new man, it will be
finished at the appearing of Jesus in the heavenlies.

If the devil tries to tell you you're going to stay
the way you are forever, he is lying. God promises in
His word that He has begun a good work in you and
He also will finish it (see Philippians 1:6).

Retire from Self-Care

*Believe in the Lord Jesus Christ [give yourself
up to Him, take yourself out of your own keeping
and entrust yourself into His keeping] and you
will be saved.*

ACTS 16:31

God wants to take care of you, and He can do a much better job of it if you will avoid a problem called *independence*, which is really self-care.

The desire to take care of yourself is based on fear. You are afraid of what might happen if you entrust yourself totally to God and He doesn't come through for you. The root problem of independence is you trust yourself more than you trust God.

People love to have a back-up plan. You may ask God to get involved in your life, but if He doesn't respond as quickly as you'd like, you take control back into your own hands.

But God has a plan for you—and His plan is much better than yours. So give yourself to Him and see what happens. I promise you won't be disappointed.

Stand Strong Against the Adversary

For a wide door of opportunity for effectual [service] has opened to me [there, a great and promising one], and [there are] many adversaries.

1 CORINTHIANS 16:9

It is true that whenever you do anything for God, the adversary will oppose you. But you must remember that greater is He who is in you than he who is in the world (see 1 John 4:4).

You should not have to spend your life struggling against the devil in order to serve God. Instead of wearing yourself out trying to fight spiritual enemies, you should learn to stand strong in the authority given to you by Jesus.

The best way to overcome the devil and his demons is simply to stay in God's will by obeying His Word and God will work things out according to His divine plan and purpose.

Depend on the Spirit

It is the Spirit Who gives life [He is the Life-giver]; the flesh conveys no benefit whatever.

JOHN 6:63

If you are to fulfill God's will for you in this life, the flesh—the selfish, rebellious sin nature—must die. It must lose its power.

Often you are not fully aware of sinful thoughts, actions, and attitudes in your heart because you are so caught up in the outer life. These things must be faced and dealt with if you are to enjoy the good life God has planned for you.

Paul said he wanted to do good things, but found himself always doing wrong things. He described how miserable this made him. He wanted to be free, and after much struggling realized that only God could set him free and that through Jesus Christ He would. (see Romans 7:18-25).

As you face seasons of testing you must learn that your flesh benefits you nothing. Only then can you deny the flesh and depend on the Life-giver to build His character in you.

Let Go and Let God

Abstain from evil . . . whatever kind it may be.
And may the God of peace Himself sanctify you
through and through . . . and may your spirit
and soul and body be preserved sound and
complete . . . Faithful is He Who is calling
you . . . and utterly trustworthy.

1 THESSALONIANS 5:22-24

These are God's instructions to you for finding peace and joy: Stay away from wrong behavior and allow the Lord of peace to sanctify you, preserve you, complete you, hallow you, and keep you.

These verses are your call from God to a certain kind of holy living. They are also your assurance that it is not you who brings about this holy life but God Himself, who can be trusted utterly to do the work in you and for you.

What then is your part? What is the work that you are to do? What does God require of you? Your part is to believe and to trust the Lord. So let go and let God!

Choose to Please God

*Now am I trying to win the favor of men, or of
God? Do I seek to please men? If I were still seeking
popularity with men, I should not be a bond servant
of Christ (the Messiah).*

GALATIANS 1:10

The apostle Paul said that in his ministry
he had to choose between pleasing men
and pleasing God. That is a choice you also must
make.

If your goal is to build a name for yourself and
win favor with people, it will cause you to live in fear
of man rather than in fear of God.

For years I tried to build my own reputation
among believers by striving to win the favor of men.
But through bitter experience I learned I was submitting to a sort of slavery to people. God helped
me realize I could only be truly free in Him.

If you are trying to build your reputation with
people, it's time to give up all your own human efforts and simply trust God. He will give you supernatural favor with the people that are right for you.

Gifts of Grace

For by the grace (unmerited favor of God) given to me I warn everyone among you not to estimate and think of himself more highly than he ought [not to have an exaggerated opinion of his own importance], but to rate his ability with sober judgment, each according to the degree of faith apportioned by God to him.

ROMANS 12:3

Proud people compare themselves to others and feel superior if they are able to do something others cannot do. In 1 Corinthians 15:10, the apostle Paul wrote, "But by the grace (the unmerited favor and blessing) of God I am what I am." If you do not realize you are what you are by the grace of God, you will think more highly of yourself than you should.

You should judge yourself soberly, knowing that without God you can do nothing of value. Success only comes by His grace. Your accomplishments and abilities are not yours to take credit for—they are gifts from a loving Father.

The I Am

And God said to Moses, I AM WHO I AM and WHAT I AM, and I WILL BE WHAT I WILL BE; and He said, You shall say this to the Israelites: I AM has sent me to you!

EXODUS 3:14

This awesome scripture holds much more than you may realize at first glance. God is so great there is no way for us to describe Him properly. What was God really saying when He referred to Himself as I AM?

Moses asked a question about God's identity, and evidently the Lord did not want to get into a long dissertation about who He was. It was as if God was saying, "You don't have to worry about Pharaoh or anybody else, I AM able to take care of anything you encounter. Whatever you need, I AM it. Either I have it or I can get it. If it doesn't exist, I will create it. I have everything covered, not only now but for all time. Relax!"

God Approves of You!

Before I formed you in the womb I knew [and] approved of you [as My chosen instrument].

JEREMIAH 1:5

Nobody knows you as well as God does. Yet even though He knows everything about you, including all of your faults, He still approves of you and accepts you. God sees your heart, not just the exterior shell (the flesh) that seems to get you into so much trouble. He does not approve of your wrong behavior, but He is committed to you as an individual. God can hate what you do and yet love you. He has no trouble keeping the two separated.

God never intended for you to feel bad about yourself. He wants you to know yourself well and yet accept yourself. You must be able to say, "I can love what God can love. I don't love everything I do, but I accept myself because God accepts me." God is changing you daily. Ask Him to help you accept and love yourself in spite of your imperfections.

Not In Vain

*You shall not use or repeat the name of the Lord
your God in vain [that is, lightly or frivolously, in
false affirmations or profanely]; for the Lord will not
hold him guiltless who takes His name in vain.*

EXODUS 20:7

Malachi 1:14 says, "For I am a great King,
says the Lord of hosts, and My name is
terrible and to be [reverently] feared among the nations." As a Christian, you need to have such reverence for the Lord that you are afraid to speak any of
His holy names without purpose. But we often say
things like, "Oh God," "My God," and "Dear God" as
casual terms of expression.

According to the Bible, we have been given authority to cast out demons, pray for the sick, and
preach the gospel in the name of Jesus. How can we
expect to see God's power manifested if we use His
name seriously one time and frivolously another? If
we mix positives with negatives, we will operate
with zero power.

A Victorious Church

And the Lord shall make you the head, and not
the tail; and you shall be above only, and you shall
not be beneath, if you heed the commandments of the
Lord your God.

DEUTERONOMY 28:13

Surely we are living in the last days, and the Bible teaches that Satan's attacks will intensify during these perilous times. The enemy is a master of deception. He lies, cheats, and steals. Satan launches personal attacks on your marriage, your children, your job, and your personal property. He also targets your mind, your emotions, and your physical body.

How do you defend yourself? Ephesians 3:10 says, "Through the church the complicated, many-sided wisdom of God . . . might now be made known to the angelic rulers and authorities (principalities and powers) in the heavenly sphere." God intends to work through the church to defeat the enemy. He will do it through us! He will grant us wisdom in what action to take and strength to take it. The greater One lives in us as believers; therefore we have power over Satan.

Thoughts of the Heart

*Either make the tree sound (healthy and good),
and its fruit sound (healthy and good), or make the
tree rotten (diseased and bad), and its fruit rotten
(diseased and bad); for the tree is known and
recognized and judged by its fruit.*

MATTHEW 12:33

The Bible says a tree is known by its fruit, and the same is true of you. You can look at a person's attitude and know what kind of thinking is prevalent in his life. A sweet, kind person does not have mean, vindictive thoughts. By the same token, a truly evil person does not have good, loving thoughts.

Your thoughts bear fruit. Think good thoughts and the fruit in your life will be good. Think bad thoughts and the fruit in your life will be bad. Remember Proverbs 23:7 and allow it to have an impact on your life: for as you think in your heart, so are you.

The Paraclete

But when He, the Spirit of Truth (the Truth-giving Spirit) comes, He will guide you into all the Truth (the whole, full Truth). For He will not speak His own message [on His own authority]; but He will tell whatever He hears [from the Father; He will give the message that has been given to Him], and He will announce and declare to you the things that are to come [that will happen in the future].

JOHN 16:13

God knew you would need help in understanding His plan for you, so He sent the Holy Spirit to dwell inside you. He is your Guide, your Teacher of truth, your Comfort, and your Helper. He is also the Parakletos (Paraclete), which means counselor, advocate, and intercessor.

Jesus was confined to a body and could be only one place at a time. But He knew the Holy Spirit would be with you everywhere you go, all the time, leading and guiding you. Trust the Holy Spirit in you, resting in the knowledge that in Him you are becoming everything God planned for you to be.

Choose Life

I call heaven and earth to witness this day against you that I have set before you life and death, the blessings and the curses; therefore choose life, that you and your descendants may live.

DEUTERONOMY 30:19

In this Scripture *life* means, "fresh, strong, lively, and merry." In John 10:10, Jesus said He came that you might have life. According to *Vine's Expository Dictionary of Biblical Words*, in this verse *life* is translated as, "life as God has it, that which the Father has in Himself, and which He gave to the Incarnate Son to have in Himself . . . and which the Son manifested in the world."

Life is not simply a span of time. It is a quality of existence—life as God has it. His life is not filled with fear, stress, worry, or depression. God takes time to enjoy His creation. Adam lost that kind of life due to sin, but you can have it back through Christ Jesus. Choose God's kind of life.

The Real Thing

You are the salt of the earth, but if salt has lost its taste (its strength, its quality), how can its saltness be restored? . . . You are the light of the world. A city set on a hill cannot be hidden.

MATTHEW 5:13-14

When people learn you're a Christian, they want to know if you are "for real." Many people have tried "religion" and had a bad experience. God uses us to reach the world. If you are to be effective salt, you must allow Jesus to shine through your life.

You probably know someone who just lights up a room. In the same way, Christians who let the light of Jesus shine can change the whole atmosphere around them. Unbelievers ought to feel as though the power has suddenly come on—even if they don't understand why. When you arrive at your job in the morning, be salt and light so those around you know that your relationship with Jesus is the real thing.

A Balancing Act

*I came that they may have and enjoy life, and
have it in abundance (to the full, till it overflows).*

JOHN 10:10

For years I felt that everything in my life should be work, work, work. As long as I was accomplishing something, as long as I was doing what everyone expected of me, I believed I was pleasing God. Unfortunately I wasn't enjoying my life!

I'll never forget the day my kids wanted me to watch a movie with them. They kept saying, "Mom, come on! You don't have to work all day and either read the Bible or pray the rest of the time. We know you love God. Let's have some fun." I finally decided to watch a movie with them but found myself feeling guilty for doing so.

God had to teach me that there is nothing wrong with spending time with family, taking a day off, or having fun. You can work yourself to death and miss some of God's greatest blessings. Allow Him to bring balance to your life.

Mumbles and Murmurs

These are inveterate murmurers (grumblers) who complain [of their lot in life], going after their own desires [controlled by their passions].

JUDE 1:16

Sometimes it seems the whole world is complaining. There is so much grumbling and murmuring and so little gratitude and appreciation. People complain about their job and their boss when they should be thankful to have regular work and appreciate the fact they are not living in a shelter for the homeless or standing in a soup line. Many people would be thrilled to have that job, despite its imperfections. They would be more than willing to put up with a not-so-perfect boss in order to have a regular income, live in their own home, and cook their own food.

Maybe you need a better paying job or perhaps you have a boss who treats you unfairly. That is unfortunate, but the way out is not through complaining. Give God thanks tonight for every blessing He has given you.

Standing in Big Shoes

No man shall be able to stand before you all the days of your life. As I was with Moses, so I will be with you; I will not fail you or forsake you.

JOSHUA 1:5

Imagine how Joshua must have felt when God told him he was to take Moses' place and lead the Israelites into the promised land. Moses was an amazing leader. Who would want to try to fill his shoes?

God told Joshua he would succeed not because of anything he had in the natural but because He was with him. Moses was successful only because God was with him. God told Joshua the same thing would hold true for him if he believed. God kept encouraging Joshua to be strong and confident, to take courage and not be afraid. In other words, He told him to believe!

Put your faith and trust in God. He will give you the strength to stand and accomplish whatever He asks you to do.

Blessed Assurance

For I am persuaded beyond doubt (am sure) that
neither death nor life, nor angels nor principalities,
nor things impending and threatening nor things to
come, nor powers, nor height nor depth, nor anything
else in all creation will be able to separate us from the
love of God which is in Christ Jesus our Lord.

ROMANS 8:38-39

You cannot trust unless you believe you are loved. To grow in God and be changed you must trust Him. Often He will lead you in ways you cannot understand. During those times you must have a tight grip on His love for you. The apostle Paul was convinced that nothing would ever be able to separate him from the love of God in Christ Jesus. You need to have that same absolute assurance of God's undying love for you.

Accept God's love for you and make that love the basis for your love for others. Receive His affirmation, knowing that you are changing and becoming all He desires you to be.

A Perfect Love

And we know (understand, recognize, are conscious
of, by observation and by experience) and believe
(adhere to and put faith in and rely on) the love God
cherishes for us. God is love, and he who dwells and
continues in love dwells and continues in God, and
God dwells and continues in him.

1 JOHN 4:16

Most people can believe God loves them if they think they deserve it. Problems arise when you feel you do not deserve God's love and yet desperately need it. God's love for you is perfect—and unconditional. When you fail He keeps loving you because His love is not based on you but on Him.

Sin separated you from God, but He loved you so much He sent His only Son, Jesus, to die for you so He could lavish His great love upon you. If you can believe that God, who is so perfect, loves you, then you can believe you are worth loving! When that happens you can accept yourself in a new way that will be life changing. You're special; you have worth and value . . . believe it, receive it, and be all you can be in Christ.

The Narrow Path

Enter by the narrow gate; for wide is the gate and
broad is the way that leads to destruction, and there
are many who go in by it. Because narrow is the gate
and difficult is the way which leads to life,
and there are few who find it.

MATTHEW 7:13-14 NKJV

Life as a Christian can sometimes feel like a pressure cooker. God speaks to us about issues and works to bring correction. There are things in our lives that hinder us from being all God wants us to be and He deals with them because He loves us and wants to release His best into our lives.

This is an ongoing process. God shows us something, we usually wrestle with Him for awhile, and then we finally change. He lets us rest awhile and then shows us something new that needs to be dealt with.

We once walked on a wide and reckless road that led to destruction, but now we are guided down a narrow path that leads to life. There is no room on the narrow path for our old fleshly, selfish ways. No wonder Paul said, "It is no longer I who live, but Christ . . . lives in me" (Galatians 2:20).

Shake It Off!

Now Paul had gathered a bundle of sticks, and he was laying them on the fire when a viper crawled out because of the heat and fastened itself on his hand. When the natives saw the little animal hanging from his hand, they said to one another, Doubtless this man is a murderer, for though he has been saved from the sea, Justice [the goddess of avenging] has not permitted that he should live. Then [Paul simply] shook off the small creature into the fire and suffered no evil effects.

ACTS 28:3-5

When Paul was shipwrecked on the island of Malta, a deadly snake that was driven out by the heat of the fire bit him. He simply shook the creature off into the flames. You should follow Paul's example and do the same in your own life.

Whatever may be troubling you, shake it off! God has great things planned for you. The dreams of the future leave no room for the snakebites of the past.

A Heart of Flesh

*I will give them one heart [a new heart] and I
will put a new spirit within them; and I will take the
stony [unnaturally hardened] heart out of their flesh,
and will give them a heart of flesh [sensitive and
responsive to the touch of their God].*

EZEKIEL 11:19

God puts a sense of right and wrong deep within your conscience, but if you rebel too many times, you can become hard-hearted. If that happens, you need to let Him soften your heart so you can be sensitive to the leadership of the Holy Spirit.

The only way to develop a heart of flesh is to spend time with God. You must be in His presence on a regular basis to hear what He is saying. God often speaks gently, and those who are busy doing their own thing will not hear His still, small voice. Tonight as you spend time in the Lord's presence, ask Him to soften your heart so you can receive His direction at all times.

Sanctification of the Soul

So get rid of all uncleanness and the rampant outgrowth of wickedness, and in a humble (gentle, modest) spirit receive and welcome the Word which implanted and rooted [in your hearts] contains the power to save your souls.

JAMES 1:21

Once you are born again, your spirit has been reborn and you will go to heaven when you die. But God is not finished—He is just beginning. You need to "work out your own salvation with fear and trembling" (Philippians 2:12 KJV). In other words, your soul needs to be saved. The soul is often defined as the mind, the will, and the emotions. Each of these areas needs salvation.

The Holy Spirit works relentlessly to transform the whole man into God's perfect will. This process is called sanctification. When your soul is renewed with His Word, you think His thoughts and not your own. Submit yourself to the Holy Spirit and allow Him to change every thought and motive.

Resist Rejection

If God is for us, who [can be] against us? [Who
can be our foe, if God is on our side?]

ROMANS 8:31

Do you feel as though the world is against you? Does it seem that no matter how hard you try no one is pleased? Maybe you have conflict with a family member. Perhaps your boss finds fault with your work.

Sooner or later you will experience some form of rejection. Not everybody will like you. Some may even aggressively dislike you. No one enjoys being rejected, but you can learn to handle rejection and get on with your life if you remember that Jesus was also rejected and despised. If you feel rejected, give your hurt to God:

Lord, I can't please everyone all of the time. I will concentrate on being a God pleaser and not a man pleaser. The rest I leave in Your hands, Lord. Grant me favor with You and with men, and continue transforming me into the image of Your Son. Thank You, Lord.

Play Your Part

So they came to John and reported to him, Rabbi,
the Man Who was with you on the other side of the
Jordan . . . notice, here He is baptizing too, and
everybody is flocking to Him!

JOHN 3:26

John the Baptist came to prepare the way for the Lord. That was his purpose on earth and he knew it. But John's disciples tried to incite him to jealousy over Jesus' ministry! John replied, "A man must be content to receive the gift which is given him from heaven; there is no other source" (John 3:27).

You have a unique role in the body of Christ. There is no point in being jealous of someone else's spiritual gifts or ministry. God is the only source for gifts and His plan is perfect for each of us. If your gift is giving, then give with zeal. If your gift is helping, then help somebody! Rather than worrying about what others are doing, figure out what God wants and go do it!

An Attitude of Gratitude

> *Rejoice in the Lord always [delight, gladden*
> *yourselves in Him]; again I say, Rejoice! Let all men*
> *know and perceive and recognize your unselfishness*
> *(your considerateness, your forbearing spirit) . . . Do*
> *not fret or have any anxiety about anything, but in*
> *every circumstance and in everything, by prayer and*
> *petition (definite requests), with thanksgiving,*
> *continue to make your wants known to God.*
>
> PHILIPPIANS 4:4-6

We all need to develop an "attitude of gratitude." This doesn't mean we should live pretending nothing negative exists. It simply means we make it our goal in life to be as positive as possible. A positive approach opens the door for God to work.

Go to bed tonight pondering everything you have to be thankful for. Do the same first thing tomorrow morning. Thank God for everything—a convenient parking place; the fact you can walk, see, or hear; your children. Don't become discouraged with yourself when you fall short, and don't quit. Keep at it until you have developed new habits.

Encourage Yourself in the Lord

*David was greatly distressed, for the men spoke of
stoning him because the souls of them all were
bitterly grieved, each man for his sons and
daughters. But David encouraged and
strengthened himself in the Lord his God.*

1 SAMUEL 30:6

When David found himself in a seemingly hopeless situation with no one to support him, he encouraged and strengthened himself in the Lord. Later on, that situation was totally turned around (see 1 Samuel 30:1-20).

If you don't believe in yourself, who is going to? God believes in you, and it is a good thing too; otherwise, you might never make any progress. You cannot always wait for someone else to come along and encourage you to be all you can be. Confidence is something you decide to have. You learn about God—about His love, His ways, and His Word— then ultimately you must decide whether you believe it or not. You will not go forward until you decide to believe in God and yourself.

Possess the Land

> *The Lord our God said to us in Horeb, You have*
> *dwelt long enough on this mountain . . . Behold, I*
> *have set the land before you; go in and take possession*
> *of the land which the Lord swore to your fathers, to*
> *Abraham, to Isaac, and to Jacob, to give to them and*
> *their descendants after them.*
>
> DEUTERONOMY 1:6,8

In Deuteronomy 1:2, Moses pointed out to the Israelites that it was only an eleven-day journey to the border of Canaan (the promised land), yet it had taken them forty years to get there. Forty years is long enough on any mountain! We shouldn't judge the Israelites harshly, because we do the same thing they did. We keep going around and around the same mountains instead of making progress. The result is it takes us years to experience victory over something that could have been dealt with quickly.

Have you spent forty years trying to make an eleven-day trip? Leave the old bondage behind and make up your mind you will not quit until you have taken possession of your rightful inheritance.

Unshakeable Peace

And God's peace [shall be yours, that tranquil state of a soul assured of its salvation through Christ, and so fearing nothing from God and being content with its earthly lot of whatever sort that is, that peace] which transcends all understanding shall garrison and mount guard over your hearts and minds in Christ Jesus.

PHILIPPIANS 4:7

Even in these confusing and frightening times, God wants you to lead an abundant life. Peace and joy and the other fruit of the Spirit are given to you to draw on all the time. When you work on developing fruit in the good times, you have a reserve for difficult times. Mature Christians know how to draw on the peace that can only come from the Prince of Peace who lives inside them.

As a child of God, you need to know how to be steady and stable no matter what the circumstances. Allow His peace to guard your heart and mind so you are prepared to handle times of crisis when they come.

No Regrets

*For godly grief and the pain God is permitted to
direct, produce a repentance that leads and
contributes to salvation and deliverance from evil,
and it never brings regret; but worldly grief (the
hopeless sorrow that is characteristic of the pagan
world) is deadly [breeding and ending in death].*

2 CORINTHIANS 7:10

Regret is ruining the lives of countless people by stealing their joy. Certainly you have things you wish you had done differently. But there is no sense becoming burdened with regret over something you have no power to change. You need to understand this is the way the devil works. God will warn you so you can change your mind before you make a mistake. Satan waits until it's too late, when you can no longer do anything about it, and then tries to heap regret and condemnation upon you.

Don't allow Satan to steal from you any longer. Ask God for forgiveness, if you haven't already, and leave your regrets in the past.

The Right Words

*Nor shall your name any longer be Abram [high,
exalted father]; but your name shall be Abraham
[father of a multitude], for I have made you the father
of many nations . . . As for Sarai your wife, you shall
not call her name Sarai; but Sarah [Princess] her name
shall be. And I will bless her and give you a son also by
her. Yes, I will bless her, and she shall be a mother of
nations; kings of peoples shall come from her.*

GENESIS 17:5, 15-16

God gave Abram and Sarai new names that carried significant meaning. Each time their names were called, the future was prophesied: Abraham would be father of a multitude and his princess, Sarah, would be a mother of nations and kings.

Now the right things were spoken over Abram and Sarai. Words proclaimed in the natural realm reached into the realm of the spirit where their miracle was. Those words came into agreement with God's Word and called forth the miracle God had promised.

Words are containers for power. Carefully watch over your words and walk through life with abundant joy!

Tests and Trials

For no temptation (no trial regarded as enticing to sin), [no matter how it comes or where it leads] . . . [has come to you that is beyond human resistance and that is not adjusted and adapted and belonging to human experience, and such as man can bear]. But God is faithful [to His Word and to His compassionate nature], and He [can be trusted] not to let you be tempted and tried and assayed beyond your ability and strength of resistance and power to endure, but with the temptation He will [always] also provide the way out (the means of escape to a landing place), that you may be capable and strong and powerful to bear up under it patiently.

I CORINTHIANS 10:13

Hard times can bring the temptation to give up and become negative, depressed, and angry with God. Life can be difficult, but God will always intervene and His help will always arrive on time. Tonight, purpose in your heart to keep pressing on and rest in His presence. God has promised to deliver you before it is too late!

Hope in God

Why are you cast down, O my inner self? And why should you moan over me and be disquieted within me? Hope in God and wait expectantly for Him, for I shall yet praise Him, my Help and my God.

PSALM 42:5

Discouragement destroys hope, so naturally the devil always tries to discourage you. Without hope you give up, which is what Satan wants you to do. The Bible repeatedly tells you not to be discouraged or dismayed. God knows you will not come through to victory if you get discouraged—He wants you to be encouraged, not discouraged.

When discouragement or condemnation tries to overtake you, ask the Lord for strength and courage. Tomorrow is a new day. God loves you and His mercy is new every morning. Say, "I refuse to be discouraged. Father, the Bible says You love me. You sent Jesus to die for me. I'll be fine—tomorrow will be a great day." Hope in Him!

A Spiritual Sabbath

*Let us therefore be zealous and exert ourselves and
strive diligently to enter that rest [of God, to know
and experience it for ourselves], that no one may fall
or perish by the same kind of unbelief and disobedience [into which those in the wilderness fell].*

HEBREWS 4:11

If you read the entire fourth chapter of the
book of Hebrews, you will find it speaking
about a Sabbath rest that is available to God's people.
Under the Old Covenant, the Sabbath was observed
as a day of rest. Under the New Covenant, this Sabbath rest spoken of is a spiritual place of rest. It is the
privilege of every believer to refuse to worry or have
anxiety. As a believer, you can enter the rest of God.

The only way to enter that rest is through believing. You will forfeit it through unbelief and disobedience. Unbelief will keep you in the wilderness,
but Jesus has provided a permanent place of rest that
can be inhabited exclusively through living by faith.

Start Where You Are

Do not say to your neighbor, Go, and come again;
and tomorrow I will give it.

PROVERBS 3:28

When God tells you to help someone, it's easy to put it off. You intend to obey God; it is just that you are going to do it later—when you have more money, when you're not so busy, when Christmas is over, when the kids are back in school, or when vacation is over.

There is no point in praying for God to give you money so you can be a blessing to others if you are not being a blessing with what you already have. Satan will try to tell you that you don't have anything to give—but don't believe Him.

Even if it is only small amounts of money, a pack of gum or a ballpoint pen, start using what you have. As you begin giving what you have, God will bring increase into your life and you will be able to give on an even larger scale.

Bless and Be Blessed by Loving

But earnestly desire and zealously cultivate the
greatest and best gifts and graces (the higher gifts
and the choicest graces). And yet I will show you a
still more excellent way [one that is better by far and
the highest of them all—love].

1 CORINTHIANS 12:31

Love should be number one on your spiritual priority list. You should learn about love, pray about love, and develop love by loving others.

God is love, so when you walk in His love you abide in Him, He is present. Because we walk in God's love by receiving and expressing it, we should not deceive ourselves into thinking we can love God while we hate other people (see 1 John 4:20).

We seek many things in the course of our lifetime hoping to find fulfillment. But most of these things disappoint. When we decide to walk in love we discover it not only blesses others, it also blesses us.

Calm Down and Use Your Gifts

*Peace I leave with you; My [own] peace I now give
and bequeath to you.*

JOHN 14:27

Do you know there's a right and wrong way to handle times of distress? I didn't know that until I became a Christian and began to learn that God's power and peace are available to me.

As a Christian, you have God's peace. He has bequeathed it to you—it is your inheritance. In addition, Luke 10:19 tells you He has given you power. Peace and power, what wonderful gifts . . . and God gave them to you for a reason—He wants you to use them.

If you haven't been putting these gifts to work in your life you're cheating yourself. So make a decision to start using them now. Don't waste your time whining, crying, or throwing a fit when problems come. Instead, calm down and think about the peace and power of God that are yours . . . and then put them to work!

Choose Life

I call heaven and earth to witness this day against
you that I have set before you life and death, the
blessings and the curses; therefore choose life, that you
and your descendants may live.

DEUTERONOMY 30:19

Happiness and joy do not come from the outside but from within you. They are the result of a conscious decision, a deliberate choice—one we make each day.

There are many people living in bad situations they would like to see changed. But despite the challenges they choose to be happy and joyous. You face that same choice every day of your life.

Either you choose to passively listen to the devil and allow him to ruin your life and make you miserable, or you choose to aggressively withstand him so you can live in the fullness of life God provided for you through His Son Jesus Christ.

Make the right choice and enjoy life like never before!

Make Love a Habit

*And let us consider and give attentive, continuous
care to watching over one another, studying how we
may stir up (stimulate and incite) to love and helpful
deeds and noble activities.*

HEBREWS 10:24

If you intend to make love a habit, you must develop the habit of loving people with your words. Your fleshly (lower, sensual) nature points out flaws, weaknesses, and failures. It seems to feed on the negatives in life. It sees and magnifies all that is wrong with people and things. But the Bible says you are to overcome evil with good (see Romans 12:21).

Walking in the Spirit—continually following the leading, guiding, and working of the Holy Spirit through your own spirit instead of being led by your emotions—requires being positive.

It is easy to find something wrong with everyone. But love does not expose faults—it covers them. Ask God to help you share His love with others.

Be a Believer, Not an Achiever

*Are you so foolish and so senseless and so silly?
Having begun [your new life spiritually] with the
[Holy] Spirit, are you now reaching perfection [by
dependence] on the flesh?*

GALATIANS 3:3

Trying to make things happen on your own without God's help is foolish and often causes feelings of frustration and condemnation. It makes no sense for you to try to do what only God can do.

God wants you to realize it is impossible for you to change yourself—only He can do that through the marvelous wonder of His grace, which is a free gift to everyone who will receive it.

If you have been struggling to achieve good results on your own it's time to make a change. God wants you to struggle less and believe more. Accept the free gift of God's grace and allow Him to change your life into the peaceful, abundant life He has planned for you.

Be Led by Peace

And let the peace (soul harmony which comes)
from Christ rule (act as umpire continually) in your
hearts [deciding and settling with finality all ques-
tions that arise in your minds].

COLOSSIANS 3:15

The umpire in a baseball game decides whether you are in or out. Peace in your heart should be the umpire that decides whether something should be out of your life, or allowed to remain.

Many people do not enjoy peace because they are out of the will of God. They follow their own will rather than God's will. They do what they feel like or what they think is right rather than following God's Word and being led by peace.

I've learned something can sound good, feel good, and even be a good thing . . . but if I don't have peace about it, I need to leave it alone.

If you want to be sensitive to God's leading, learn to follow peace!

Experience Joy as a Calm Delight

> *I have told you these things, that My joy and delight may be in you, and that your joy and gladness may be of full measure and complete and overflowing.*
>
> JOHN 15:11

Are you like some believers who think that in order to be filled with the joy of the Lord they must be turned on, fired up, and superhyped?

God wants your joy to be full and complete, but that doesn't mean you have to swing from chandeliers!

Some define *joy* as "hilarity," and there is some basis for that definition. But according to *Strong's Concordance*, the Greek word *chara*, translated *joy* in the above verse, means "calm delight."

My husband, Dave, likens this calm delight to a bubbling brook that just flows along quietly and peacefully, bringing refreshment to everything and everyone along its path. Doesn't that sound appealing?

Of course there will be times when your joy will be supercharged and exciting, but most of the time we will live with a simple "calm delight."

Refuse to Be Confused

God is not the author of confusion, but of peace.

1 CORINTHIANS 14:33 KJV

Are you confused? Is there something happening in your life right now you don't understand? Or perhaps you're baffled about the way things happened in your past.

Many people today suffer tremendously with confusion, but that was never God's plan. He doesn't cause your confusion—He wants to stop it.

He doesn't want you to try to figure out everything that happens in your life. He knows what is going on and why, and He is in control.

That means you don't have to worry and live in confusion. It almost sounds too easy, but you can have total freedom from the torment of confusion just by refusing the temptation to figure things out. So trust God to take care of everything that concerns you and enjoy a peaceful, happy life.

Rejoice in Today

This is the day which the Lord hath made; we will rejoice and be glad in it.

PSALM 118:24 KJV

The Lord once told me anxiety is caused by trying to mentally and emotionally get into things that are not here yet or that have already passed—mentally leaving today and getting into an area of the past or the future.

Since then I have been trying to learn to lighten up and enjoy life. I try to live life one day at a time and not worry about the past or future. We need to be responsible, but we also need to relax and take things as they come without getting all nervous and upset.

Learn to enjoy the good life God provided for you. In spite of all the troubling things going on in the world, make this daily confession: "This is the day the Lord has made, and I will rejoice and be glad in it."

Don't Fret—Rejoice!

Rejoice in the Lord always . . . again I say,
Rejoice! . . . Do not fret or have any anxiety about
anything, but in . . . everything, by prayer and
petition, . . . with thanksgiving, continue to
make your wants known to God.

PHILIPPIANS 4:4,6

Twice in this passage the apostle Paul tells us to rejoice. He urges us not to fret or have any anxiety about anything but to pray and give thanks to God in everything—not after everything is over.

If you wait until everything is perfect before rejoicing and giving thanks you won't have much fun. Learning to enjoy life even in the midst of trying circumstances is one way to develop spiritual maturity.

Live in the fullness of the joy of the Lord by finding something to be glad about besides your current circumstances. You must learn to derive your happiness and joy from the Lord who lives inside you.

Decide you will not fret or have anxiety about anything but will give thanks and praise to God, rejoicing in Him always.

Accept God's Great Grace

*But where sin increased and abounded, grace
(God's unmerited favor) has surpassed it and
increased the more and superabounded.*

ROMANS 5:20

God conquers evil with good by pouring out His limitless grace upon you so that if you sin, His grace becomes greater than your sin. God's love is the power that forgives your sins, heals your emotional wounds, and mends your broken heart.

Once you realize you are loved by God—not because of anything you are or anything you have done—you can quit trying to earn His love and simply receive and enjoy it.

Start by confessing aloud several times a day that God loves you. Speak it out and get comfortable with the thought of it. Bask in His love and let it saturate your soul. Once your heart is filled with the knowledge of God's love you can begin to love Him in return: We love Him because He first loved us.

Enjoy Your Inheritance

In Him we also were made [God's] heritage . . .
and we obtained an inheritance . . . so that we who
first hoped in Christ [who first put our confidence in
Him have been destined and appointed to] live for the
praise of His glory!

EPHESIANS 1:11-12

As a believer, you are meant to enjoy your spiritual inheritance. Life presents many challenges, but you must recognize what is rightfully yours through placing your confidence in Christ. You don't have to live on an emotional roller coaster, feeling up one day and down the next. Instead, you can live as Christ lived, with a sense of peace and security that comes from knowing who you are and whose you are.

Until you make the decision to claim and live in your inheritance, the enemy will continue to rob you of what Jesus died to provide you—His righteousness, peace, and joy that prevail even in the midst of turmoil and confusion.

So calm down, cheer up, and learn to enjoy the inheritance that is yours through Christ.

Simplify Your Life

You were wearied with the length of your way [in trying to find rest and satisfaction in alliances apart from the true God], yet you did not say, There is no result or profit.

ISAIAH 57:10

There seems to be a great lack of simplicity in society today, even among Christians. Somehow life gets so complicated it eventually drains you of your energy and produces frustration and fatigue.

One translation of the first line of this verse from Isaiah is, "You are wearied out through the multiplicity of your ways." The answer for the problem of multiplicity is a return to simplicity.

In our modern society, we think that more is always better. But the writer of Ecclesiastes warns that the more your goods increase, the more complicated your life becomes (see Ecclesiastes 5:11-12).

Instead of making everything so difficult, why don't you decide to simplify your life and enjoy the rest and satisfaction that comes through following God's plan?

Have an Attitude of Faith

Faith is the assurance . . . of the things [we] hope
for, being the proof of things [we] do not see.

HEBREWS 11:1

Faith can be described in many ways, but a very simple way to look at faith—even to examine whether or not you are operating in it— is to say that "faith has an attitude."

Hebrews 4 says that those who have believed God—those who have an attitude of faith—enter His rest and cease from the weariness and pain of human labors.

The attitude of faith does not worry, fret, or have anxiety concerning tomorrow, because faith understands that wherever it needs to go, even into the unknowns of the future, Jesus has already been there.

Remember, He is the Alpha and the Omega. Not only is He the Beginning and the End, He is everything in between. So have an attitude of faith as you pray tonight, placing your trust completely in the one who was, who is, and who is to come.

Exchange Ashes for Beauty

[Cast] all your care upon him; for he careth for you.

1 PETER 5:7 KJV

Do you know God wants to take care of you? It's true. He wants you to give Him all your cares, your problems, your failures—your "ashes"—and in exchange He will give you beauty.

Many people want God to take care of them, but they continue worrying or trying to figure out the answers to their problems instead of waiting for His direction. They continue to wallow in their "ashes" and expect God to give them beauty. But it doesn't work that way—God can only give you beauty when you give Him the ashes.

It's a great privilege to be cared for by the King of kings, so give up your worries and concerns to Him and enjoy His protection, stability, and fullness of joy.

Are You Lovable?

*God shows and clearly proves His [own] love for us
by the fact that while we were still sinners, Christ (the
Messiah, the Anointed One) died for us.*

ROMANS 5:8

When you read the title on this page—
Are You Lovable?—you may have immediately thought, "No, I'm not!"

I would have probably responded the same way
before I came to understand the true nature of God's
love and His reason for loving me.

How can God love you as imperfect as you are?
He loves you because He wants to. It pleases Him.
God loves you because that is His nature. God is love
(see 1 John 4:8). If He were otherwise, He wouldn't
be who He is.

God may not always love everything you do, but
He does love you. His love is unconditional—it is
based on Him, not you.

Live According to God's Plan

*Cursed [with great evil] is the strong man who
trusts in and relies on frail man, making weak
[human] flesh his arm, and whose mind and heart
turn aside from the Lord.*

JEREMIAH 17:5

The Bible speaks of the arm of the flesh and the arm of the Lord. One is based on human ideas and effort; the other is based on God's plan and power.

It is hard work to carry out the plans and schemes you yourself devise because you are operating in the flesh. But when God starts something, He carries it through to completion without any struggle on your part.

If you are facing struggles, it may be because you are taking matters into your own hands instead of being patient and waiting on the Lord to work things out according to His perfect will.

So stop struggling—turn away from the arm of the flesh and learn to live victoriously according to God's divine plan and purpose for your life.

Succeed at Being Yourself

The [Holy] Spirit . . . bears us up in our weakness.

ROMANS 8:26

Are you tired of playing games, wearing masks, and trying to be someone other than who you are? Wouldn't you like the freedom just to be accepted as you are, without pressure to be someone you really don't know how to be? Would you like to learn how to succeed at being yourself?

God wants you to accept yourself, to like who you are, and to learn to deal with your weaknesses. Everyone has weaknesses, but God doesn't want you to reject yourself because of them.

If you base your value on your weaknesses, you will underestimate your value. Your worth is not based on anything you do but on what God has already done.

So if the devil has been trying to convince you that you don't measure up to the proper standard, remind him tonight that everyone is imperfect and that God loves you just the way you are.

Give Away What You Have

Beloved, if God loved us so [very much], we also
ought to love one another.

1 JOHN 4:11

What a blessing it is to have God's love in you—but you must not hoard it for yourself. God wants you to give it away . . . to love others lavishly and unconditionally as He has loved you.

Everyone in the world desires to be loved and accepted. God's love is the most wonderful gift He could give you. And you have the privilege of sharing that love by allowing it to flow through you into the lives of others.

Many people try to find happiness in getting, but true happiness can only be found in giving. Think of yourself as a dispensary of blessings. Be the kind of person others come to looking for love and blessings. You'll discover that as you give love away, you'll reap happiness and love in your own life.

Isn't it comforting to know you are lovable? Now share your love with someone else.

Little Things Mean a Lot

For who has despised the day of small things?
ZECHARIAH 4:10 NKJV

Little things are often viewed as being insignificant, but in reality they are very important. They are the spice of life.

It is a mistake to be interested only in the main course (big things), disregarding the need for the little things (spices). The main course without spice is bland, tasteless, and unsatisfying.

Parents may feel they are showing love for their family by working long hours and bringing home plenty of money to assure financial security. But if working long hours and making lots of money (the seemingly big thing) means they have little time at home for the little things like talking and laughing with the family and doing fun things together, the marriage and family relationships become dull and unsatisfying.

So if you've been overlooking the importance of the little things in life, it's time to add some spice to your life. Why not start tonight?

Freedom from the Pit

I waited patiently and expectantly for the Lord;
and He inclined to me and heard my cry. He drew me up
out of a horrible pit . . . and set my feet upon a rock.

PSALM 40:1-2

When the Bible speaks of "the pit," I always think of the depths of depression.

David spoke of feeling as though he were in a pit, calling out to the Lord to rescue him and set his feet on solid ground.

Nobody wants to be in the pit of depression. Satan takes advantage of your situation by reminding you of painful memories.

When you are depressed, the devil's goal is to make you so miserable and hopeless you will never rise up to cause him any problems or to fulfill the call of God on your life.

So if you're struggling in a pit that keeps you from being all God wants you to be, cry out to the Lord and allow Him to draw you out of the pit and set you free. God has a great life planned for you, don't let Satan steal it through depression.

Eliminate the Negative

*The communication of thy faith may become
effectual by the acknowledging of every good thing
which is in you in Christ Jesus.*

PHILEMON 1:6 KJV

The communication of your faith is made effectual by acknowledging every good thing that is in you through Christ Jesus, not by acknowledging every thing that is wrong with you.

The devil wants you to spend every waking moment acknowledging in your mind and out of your mouth how awful you are. He continually tries to redirect your focus from who you are in Christ, back to your shortcomings. He wants to deceive you into believing that because of your faults, you are worthless.

But you can increase your self-acceptance and improve your opinion of yourself by deciding right here and now you will not entertain one more negative thought or allow one more negative word about yourself to come out of your mouth.

Start acknowledging the good things that are in you because of Christ.

There Is a Way Out

We are hedged in (pressed) on every side
[troubled and oppressed in every way], but not
cramped or crushed; we suffer embarrassments and are
perplexed and unable to find a way out,
but not driven to despair.

2 CORINTHIANS 4:8

Despair is a state in which a person feels so overcome by a sense of futility or defeat they don't know what to do. At such times it seems there is no way out. But for believers there is always a way out of every situation because Jesus has told us, "I am the Way" (John 14:6).

It is very comforting to know that although there are times when you are pressed on every side and perplexed because there seems to be no way out, the Lord has promised He will not forsake you.

So when it seems you've come to a dead end, don't be driven to despair. God will show you the way to go and lead you through to victory.

Let the Master Builder Complete the Job

For [of course] every house is built and furnished by someone, but the Builder of all things and the Furnisher [of the entire equipment of all things] is God.

HEBREWS 3:4

God is the Master Builder—the one who builds and equips you for the work of the Lord Jesus Christ. The Bible tells you it is God who starts a good work in you, and it is God who will finish it!

This means you should let Him do His work in you. There are certain things only God can do, and your part is to let Him do it. You are to handle your responsibility but cast your care on Him.

Confess your sins and failures to the Lord, confident that He will forgive you. Then trust Him with the job of perfecting you for the work He wants you to do in this life. This will take the pressure off of you and relieve you of the anxiety of trying to perfect yourself.

Have No Fear

There is no fear in love; but perfect love casteth
out fear: because fear hath torment. He that feareth is
not made perfect in love.

1 JOHN 4:18 KJV

Have you ever started to step out in faith and, even at the thought of it, felt fear rising up in you? It happens to everyone, but it is important to realize that the source of fear is Satan.

Satan doesn't want you to do what God wants you to do and receive all God has for you, so he sends fear to try to torment you into being doubtful and miserable. Fear is an evil spirit that hinders progress.

But you can live without fear by building your faith on what God has said in His Word. There is great power in confessing the Word of God.

So when Satan attempts to torment you with fear, confess what the Word says—that the Lord is with you and "will not fail you or forsake you" (Deuteronomy 31:6). Take steps of faith even if you have to "do it afraid."

Do It Afraid!

The Lord said to Abram, Go . . . away from your country, from your relatives and your father's house, to the land that I will show you.

How would you feel if God told you to leave your home, your family, and everything that is familiar and comfortable and head out to who knows where?

That is the challenge Abram faced, and it frightened him. But God kept saying to him, "Fear not." That's the same message He gave to Joshua when He called him to lead the children of Israel to the promised land.

You want to wait until you're not afraid before you do anything, but if you do that, you will accomplish very little for God. Abram and Joshua had to step out in faith and obedience to do what God had commanded them to do—and they had to do it afraid. They took "steps of faith" even though they had "feelings of fear."

That's what you will have to do to accomplish the job God wants you to do. But He'll be with you, saying, "Fear not."

Ending Your Day Right ~ 87

You Are Not of This World

These are [still] in the world . . . [but] they are
not of the world . . . just as I am not of the
world . . . Keep and protect them from the evil one.

JOHN 17:11,14-15

People in the world are under such intense pressure they are often hurried, rude, short-tempered, and frustrated. They experience financial and marital stress and the stress of raising children in a changing and uncertain world. Because of mental stress on the job and physical stress from overwork and frayed nerves, some people seem to be time bombs on the verge of explosion.

As a believer, you do not need to succumb to the stress that affects people who do not know Jesus as their Savior. You do not have to operate in the world's system.

God has provided ways for you to live in the world without being affected by that type of stress. Jesus is the Prince of Peace, and following the leading of the Holy Spirit will always lead you to peace and joy, not to anxiety and frustration.

Refuse to Lose

*Behold, the Lord thy God hath set the land
before thee: go up and possess it, as the Lord God
of thy fathers hath said unto thee; fear not, neither
be discouraged.*

DEUTERONOMY 1:21 KJV

All of us become disappointed when we
have plans that fail, hopes that don't mate-
rialize, and goals that are not reached. When this continues for a while, we become discouraged, a condition
that can lead to depression if not handled properly.

When you get discouraged, you must make a decision to adapt and adjust, to take a new approach, to
just keep going despite your feelings. That's when you
must remember the Greater One resides within
you and decide you won't let discouragement keep
you from realizing your dreams and goals.

When you feel discouraged it is sometimes difficult to be positive. That's when you must rise above
the discouragement through Him who lives in you.
He is always available to help you find renewed direction and hope. I always say, "When you're discouraged, get encouraged, and when you're disappointed,
get reappointed."

Are You Lonely Tonight?

For I will turn their mourning into joy and will
comfort them and make them rejoice after their sorrow.

JEREMIAH 31:13

One of the many sources of sorrow is loneliness. Some who suffer most from loneliness, which is a form of grief, are the shy or extremely timid; those who feel misunderstood; the divorced and unmarried; the widowed; the elderly . . . the list goes on and on.

Loneliness can manifest as an inner ache, a vacuum, or a craving for affection. Its side effects include feelings of emptiness, uselessness, or purposelessness. But loneliness can be cured, no matter what the cause.

If you are lonely, you must realize you can confront it in the name of Jesus Christ.

God has promised to be with you always and to never leave or forsake you. Ask Him to reveal His precious Presence to you. Also, ask Him for what I call "divine connections"—right friends who will be real friends that God Himself has chosen for you. Stand on His promise that He will comfort you and cause you to rejoice. Then get ready for the joy!

Be Willing and Yielded

If God is for us, who [can be] against us? [Who can be our foe, if God is on our side?]

ROMANS 8:31

You do not have to depend on your own human efforts to overcome adversity and opposition or to earn favor and win promotion. When God is ready to move in your life, He will give you favor and promotion—and no devil in hell or person on earth will be able to prevent it from happening.

It doesn't matter what people think of you. Your weaknesses and inabilities don't make any difference to God. His criteria for using people is not their talents, gifts, and abilities. He is looking for people who are willing and yielded. God looks for availability, not ability.

Let God build you, your reputation, and your career. When the time is right He will deliver you out of adversity, and then you'll see the fulfillment of your dreams.

Honor Him First

> *But as for you, the anointing (the sacred*
> *appointment, the unction) which you received from*
> *Him abides [permanently] in you; [so] then you*
> *have no need that anyone should instruct you.*
>
> I JOHN 2:27

This verse isn't suggesting you don't need anyone to teach you the Word. Otherwise God wouldn't appoint some to teach in the body of Christ. But it does say if you are in Christ you have an anointing that abides on the inside of you to guide and direct your life.

Sometimes you give more consideration to what people tell you than to what God has said. You might occasionally ask somebody for their wisdom, but if you hear from God and then start asking everybody else what they think, you are honoring people's opinions above the Word of God. You need to say, "God, no matter what anybody else says, no matter what my own plan is, if You say something to me, I am going to honor You above anything else."

Seek the Truth

*The sower sows the Word. The ones along the path
are those who have the Word sown [in their hearts],
but when they hear, Satan comes at once and [by
force] takes away the message which is sown in them.*

If you hear or study the Word, the devil will immediately attempt to steal it from you. He does not want the Word to take root in your heart and begin to produce good fruit in your life. When you learn the truth, deception is uncovered and you are set free. Satan hates and fears the Word. He will do anything possible to prevent you from learning God's Word.

The reason Satan works so hard to keep you from the Word is simple: he knows the Word of God is a powerful weapon against him. It assures his defeat! That is why it is imperative that you learn to wield the spiritual sword. Reading, hearing, believing, meditating on, and confessing the Word cancels Satan's evil plan. Tonight, determine to make the Word of God a priority in your life.

Little by Little

But we do [strongly and earnestly] desire for each of you to show the same diligence and sincerity [all the way through] in realizing and enjoying the full assurance and development of [your] hope until the end.

HEBREWS 6:11

In some ways, spiritual growth can be compared to physical growth. Sadly, many people do not enjoy their children while they are raising them. At each stage of growth the parents wish the child was in another stage. If the child is crawling, they wish he was walking, out of diapers, in school, getting married, and on and on.

In Deuteronomy 7:22, Moses told the children of Israel the Lord would drive out their enemies before them "little by little." Between each victory in your life there is a time of waiting, but it is usually difficult because you want everything now! As a Christian you grow throughout your lifetime and never stop progressing. Learn to enjoy each stage of life as it comes because each has joys uniquely its own.

Dream Big Dreams

*Through skillful and godly Wisdom is a house (a
life, a home, a family) built, and by understanding it
is established [on a sound and good foundation]. And
by knowledge shall its chambers [of every area] be
filled with all precious and pleasant riches.*

PROVERBS 24:3-4

Do you have a dream or a vision in your
heart for something greater than what
you have now? Ephesians 3:20 tells us God is able to
do exceedingly abundantly above and beyond all we
can hope, ask, or think. If you are not thinking, hoping, or asking—you are cheating yourself. You need
to think big thoughts, dream big dreams, and ask for
big things.

There is a gold mine of dreams, visions, abilities, and strength hidden in every life, but you have
to dig to get to it. You must be willing to dig deep
and go beyond how you feel or what is convenient.
If you will dig down deep into the spirit, you will do
greater things than anyone could ever imagine.

An Effective Prayer

And when you pray, do not heap up phrases
(multiply words, repeating the same ones over and
over) as the Gentiles do, for they think they will be
heard for their much speaking.

Too often we get caught up in our own
works concerning prayer. Sometimes we
try to pray so long, loud, and fancy that we lose sight
of the fact that prayer is simply conversation with
God. The length or loudness or eloquence of our
prayer is not the issue—it is the sincerity of our heart
and our faith God hears that is important.

We must develop simple, believing prayer. We
need the confidence that even if we only say, "God,
help me," He hears and will answer. We should believe that God wants to help us because He is our
Helper (see Hebrews 13:6). We can depend on God
to be faithful to do what we have asked Him to do,
as long as our request is in accordance with His will.

Run On Through

Let us strip off and throw aside every encumbrance
(unnecessary weight) and that sin which so readily
(deftly and cleverly) clings to and entangles us, and
let us run with patient endurance and steady and
active persistence the appointed course of the race
that is set before us.

HEBREWS 12:1

When you begin your journey to whole-
ness with the Lord, you are usually all
knotted up inside. As you allow Him to do so, He
begins to straighten up your life by untying one knot
at a time. The temptation is to run away from your
problems, but the Lord says that you are to go through
them.

The good news is that Jesus has promised that
you will never have to go through them alone. He
will always be there to help you in every way. He
said, "I am the way, follow Me." When you decide to
follow Jesus, you will soon learn He never turns
back in fear. His path is always straightforward to
the finish line.

These Perilous Times

*But understand this, that in the last days will come
(set in) perilous times of great stress and trouble [hard
to deal with and hard to bear]. For people will be
lovers of self and [utterly] self-centered, lovers of
money and aroused by an inordinate [greedy] desire for
wealth, proud and arrogant and contemptuous boast-
ers. They will be abusive (blasphemous, scoffing),
disobedient to parents, ungrateful, unholy and profane.*

2 TIMOTHY 3:1-2

Just as Paul predicted long ago, these are
perilous times. There has now arisen a
new generation of people, many of whom have not
been taught anything about God in school, nor have
they been taught to pray at home. They have seen
some sad examples of spiritual leaders who have
publicly fallen, and having no solid foundation, it is
easy for them to conclude that "religion" is a bunch
of junk.

As a believer, you must strive to be different than
the world. Be a good example. Walk in love, being
honorable in all your conduct. People are watching
you. Show them that Christ lives in you.

Why Worry?

Cease from anger and forsake wrath; fret not yourself—it tends only to evildoing.

PSALM 37:8

Anxiety and worry are both attacks on the mind intended to keep you from serving the Lord. The enemy uses these weapons to press your faith down so you cannot live in victory. Many people are worriers but don't even realize it. They may call it something else—but it is still worry. In addition to telling you to "fret not," other passages warn you to "take no thought" (Matthew 6:25), "be careful for nothing" (Philippians 4:6), and "cast . . . all your care" (1 Peter 5:7).

Matthew 6:27 says, "And who of you by worrying and being anxious can add one unit of measure (cubit) to his stature or to the span of his life?" The obvious point is that worry is useless. It does not accomplish any good thing. In that case, why worry and why be so anxious?

Praying His Will

[Yes] I will grant [I Myself will do for you]
whatever you shall ask in My Name [as presenting
all that I Am].

JOHN 14:14

Some Christians read this passage and take its meaning out of context. What a statement! Wouldn't it be wonderful if this gave you license to have anything and everything you want? But the name of Jesus is not simply a "magic word" to tack on at the end of your wish list.

You must realize that all effective prayer involves praying the will of God, not the will of man. There are many things in the Word that clearly reveal God's will, and these you may certainly ask for boldly without any hesitation or concern about whether you should have them. Yet there are many other things you need to pray about without knowing the exact will of God in the situation. It is at these times you should pray that His perfect will be done and not your own.

Small Beginnings

Who [with reason] despises the day of small things?

ZECHARIAH 4:10

You are probably believing God for something to come to pass in your life. If you look, you will find evidence of a small beginning. God gives you seed—perhaps only a little, tiny seed—something that causes you to hope. Rejoice over that seed. It is a sign of greater things to come.

When you despise something you regard it lightly. You count it as nothing and don't take care of it. But if you don't take care of what God gives you, you will lose it. You need to be content during the small things. You know the Lord is the Author and the Finisher (see Hebrews 12:2). What He begins, He completes (see Philippians 1:6). Don't curse your seed by complaining or proclaiming negative things over it. Instead say, "Lord, this is only a little thing, but thank You for giving me some hope, something to hold on to. Thank You, Lord, for a beginning."

A Strong Fortress

I will say of the Lord, He is my Refuge and my
Fortress, my God; on Him I lean and rely, and in Him
I [confidently] trust! . . . You shall not be afraid of
the terror of the night, nor of the arrow (the evil
plots and slanders of the wicked) that flies by day, nor
of the pestilence that stalks in darkness, nor of the
destruction and sudden death that surprise and lay
waste at noonday.

PSALM 91:2,5-6

You need to remember you are ready for anything through Christ who infuses inner strength into you. Paul prayed for the Church at Ephesus to be strengthened with all might and power in the inner man (see Ephesians 3:16). He knew if they stayed strong inwardly, they would be able to handle whatever came against them.

When you trust God, you don't have to be afraid of the devil's sudden surprises that stalk you. He is your strong fortress. No matter what may come against you, you will not be defeated.

Hear and Obey

*Sacrifice and offering You do not desire, nor have
You delight in them; You have given me the capacity
to hear and obey [Your law, a more valuable service
than] burnt offerings and sin offerings [which] You
do not require.*

PSALM 40:6

God delights in your obedience. Naturally, it doesn't do Him any good to speak
to you if you aren't going to listen and obey. For
many years, I wanted God to talk to me, but I wanted
to pick and choose what to obey. I wanted to do what
He said if I thought it was a good idea. If I didn't like
what I was hearing, I would act like it wasn't from
God.

Some of what God says will be exciting. Some
things might not be so thrilling to hear. But that
doesn't mean what He tells you won't work out for
good if you will just do it His way. God does not require a higher sacrifice than obedience.

Sufficient Grace

My grace (My favor and loving-kindness and
mercy) is enough for you [sufficient against any
danger and enables you to bear the trouble
manfully]; for My strength and power are made
perfect (fulfilled and completed) and show
themselves most effective in [your] weakness.

2 CORINTHIANS 12:9

Do you ever wonder why God does not always deliver you from your bondage and problems immediately? The reason is because only the Lord knows everything that needs to be done in the lives of His children—and the perfect timing for it to be done.

You are not always delivered from your distress at the precise moment you call on the name of the Lord. Sometimes you must endure for a while, be patient and continue in faith. Thank God, during those times in which the Lord decides for whatever reason not to deliver you right away, He always gives the grace and strength you need to press on toward eventual victory.

Great Expectations

And therefore the Lord [earnestly] waits [expecting, looking, and longing] to be gracious to you; and therefore He lifts Himself up, that He may have mercy on you and show loving-kindness to you. For the Lord is a God of justice. Blessed (happy, fortunate, to be envied) are all those who [earnestly] wait for Him, who expect and look and long for Him [for His victory, His favor, His love, His peace, His joy, and His matchless, unbroken companionship]!

ISAIAH 30:18

What a wonderful promise. God is earnestly looking for someone to be good to—but there is one requirement. You must be expecting, looking, and longing for God's goodness.

Hebrews 6:19 says hope is the anchor of the soul. Hope is the force that keeps you steady in a time of trial. Don't ever stop hoping. Things may not always turn out the way you want them to, but even in disappointing times there is still reason to hope. Expect a miracle in your life. Expect good things!

Peculiar Treasure

*Now therefore, if you will obey My voice in truth
and keep My covenant, then you shall be My own
peculiar possession and treasure from among and
above all peoples; for all the earth is Mine. And you
shall be to Me a kingdom of priests, a holy nation
[consecrated, set apart to the worship of God].*

EXODUS 19:5-6

Self-rejection and self-hatred can almost
seem pious in a sense. They can become a
way of punishing yourself for your mistakes, failures, and inabilities. People cannot be perfect, so they
sometimes reject and despise themselves.

Do you lack appreciation for your own worth
and value? You may not feel treasured or even acceptable, but you are. In Ephesians 1:6, Paul says
that all who believe in Christ have been "accepted in
the beloved." What joyous and amazing affirmation!
Surely you are valuable; otherwise your heavenly Father would not have paid such a heavy price for your
redemption.

Confidence in Christ

Do not, therefore, fling away your fearless
confidence, for it carries a great and glorious
compensation of reward. For you have need of steadfast
patience and endurance, so that you may perform and
fully accomplish the will of God, and thus receive and
carry away [and enjoy to the full] what is promised.

HEBREWS 10:35-36

What is confidence? It has been defined as the quality of assurance that leads one to undertake something; the belief that one is able and acceptable; the certainty that causes one to be bold, open, and plain.

The devil begins his assault on personal confidence wherever he can find an opening, especially during the vulnerable years of childhood. His goal is to undermine the person because an individual without confidence will never fulfill the plan of God for his life.

Christ is in you, ready to help with everything you do for Him. Jesus can restore your confidence and give you the strength, power, and boldness to do what you could never do on your own. Be confident—it is part of your spiritual inheritance!

Seeing in the Darkness

God is faithful (reliable, trustworthy, and therefore
ever true to His promise, and He can be depended
on); by Him you were called into companionship and
participation with His Son, Jesus Christ our Lord.

1 CORINTHIANS 1:9

There are times you just can't see through
the darkness that seems to be closing in
around you. It is in those times of endurance and patience that your faith is stretched and you learn to
trust God even when you can't hear His voice.

You can grow in your confidence level to the
point where "knowing" is even better than "hearing."
You may not know what to do, but it is sufficient to
know the one who does know. Everyone likes specific direction; however, when you don't have it,
knowing God is faithful and ever true to His promise, and that He has promised to be with us always,
is comforting and keeps us stable until His timing
comes to illuminate the situation.

The Lie of Self

For we [Christians] are the true circumcision, who
worship God in spirit and by the Spirit of God and
exult and glory and pride ourselves in Jesus Christ,
and put no confidence or dependence [on what we
are] in the flesh and on outward privileges and
physical advantages and external appearances.

PHILIPPIANS 3:3

Self-confidence is the buzzword of to-day's culture. Society proclaims a basic need to believe in oneself and that you need to feel good if you are ever going to accomplish anything in life. Too many believe that lie.

Many people spend their lives climbing the ladder of success only to reach the top and discover their ladder was propped against the wrong building. Others strive to perform perfectly, only to endure repeated failures. The result is always the same—emptiness and misery.

You don't need to believe in yourself—you need to believe in Jesus in you. You do not need self-confidence. You need God-confidence!

Be Who You Are

Let us not become vainglorious and self-conceited,
competitive and challenging and provoking and
irritating to one another, envying and being jealous
of one another.

GALATIANS 5:26

In Galatians 6:4 the apostle Paul exhorts you to grow in the Lord until you come to the point you can have the personal satisfaction and joy of doing something commendable in itself alone without resorting to boastful comparison with other people.

Thank God, once you know who you are in Christ, you are set free from the stress of comparison and competition. You know you have worth and value apart from your works and accomplishments. Therefore you can do your best to glorify God, rather than just trying to be better than someone else. What a glorious, wonderful freedom to be secure in Christ and not have to be controlled by strife, envy, or jealousy. You can be who God created you to be! He doesn't make mistakes!

From Pit to Palace

When Joseph had come to his brothers, they
stripped him of his [distinctive] long garment which
he was wearing; Then they took him and cast him
into the [well-like] pit which was empty; there
was no water in it.

GENESIS 37:23-24

When Joseph's brothers threw him in the pit to die, God had other plans. Scripture says that even though Joseph was sold as a slave, he did not have a slave mentality. He still believed he could do great things. Ultimately he ended up second in command to Pharaoh, the ruler over all Egypt. How did Joseph get from the pit to the palace? It was by remaining positive, refusing to be bitter, being confident, and trusting God.

Make up your mind right now to do something great for God. No matter where you started, you can have a great finish. If people have mistreated you, don't waste your time trying to get revenge— leave them in God's hands and trust Him to bring justice in your life.

The Stress-Free Life

Come to Me, all you who labor and are heavy-laden and overburdened, and I will cause you to rest. [I will ease and relieve and refresh your souls.]

MATTHEW 11:28

Many people today are stressed out beyond anything a human being was ever meant to endure. Every person is very different, uniquely created by God's design. What is complicated for one may be simple for another. Don't compare yourself with other people. But when faced with a problem or difficult circumstance you must ask yourself, "What would Jesus have me do in this situation? How would He handle it?"

Jesus was not stressed out or burned out. He was not controlled by circumstances or the demands of other people. In John 14:6, Jesus said, "I am the Way." His way is the right way—the way that will lead you into righteousness, peace, and joy. Jesus prayed that His enjoyment would fill your soul, and it will when you learn to take His approach to life and its many different challenges.

No Condemnation

*He who believes in Him [who clings to, trusts in,
relies on Him] is not judged [he who trusts in Him
never comes up for judgment; for him there is no rejection, no condemnation—he incurs no damnation].*

JOHN 3:18

The Holy Spirit works to convict you of sin and convince you of righteousness (see John 16:7-11). His conviction is intended to convince you to repent, which means to turn around and go in the right direction.

It is normal to feel guilty when you are initially convicted of sin; but to keep feeling guilty after you have repented is not healthy, nor is it God's will. Conviction is entirely different from condemnation. Condemnation presses you down and puts you under a burden of guilt, but conviction is meant to lift you out of something, to help you move up higher in God's plan for your life. If you are suffering under a burden of condemnation, lay your guilt before the throne of God tonight and receive His forgiveness and mercy.

The Sword of the Spirit

*Stand therefore [hold your ground], having
tightened the belt of truth around your loins and
having put on the breastplate of integrity and of
moral rectitude and right standing with God, and
having shod your feet in preparation [to face the
enemy with the firm-footed stability, the promptness,
and the readiness produced by the good news] of the
Gospel of peace. Lift up over all the [covering] shield
of saving faith, upon which you can quench all the
flaming missiles of the wicked [one]. And take the
helmet of salvation and the sword that the Spirit
wields, which is the Word of God.*

EPHESIANS 6:14-17

This passage instructs you to wear armor
that serves as protection against the principalities and powers of the enemy. You have defensive armor and a powerful offensive weapon—the
sword of the Spirit. A sword kept in the sheath has
no value. It must be wielded—taken from the sheath
and used. The Word of God is your sword. When
Satan attacks your mind say, "It is written" and quote
a Scripture that opposes his lie.

The Written Word

*Your word is a lamp to my feet
and a light to my path.*

PSALM 119:105

The Bible is written as a personal letter to you. God speaks to you, ministers to your needs, and directs you in the way you should go in His written Word. He tells you what you should do and how you should live.

It is a mistake to think we can hear clearly from God without spending time in the Word. Knowing the written Word protects you from deception. Listening for God's voice without being dedicated to spending time in the Word on a regular basis opens you up to hearing voices that are not from God. There may be times when God speaks something to you that is outside a specific chapter and verse of the Bible, but it will always be in agreement with His Word. Tonight, spend time reading a portion of God's personal letter to you and allow Him to speak to your heart. God's Word is one of the most precious gifts we have. Treasure it.

Yearnings in the Night

My soul yearns for You [O Lord] in the night, yes,
my spirit within me seeks You earnestly.

ISAIAH 26:9

Nothing can satisfy your longing for God except communion and fellowship with Him. The apostle John wrote, "And the world passes away and disappears, and with it the forbidden cravings (the passionate desires, the lust) of it; but he who does the will of God and carries out His purposes in his life abides (remains) forever" (1 John 2:17).

The world makes it easy for you to fill your ears with all kinds of things that drown out the voice of God and push Him far into the background of your life. However, the day comes for every person when only God remains. Everything else in life eventually passes away; when it does, God will still be there. Seek God earnestly tonight and He will abide in you.

Tame the Tongue

Look at the ships: though they are so great and
are driven by rough winds, they are steered by a very
small rudder wherever the impulse of the helmsman
determines. Even so the tongue is a little member,
and it can boast of great things. . . . But the
human tongue can be tamed by no man. It is a
restless (undisciplined, irreconcilable) evil, full
of deadly poison.

JAMES 3:4-5,8

Anything undisciplined will be wild and uncontrollable, always wanting to do its own thing. A child is that way. So is a wild animal. So is appetite. The human tongue is no different. No man can tame the tongue—not by himself. You need the Holy Spirit's help, but God will not do it all for you. You must discipline your mouth and take responsibility for what comes out of it.

How do you talk about your future? If you are not satisfied with your life and want to see it change, begin speaking over yourself according to God's Word. Let your words be in agreement with God's Word and you will be blessed greatly.

The Perfect Plan

*For I know the thoughts and plans that I have
for you, says the Lord, thoughts and plans for welfare
and peace and not for evil, to give you hope in your
final outcome.*

JEREMIAH 29:11

God has a perfect plan for all those who put their faith in Jesus Christ as Lord of their lives. His plan is complete in great detail, and it will lead all who follow Him to an abundant life. But only a few ever enjoy the fulfillment of God's plan because most don't know how to listen to God's leading and follow Him. Instead they choose (either willfully or ignorantly) to go their own way.

You can walk in the perfect will of God if you will learn how to hear from Him and follow His instructions. But listening to Him is your decision. God won't force you to choose His will. However, He will do everything He can to encourage you to say yes to His direction.

Uncommon Wisdom

*If any of you is deficient in wisdom, let him ask of
the giving God [Who gives] to everyone liberally and
ungrudgingly, without reproaching or faultfinding,
and it will be given him.*

JAMES 1:5

Surprisingly, many sophisticated and intelligent people lack wisdom and common sense. Wisdom and common sense are closely
linked—wisdom discerns truth in a situation, while
common sense provides good judgment regarding
what to do about the truth. Wisdom is supernatural—it isn't taught by men, it is a gift from God.

It is amazing how many people seem to think
that common sense is incompatible with being "spiritual." Spiritual people don't float around all day on
clouds of glory, seeing angels and hearing disem-
bodied voices. You live in a real world with real issues and need real answers. You do the seeking and
He does the speaking, but He is the Spirit of Wisdom and will not tell you to do things that are unwise. If you need real answers in your life, wisdom
and common sense are yours for the asking.

Get Off the Treadmill

But to one who, not working [by the Law], trusts (believes fully) in Him Who justifies the ungodly, his faith is credited to him as righteousness (the standing acceptable to God). Thus David congratulates the man and pronounces a blessing on him to whom God credits righteousness apart from the works he does.

ROMANS 4:5-6

If you spend years on the performance treadmill of the world, it is hard to get off. When you are addicted to feeling good about yourself only when you perform well, you are in for a life of misery. It is a cycle of trying and failing, trying harder and failing again, and feeling guilty and rejected.

God does not want you on the performance treadmill. He wants you to feel good about yourself whether you perform perfectly or not. He doesn't want you to be filled with pride, but He certainly did not create you to reject yourself. If you are trapped on the performance treadmill, ask God to break the cycle in your life. Let your confidence be based on who you are in Christ.

Spirit, Mind, and Body

*And may the God of peace Himself sanctify you
through and through [separate you from profane
things, make you pure and wholly consecrated to
God]; and may your spirit and soul and body be
preserved sound and complete [and found] blameless
at the coming of our Lord Jesus Christ (the Messiah).*

I THESSALONIANS 5:23

Many people do not understand they are a tri-part being: a spirit, soul, and body. You are a spirit, you have a soul, and you live in a body. God promises to take care of all three parts that make you who you are.

You are to work with the Holy Spirit to carry out the plan that began to operate in you when you accepted Jesus as your Lord and Savior. Your new birth begins in your spirit, is carried out through your soul (mind, will, and emotions), and is finally visible to other people through a demonstration of His glory in your physical life. God is working in you as long as you believe. He has begun a good work and He will also finish it.

You Are Not Alone

Because he has set his love upon Me, therefore
will I deliver him; I will set him on high, because
he . . . [has a personal knowledge of My mercy,
love, and kindness—trusts and relies on Me,
knowing I will never forsake him].

PSALM 91:14

God wants you to know you are not alone. Satan wants you to believe you are all alone, but you are not. He wants you to believe no one understands how you feel, but that is not true.

In addition to God being with you, many believers know how you feel and understand what you are experiencing mentally and emotionally.

As God's child, you can claim His wonderful promises. No matter what you are facing or how lonely you may feel, know that you are not alone.

As you meditate on God tonight, draw strength and encouragement from knowing He is always faithful and He will never forsake you.

Lift Up Your Eyes

But You, O Lord, are a shield for me,
my glory, and the lifter of my head.

PSALM 3:3

When you feel down, everything around you seems to fall apart, and you begin to lose your strength. Your head and hands and heart begin to droop. Even your eyes and your voice are lowered.

You are downcast because you are looking at your problems, and this only makes you feel worse. Sometimes you are tempted to say, "Oh, what's the use?" and just give up. But God is waiting for you to lift up your eyes and look to Him for help.

Life will always bring discouraging situations, but you don't have to let them get you down. Despite life's distressing circumstances, you can be confident in the Lord, the lifter of your head.

Lift up your eyes, hands, head, and heart and look not at your problems, but at the one who has promised to see you through to victory. Smile . . . it will lift your spirit.

Expect a Turnaround

*As for you, you thought evil against me, but God
meant it for good, to bring about that many people
should be kept alive, as they are this day.*

GENESIS 50:20

This verse is part of the story of how
God promoted Joseph to a place of power
after his brothers had sold him into slavery. It is a
great testament to God's desire and ability to overcome evil with good.

Joseph's brothers meant to destroy him, but
Joseph became second in command to Pharaoh and
was used by God to save not only his own family but
many thousands of others.

Sometimes you forget how big your God is.
Whatever may have happened to you in the past, you
must understand it doesn't have to dictate your future. Set your faith and trust in God and watch to
see how He will turn it around for your good. Rejoice! God has a good plan for your life.

Love by Giving

*But if anyone has this world's goods . . . and sees
his brother . . . in need, yet closes his heart of compassion against him, how can the love of God live and
remain in him? . . . Let us not love [merely] in theory
or in speech but in deed and in truth.*

I JOHN 3:17-18

Many people love things and use people
to get them. But God intends for you to
love people and use things to bless them. Sharing
your possessions with others is one way to move
love from the "talking about it stage" to the "doing it
stage."

God has given you a heart of compassion, but
you choose whether to open or close it. There are
hurting people all around you, and simple acts of
kindness can make these individuals feel loved and
valuable.

Don't just strive to have more prosperity; strive
to excel in giving. If you do, you will discover God
makes sure you have enough to meet your own
needs, with plenty to give away.

Live One Day at a Time

So do not worry or be anxious about tomorrow, for tomorrow will have worries and anxieties of its own. Sufficient for each day is its own trouble.

MATTHEW 6:34

Most of us have enough to handle today without worrying about tomorrow. God will give you grace for today, but He will not give you grace for tomorrow until tomorrow arrives.

So often people worry about something that never happens. When you begin to think about the "what ifs," the door opens for fear and worry. Some people worry so much that their worries become fear, and often the things people fear manifest in their life.

Do not allow yourself to dread tomorrow. Just know that God is faithful. It is comforting to know that whatever tomorrow may hold, He holds tomorrow. His grace is sufficient to meet the need. Do not waste today's grace by worrying about tomorrow. Live one day at a time and you'll be amazed at how much you can accomplish for Christ.

Change Your Focus

I pray: that your love may abound yet more and more and extend to its fullest development . . . so that you may surely learn to sense what is vital, and approve and prize what is excellent and of real value.

PHILIPPIANS 1:9-10

Paul prayed this prayer for the believers at the church in Philippi, knowing they could not have powerful, victorious lives unless they learned the real value of loving others.

You too must make a true commitment to walk in love, which may require you to readjust your priorities and change your focus.

You should have your mind renewed to what love really is. It is not a feeling you have; it is a decision you make—a decision to treat people the way Jesus would treat them.

A true love walk does not come easily or without personal sacrifice, but the benefits are great. God will enrich your life like never before. Loving others is the pathway to true joy.

Let God Increase Your Strength

He gives power to the faint and weary, and to
him who has no might He increases strength
[causing it to multiply and making it to abound].

ISAIAH 40:29

When I feel myself starting to get weary, I go to the Lord. I have learned it's better to keep up regular maintenance than to wait until a breakdown occurs and then try to repair the damage.

It is wise not to use up everything you have and totally deplete all your resources—physically, mentally, emotionally, and spiritually.

It's easy to get burned out from overwork or just being continually upset and frustrated about problems, especially when you focus on them rather than keeping your eyes on the Lord.

Don't rely on yourself and your own strength and abilities. God has promised to provide the strength, energy, and power you need to keep going. So learn to relax more and allow the Lord to restore and renew you before you start falling apart. Come apart daily and spend quality time with Jesus.

Trust God's Timing

I trusted in, relied on, and was confident in
You, O Lord; I said, You are my God. My
times are in Your hands.

PSALM 31:14-15

Trust requires you to place your time in God's hands, believing that His timing is perfect for all things in your life.

Your human nature wants good things to happen in your life now—not later. But as you mature in the Christian life you learn to believe for things not now, but in God's perfect timing.

Trusting God often means not knowing how God is going to accomplish something and not knowing when He will do it. But not knowing "how and when" stretches your faith and teaches you lessons in trust. Remember: Trust is not inherited; it is learned.

Timing plays an important part in learning to trust God. As you experience His faithfulness over and over, you will give up trusting yourself and place your life in His very capable hands. What a wonderful place to be!

Remember God and Take Action

O my God, my life is cast down upon me
[and I find the burden more than I can bear];
therefore will I [earnestly] remember You.

PSALM 42:6

When you are down, the devil wants you to remember every foul, rotten, stinking thing that has ever happened to you and every shameful, detestable, despicable thing you have ever done.

God wants you to remember Him and sing praises to Him in the midst of your miserable situation. Remember you are a new creature; old things have passed away.

When King Saul was assaulted by an evil spirit, he took action. Saul called for David to come play his harp to soothe His troubled spirit (see 1 Samuel 16).

Whenever you feel your spirit starting to sink, you need to take action immediately. Don't wait.

Remember the Lord and the good things He has done for you—it will boost your faith and lift your spirit! Lift your hands in praise and your voice in song. Satan cannot defeat a worshipper.

Don't Exceed Reasonable Limits

Do you not know that your body is the temple . . .
of the Holy Spirit Who lives within you . . .
You are not your own, you were bought with a
price . . . So then, honor God and bring
glory to Him in your body.

1 CORINTHIANS 6:19-20

In today's world, stress is a normal part of everyday life. God created you to withstand normal amounts of pressure and tension, and if you keep stress within reasonable limits, there is no problem. But if you don't, the trouble begins.

Many stressful situations are unavoidable, but too often you cause yourself extra stress by working too hard and too long, not eating and sleeping properly, and getting so involved in activities—even good works—that you exceed wise limits. If you keep adding to that mental and emotional stress, you get into trouble.

If you are pushing yourself beyond reasonable limits, it's time to remember that the Holy Spirit lives in you. You owe it to Him and to yourself to let Him help you recognize and stay within your limits. Don't burn out. Burn on!

Enjoy the Righteousness of Christ

> *[Righteousness, standing acceptable to God] will
> be granted and credited to us also who believe in
> (trust in, adhere to, and rely on) God, Who raised
> Jesus our Lord from the dead.*
>
> ROMANS 4:24

It is an awe-inspiring thing to realize you are in right standing with God simply because you believe in Him. Because Jesus who knew no sin became sin, you are the righteousness of God. What a thrilling and humbling thought.

But the devil doesn't want you to walk in the wonderful thrill of that reality. He wants to bring up all your faults and distract you from the joy of righteousness Jesus died to give you.

Don't let the devil steal the thrill of your righteousness through Christ. As you prepare for a night of rest, spend a few quiet moments thinking about that matchless gift, and worship the one who made it all possible. Go to sleep thinking, "I am the righteousness of God in Christ" (2 Corinthians 5:21).

Heed the Signposts

*And your ears will hear a word behind you, say-
ing, This is the way; walk in it, when you turn to the
right hand and when you turn to the left.*

ISAIAH 30:21

Suppose you are driving along the road.
In the middle of the road are lines. Some
are yellow double lines warning that if you cross
them, you run a high risk of being in a head-on col-
lision. Some are broken white lines that mean you
can cross into the other lane and pass the car in front
of you as long as you are cautious and check for on-
coming traffic.

There are also signposts that give specific direction
or warning: "Detour," "One Way," "Under Construc-
tion," "Curve Ahead." If you heed the instructions,
you will avoid getting into an unsafe situation.

The same is true in life. There are spiritual signposts that instruct us about how to stay under God's
protection. If you will heed these signposts, you will
be able to safely remain on course. For example, always follow peace and you will be going in the right
direction.

Love Man . . . Trust God

Many believed in His name . . . but Jesus
[for His part] did not trust Himself to them . . .
for He Himself knew what was in human nature.
[He could read men's hearts.]

JOHN 2:23-25

Jesus loved people, especially His disciples. He had great fellowship with them, traveled with them, ate with them, and taught them. But He didn't put His trust in them, because He knew human nature.

This doesn't mean He had no trust in His relationship with them; He just didn't open Himself to them in the same way that He trusted in and opened up to His heavenly Father. That is the way you should be.

Many times people form close relationships and depend on their friends to be there for them instead of looking to God. But you don't want to do that. Even in the best relationships, people will disappoint you because people are not perfect.

It is right to love and respect others, but always remember that only God can be counted on to never fail you!

Don't React—Stay Calm

As for you, be calm and cool and steady.

2 TIMOTHY 4:5

If you struggle because of all the trouble in the world and in your life, and you get upset with people who are hard to deal with—here is the solution: Be calm and cool and steady.

When trouble starts in our lives, too often we tend to get upset, saying, "What can I do? What can I do? What can I do?" We immediately react in the flesh instead of seeking the Lord for direction.

This seems to be the way of the world, and if we are not careful, we do what everyone else does. But God has a better plan for His children. Getting all upset and reacting emotionally doesn't help matters—it only causes more problems.

So when trouble rushes in and interrupts your plans, be obedient to God—ask Him to help you be calm, cool, and steady.

Give Until It Hurts

[They gave] according to their ability, yes, and
beyond their ability; and [they did it] voluntarily.

2 CORINTHIANS 8:3

There are various levels of giving, and some are less painful than others. One way to be a giver is to use your material possessions to be a blessing. Giving away things you no longer want or use is good, but you should also give away new things, or things that have value to you.

If you know someone who has been through a difficult time, go shopping for that person. Look for that special gift that seems just right. It will take time, and for busy people that is painful, but it is good to stretch yourself in new areas.

Sometimes you may need to give away one of your favorite possessions—and that can be painful. But it is good to get out of your comfort zone and give until it hurts. Jesus gave His all on the cross for your sins. Surely we can endure giving up mere worldly possessions.

Love Not the World

*Do not love or cherish the world or the things
that are in the world. If anyone loves the world,
love for the Father is not in him.*

1 JOHN 2:15

Many today are far too attached to the things of this world. Our society is filled to the brim with commerce—there are stores on almost every corner. And everyone is busy making money so they can buy more things. God wants His children to be blessed with nice things, but the Bible tells us not to love them excessively. It is important to keep things in their proper place.

If you use what you have to bless others, God will see to it that you have everything you need, and more. So your goal should be to enjoy the things God gives you and to share with others. This shows your love for the Father.

Trust God and Don't be Afraid

Fear not; stand still (firm, confident, undismayed)
and see the salvation of the Lord which
He will work for you today.

EXODUS 14:13

All of us face times when we feel fear about doing a particular thing. Perhaps the Lord has prompted you to step out and do something, and the devil is trying to keep you from doing it. This verse provides a clear and simple solution: Fear not, don't run, and God will help you.

When you are faced with fear, rather than bowing your knee to it you must stand firm, knowing that God will help you.

Even if your knees are shaking, your mouth is dry, and you feel as though you are getting weak, just keep saying, "Lord, strengthen me. This is what You have told me to do, and with Your help I am going to do it because it is Your revealed will for me. I am determined that my life is not going to be ruled by fear but by Your Word."

Pursue and Seek Love

Eagerly pursue and seek to acquire [this] love
[make it your aim, your great quest].

I CORINTHIANS 14:1

Developing a love walk like the one displayed in the life of Jesus is like digging for gold. True Christlike love is not found on the surface of life. The Bible says you must eagerly pursue and seek it. This means you must go after love with all your might, as if you cannot live without it.

You must learn all you can about love and familiarize yourself with everything Jesus and the apostles said about it. However, not only are you to learn about love, you are to walk in love, remembering to treat others the way you desire to be treated.

Tonight, ask God to help you seek and acquire His kind of love—the love that can make a meaningful difference in your life . . . and in the lives of those around you.

Trust God's Ways

For my thoughts are not your thoughts, neither are
your ways my ways . . . For as the heavens are higher
than the earth, so are My ways higher than your ways
and My thoughts than your thoughts.

ISAIAH 55:8-9

Did you know a lack of understanding of how God does things can wear you out? If you don't understand His ways, you could end up fighting and resisting things, thinking they are an attack from the devil, when in reality they are an attempt by the Lord to work something good in your life.

You know God does not do bad things. But sometimes you may fail to realize that everything that feels bad *to* you is not necessarily bad *for* you. Reminding yourself that His ways are not your ways will help you trust Him even when your circumstances are hard to understand.

As this busy day comes to a close, just put yourself in the hands of almighty God . . . and rest in the knowledge that He is good and knows what's best.

Stop Worrying

Stop being perpetually uneasy (anxious and worried) about your life . . . who of you by worrying and being anxious can add one unit of measure (cubit) to his stature or to the span of his life?

MATTHEW 6:25,27

Many people worry about everything, including what they will or will not eat or wear, or what they will do if a particular situation occurs.

Most of us have enough clothes, adequate food, comfortable houses, and serviceable cars. But when things get tough and you are faced with situations that seem impossible, the devil says, "What are you going to do now?" The temptation comes to worry but that isn't the answer.

God wants you to know that worrying doesn't add to your life—in fact, it will surely shorten it if you make it a habit.

Your heavenly Father knows about all the things you need before you ask Him. So stop worrying and focus your attention on the one who is able to provide everything you need, and more.

Live a Balanced Life

So then, whether you eat or drink, or whatever you
may do, do all for the honor and glory of God.

1 CORINTHIANS 10:31

As a Christian, you must balance your spiritual life with your earthly responsibilities. Some people have a "religious spirit" that causes them to either ignore their earthly tasks or to do them without joy. These people only feel approved by God when they are doing what they think are "spiritual" things.

God wants you to learn that you can communicate with and enjoy Him while doing any number of earthly chores. He wants you to know you can talk with Him throughout the day as well as on bended knee. He is ever-present and always available to fellowship with you and to help with your needs.

It is good to set aside special times to spend with God in prayer and study, but you can also enjoy Him while you're doing other things. This way, you can enjoy life and God at all times, not just during "spiritual times."

Watch and Pray

Keep awake (give strict attention, be cautious and active) and watch and pray, that you may not come into temptation. The spirit indeed is willing, but the flesh is weak.

MATTHEW 26:41

Suppose you knew your house was surrounded by enemy agents and at any moment they might break through the door and attack you. Do you think you would be inclined to stay awake and watch the door?

What would you do if for some reason you couldn't stay awake and watch? Wouldn't you make sure someone else in the family was awake and alerted to the danger?

You need to be just as careful to guard against any potential attacks from the enemy of your soul. The devil is out to get you, and you must watch and pray at all times, asking God to help you when you feel weak.

Ask God to provide the strength you need to overcome any temptation the devil brings your way. Guard your heart and take every thought captive.

Let Go of the Ashes

*The Lord has anointed . . . me . . . to grant
[consolation and joy] to those who mourn . . . to give
them an ornament (a garland or diadem) of beauty
instead of ashes, the oil of joy instead of mourning.*

ISAIAH 61:1,3

This passage specifically says God wants
to give consolation and joy—beauty instead of ashes—for those who mourn. But in order
for Him to do that you must let go of the ashes of
your past.

Some people have their loved ones cremated and
keep their ashes in a box or urn. Eventually they
may carry the ashes to a meaningful spot and throw
them to the wind. It's a way of letting them go—
permanently.

That is what God wants you to do if you have
been hurt in the past and are hanging on to the
ashes. If you want real joy, let go of those ashes, allowing the wind of the Holy Spirit to blow them out
of your life . . . permanently!

Wear God's Armor and Stand Your Ground

Therefore put on God's complete armor, that you may be able to resist and stand your ground on the evil day [of danger], and, having done all [the crisis demands], to stand [firmly in your place].

EPHESIANS 6:13

When the devil comes against you, you must have on the complete armor of God if you are to resist the devil and do all God wants you to do.

You must realize that what you do to overcome one crisis may not be the best way to handle the next crisis. The solution to your problem is not in a certain method or procedure, but in the power God gives you to accomplish what He directs you to do.

When you deal with a crisis, the key is not in your method but in unleashing the power of God through faith. So wear God's armor, stand your ground against the devil, lift up the shield of faith, and see how God will bring the victory!

Be a Blessing Everywhere You Go

He [the benevolent person] scatters abroad;
He gives to the poor; His deeds of justice and
goodness and kindness and benevolence will
go on and endure forever!

2 CORINTHIANS 9:9

It is both good and scriptural to give to the poor—they should be one of your primary concerns. Look for people who are needy and bless them. Share what you have with those who are less fortunate.

But it is also good to remember that *everyone* needs blessings—even the rich, the successful, and those who appear to have everything. What you buy or do for these people is not the real issue; they may not need the gift, but they need the love.

We all get weary sometimes and need to be encouraged, edified, complimented, and appreciated. This can be done with words alone, but it is a nice gesture to add a gift when appropriate.

Remember, God blesses you so you can be a blessing—not only in a few places but everywhere you go!

Discipline Your Thoughts and Words

A man's [moral] self shall be filled with the fruit
of his mouth; and with the consequence of his words
he must be satisfied [whether good or evil]. Death
and life are in the power of the tongue.

PROVERBS 18:20-21

Troubles are a part of life, but God has provided a powerful way for you to free yourself of the worry and anxiety that normally accompany your problems.

God wants good things for your life, but you must cooperate with Him by carefully choosing what you think and speak. By speaking negative words you are inviting negative experiences, but when you speak positive, faith-filled words, you can expect to receive the goodness of God.

Yes, times of trouble are inevitable, but it is during these times that you have the opportunity to discipline your thoughts and words, obey God, and exercise and stretch your faith. When you choose discipline, you are choosing life!

Stop Trying and Start Trusting

[Not in your own strength] for it is God Who is all the while effectually at work in you [energizing and creating in you the power and desire], both to will and to work for His good pleasure and satisfaction and delight.

PHILIPPIANS 2:13

Most of us desire the good life God has planned for us, but we recognize areas in our lives that need to be changed. Many times you set out to make those changes, yet in spite of your best efforts, you seem powerless to make it happen.

Trying to bring about change through your own strength and plans will always result in frustration. God is waiting for you to stop trying to change and start trusting Him to change you.

If you need to make changes in your thoughts, attitudes, and behavior, understand that you can't do it by yourself. Spend time with God and ask for His help—after all, if He can't do it, it can't be done. But He can . . . and He will!

Don't Waste Your Pain

All things work together and are [fitting into a
plan] for good to and for those who love God and are
called according to [His] design and purpose.

ROMANS 8:28

Life is full of unjust situations that can create a great deal of pain for you, especially in your relationship with other people. You will experience some hurt and pain, but you don't have to allow these experiences to destroy your happiness. You can't always choose what happens to you, but you can choose how you respond to it.

If you've been hurt, God can take your bad experiences and make them work for your good. Believing this truth is a positive decision that can help stop your pain.

Choose to learn from the hurtful experiences instead of wasting your pain by allowing them to make you bitter. One way to do this is to overcome evil with good by making sure you don't hurt others. It's a good place to start!

Hurt . . . Heal . . . Help!

God's love has been poured out in our hearts
through the Holy Spirit Who has been given to us.

ROMANS 5:5

Sometimes people say or do things that hurt you, but you have the God-given ability to love these people. One good way to start is by following the well-known golden rule. It isn't easy. In fact, it requires discipline. But God will help you if you really want to do it.

Discipline is your friend—it is the ability God gives you to walk in His ways. Although it is difficult, discipline is temporary discomfort that can lead to permanent or long-term enjoyment.

If you've been hurt and learned to overcome it, you have a valuable tool to help others. God comforts us so we can comfort others. Here's the progression: We are hurt . . . we allow God to heal us . . . and we are ready to help others. Hurt . . . heal . . . help! It's a process that can literally change your life . . . and the lives of many others around you.

Use the Word as a Weapon

No weapon that is formed against you shall prosper, and every tongue that shall rise against you in judgment you shall show to be in the wrong.

ISAIAH 54:17

Do certain situations in your life always seem to trigger thoughts you don't want and can't seem to get rid of? This is a stronghold the devil has built in your mind—a fortress that attracts and holds a certain kind of thinking. There is a battle going on, and it is taking place in your mind.

God has a great plan for your life, but if you allow yourself to be deceived by the enemy, your wrong thoughts can stop that plan. If you will attack those thoughts with the Word, using it as a weapon against the devil, God will set you free from the strongholds in your mind. He will change your thoughts—and your life—and you will start experiencing that abundance He had planned for you all along.

Let God Have Control

*Aim at and seek the [rich, eternal treasures] that
are above . . . And set your minds and keep them set
on what is above . . . not on the things that are on
the earth . . . kill (deaden, deprive of power) the evil
desire . . . [and all that is earthly in you.]*

COLOSSIANS 3:1,2,5

It is a natural desire to want to be in control of your life; however, it is not an attainable goal. Assuming you can control all the people and situations that come into your life is an unrealistic expectation—and one that leaves you frustrated, angry, and exhausted.

God has a good plan for everyone that includes a life far superior to anything the world has to offer, but attaining it involves dying to self. God relentlessly pursues the flesh—our human nature—and is intent on setting us free from its control. The process of letting go and giving up control can be painful, but the end result is worth it. So let go of control and let God be God in your life.

Meditate on Him

I will meditate on Your precepts and
have respect to Your ways [the paths of
life marked out by Your law].

PSALM 119:15

The psalmist said that he thought about or meditated on the precepts of God. In other words, he spent a lot of time pondering and thinking on the ways of God, His instructions, and His teachings. The person who does this, according to Psalm 1:3, is "like a tree firmly planted [and tended] by the streams of water, ready to bring forth its fruit in its season; its leaf also shall not fade or wither; and everything he does shall prosper [and come to maturity]."

The more time you spend meditating on God's Word, the more you will reap from it. The more Word you read and hear, the more power and ability you will have. You will get as much from the Word of God as the effort you put into it. Spend time tonight meditating on God's ways. Choose a Scripture that ministers to you and go to sleep rolling it over and over in your mind.

A Child's Heart

Truly I say to you, unless you repent (change, turn about) and become like little children [trusting, lowly, loving, forgiving], you can never enter the kingdom of heaven [at all]. Whoever will humble himself therefore and become like this little child [trusting, lowly, loving, forgiving] is greatest in the kingdom of heaven.

MATTHEW 18:3-4

Children believe what they are told. Some people say children are gullible, meaning they believe anything no matter how ridiculous it sounds. But children are not gullible—they are trusting. It is a child's nature to trust unless he has experienced something that teaches him otherwise. Your heavenly Father wants you to know that you are His precious little one—His child—and that when you come to Him as such, you show faith in Him, which releases Him to care for you.

God is not like people. If people in your past have hurt you, don't let it affect your relationship with the Lord. You can trust Him. He will care for you as a loving Father.

Don't Dread

Be strong and of good courage. Dread not and
fear not; be not dismayed.

1 CHRONICLES 22:13

Dread is like fear—it draws disaster. It is Satan's open door to bring in the thing feared or dreaded. In Deuteronomy 1:29-30, we read the words of Moses spoken to the children of Israel about their enemies dwelling in the promised land: "Then I said to you, Dread not, neither be afraid of them. The Lord your God Who goes before you, He will fight for you just as He did for you in Egypt before your eyes."

God has not given you a spirit of fear (see 2 Timothy 1:7), and since He did not give you fear, you know He did not give you dread either. Jesus is your Pioneer (see Hebrews 2:10); He goes out ahead of you and makes a way for you. When something seems impossible or unpleasant, trust your Pioneer to go before you and pave the way. Refuse to live in dread and fear.

OK and on Your Way

And I am convinced and sure of this very thing,
that He Who began a good work in you will continue
until the day of Jesus Christ [right up to the time of
His return], developing [that good work] and perfect-
ing and bringing it to full completion in you.

PHILIPPIANS 1:6

None of us has arrived. We are all in the process of becoming. In Romans 7, Paul said the good things he wanted to do, he could not do; and the evil things he did not want to do, he always found himself doing. He said he felt wretched. You can probably relate to that feeling. We all have a long way to go, and Satan seems to enjoy reminding us daily.

If you struggle with a constant sense of failure, adopt a new attitude. Tell yourself tonight, "I am not where I need to be, but thank God I am not where I used to be. I'm okay, and I'm on my way!"

A Reining Ear

*But I say, walk and live [habitually] in the
[Holy] Spirit [responsive to and controlled and
guided by the Spirit]; then you will certainly not
gratify the cravings and desires of the flesh.*

GALATIANS 5:16

Some horses have what their trainers call a "reining ear." While most horses are guided by a bit in their mouths, a few are directed by verbal command. One ear is sensitive to natural warnings; the other is attuned to the voice of the master.

God teaches you what is right, and every single day you must choose. In order to follow God the flesh must be told "no," and the flesh suffers when that happens. You must also understand there may be times when you are galloping full speed ahead in one direction and the Master will tell you to stop and go another way. Like the horse with the "reining ear," you must be willing to follow the Lord in all His leadings. You must learn to say no to self, and yes to God.

The Fruit of the Spirit

But the fruit of the [Holy] Spirit [the work which
His presence within accomplishes] is love, joy
(gladness), peace, patience (an even temper,
forbearance), kindness, goodness (benevolence),
faithfulness, gentleness (meekness, humility),
self-control (self-restraint, continence).

GALATIANS 5:22-23

When the Holy Spirit lives inside you, you have everything He has. His fruit is in you. The seed has been planted. God gives each one of us various gifts to use, but in order to use your gifts in the most powerful way as He desires, you must first allow the fruit to grow up and mature within you by cultivating it. Each time you choose to operate in the fruit of the Spirit it grows.

When you know what God has available for you and you release your faith to walk in it, His Spirit will give you the power you need to produce good fruit. If you are willing to develop the character qualities of God in your life, which is the fruit of the Spirit, you will live an exceptional type of life that is reserved only for His sons and daughters.

Raised from the Dead

*Martha then said to Jesus, Master, if You had been
here, my brother would not have died.*

JOHN 11:21

John 11 records the illness and death of
Lazarus, a close friend of Jesus. By the
time Jesus arrived Lazarus had already been dead for
four days. Like Martha, Mary also told the Lord, "If
You had been here, my brother would not have died"
(John 11:32).

We all feel like that sometimes. We feel that if
Jesus had only shown up sooner maybe things would
not be so bad. Verses 23 and 25 tell us how Jesus responded to these words of hopelessness and despair:
"Your brother shall rise again. . . . I am [Myself] the
Resurrection and the Life. Whoever believes in (ad-
heres to, trusts in, and relies on) Me, although he
may die, yet he shall live."

As He promised, Jesus called Lazarus to come
forth from the tomb and he did so, totally restored.
If Jesus can raise a dead man, surely He can raise a
dead circumstance.

Just Do It!

*Do all things without grumbling and faultfinding
and complaining [against God] and questioning and
doubting [among yourselves].*

PHILIPPIANS 2:14

When your feelings get off track, you need to keep them from running your life. You need to submit your will to what God tells you to do through His Word to you. If you don't feel like going to church, go anyway. If you don't feel like giving that special offering God told you to give, do it anyway. If God tells you to give away items you feel like keeping, give them away with joy.

If you really want to be happy and you want God's anointing on your life, you must be obedient to the voice of God—regardless of what you think about it or how you feel. We don't always have to know why God wants us to do something. We just need to know what He tells us to do—and then do it!

From the Inside Out

Bring forth fruit that is consistent with repentance
[let your lives prove your change of heart].

MATTHEW 3:8

Our society places so much importance on the way things look that appearances often take priority over true quality. One time I saw some big, perfect oranges in the grocery store and decided to buy one. I was sure the orange would taste as good as it looked, but when I peeled that beautiful thing and took a bite, it was dry and bitter.

Giving consideration to whether you are as good on the inside as you look on the outside is a serious matter. Many people are searching for God today, and there are numerous teachings about how to find Him that sound right. As Christians, we need to make sure we are "the real thing" and not a phony. Only then will people see Jesus in us and want what we have.

Light and Life

> *In the beginning God (prepared, formed, fash-*
> *ioned, and) created the heavens and the earth. The*
> *earth was without form and an empty waste, and*
> *darkness was upon the face of the very great deep.*
> *The Spirit of God was moving (hovering, brooding)*
> *over the face of the waters. And God said, Let there be*
> *light; and there was light. And God saw that the*
> *light was good (suitable, pleasant) and He approved*
> *it; and God separated the light from the darkness.*
>
> GENESIS 1:1-4

You see a spiritual principle at work in these verses—light overpowering darkness. Life overpowering death works the same way. Pour in light and darkness has to flee. Pour in life and death has to flee.

Some people fight with the devil all the time, and while they are doing so they are also speaking death to themselves and their situation. Not only can you overcome death and darkness in your own life by speaking the Word, you can be an effective intercessor in the lives of others.

A Hearing Heart

*So give Your servant an understanding mind
and a hearing heart to judge Your people, that I
may discern between good and bad.*

1 KINGS 3:9

Jesus said, "Take heed that no man deceive you" (Matthew 24:4 KJV). The Bible tells you that in the last days deception will become so rampant that even God's select people could be deceived. There will be people who say they are the Christ, the Messiah, and false prophets who will deceive and lead many people astray. They will even show great signs and wonders. It will be pretty confusing to tell who is who and what is what.

You need a great deal of discernment, and the Bible says you can have it if you seek it. God wants you to ask Him for wisdom, knowledge, and understanding. He wants to give you discretion and discernment. Seek God tonight and ask Him for these things. He will surely bless you with a heart that hears clearly and discerns what is right.

Hang Tough!

And let us not lose heart and grow weary and
faint in acting nobly and doing right, for in due time
and at the appointed season we shall reap, if we do
not loosen and relax our courage and faint.

GALATIANS 6:9

Think about Jesus. Immediately after being baptized and filled with the Holy Ghost, He was led into the wilderness to be tested and tried by the devil. He did not complain and become discouraged and depressed. He did not think or speak negatively. He went through each test victoriously.

Can you imagine Jesus traveling around the country with His disciples talking about how hard everything was? Can you picture Him complaining about how difficult going to the cross was going to be . . . or how uncomfortable it was to roam the countryside with no bed to sleep in at night? You and I have the mind of Christ, and we can handle things the way He did: by being mentally prepared through "victory thinking."

Well-Aimed Stones

*And the Word (Christ) became flesh (human,
incarnate) and tabernacled (fixed His tent
of flesh, lived awhile) among us.*

Jesus is the Word made flesh who came
to dwell among men. Scripture also refers
to Jesus as "the Rock," or a stone, as in Luke 20:17,
where He is called the chief Cornerstone. If Jesus is
the Word made flesh, and if He is the Rock, then
each portion of the Word is like a stone.

Instructions were given to the Israelites concerning how to handle their enemy in Deuteronomy
13:10, "And you shall stone him to death with
stones, because he has tried to draw you away from
the Lord your God." Remember that David defeated
Goliath with a well-aimed stone.

You too can "stone" your enemy, Satan, in accordance with Deuteronomy 30:14, "But the word is
very near you, in your mouth and in your mind and
in your heart." Learn the Word and allow the Holy
Spirit to teach you how to speak it effectively.

Fiery Trials

*Rejoice and exult in hope; be steadfast and patient
in suffering and tribulation; be constant in prayer.*

ROMANS 12:12

I've heard *patience* defined as "a fruit of the Spirit that can only be developed under trial." Really, you cannot develop patience any other way. That means the only way you can develop the fruit of patience is by being around obnoxious people who drive you crazy; waiting in backed-up traffic; waiting in endless grocery store lines; waiting for breakthroughs; waiting for your healing; waiting for people in your life to change; and waiting for yourself to change.

Be patient with yourself! Be patient with your own spiritual growth. Be patient with God if He's not coming through at the time you'd like Him to. Be patient with people; be patient with circumstances. Be patient because in patience you possess your soul. James 1:4 says that the patient man is perfect and entire, lacking in nothing.

Above Every Name

*That in (at) the name of Jesus every
knee should (must) bow, in heaven and on
earth and under the earth.*

PHILIPPIANS 2:10

Speaking the name of Jesus and having a revelation about the power in that name are two different things. Releasing the power in the name of Jesus requires a supernatural revelation. When you speak the name of Jesus in faith, His name is so powerful that every knee must bow in three realms—in heaven, on earth, and under the earth!

Think about this tonight: Jesus came from the highest heaven, He has been to the earth, and has descended to Hades, or under the earth, and now is seated at the right hand of the Father once again in the highest heaven. He has filled everything and everywhere with Himself. He is seated above everything else and has a name that is above every other name. His name is the highest name, the most powerful name—and His name has been given to us!

Cast Your Care

Therefore humble yourselves [demote, lower your-
selves in your own estimation] under the mighty hand
of God, that in due time He may exalt you, casting the
whole of your care [all your anxieties, all your worries,
all your concerns, once and for all] on Him, for He cares
for you affectionately and cares about you watchfully.

1 PETER 5:6-7

This passage of Scripture tells you to humble yourself and not worry. Worry is the mind racing around trying to find a solution to its situation. A person who worries still thinks that in some way he can solve his own problem. But only God can deliver you and in every situation your first response should be to lean on Him.

When the enemy tries to give you a problem, you have the privilege of casting it upon God. The word *cast* actually means to pitch or throw. You and I can pitch our problems to God and He will catch them. He knows exactly what to do with them.

Loving Correction

For the time being no discipline brings joy, but seems grievous and painful; but afterwards it yields a peaceable fruit of righteousness to those who have been trained by it.

HEBREWS 12:11

When we need correction—and we all need it at one time or another—it is the Lord's desire to correct us Himself. Whom the Lord loves, He chastens (see Hebrews 12:6). God's correction or chastisement is not a bad thing; it is always and ultimately only for your good.

The fact that it works toward your good does not mean it always feels good or that it is something you enjoy immediately. In fact, correction can be one of the most difficult things to receive—especially when it comes through another person. Even if you have problems, you don't want others to know you have them. Usually God prefers to correct you privately, but if you won't accept His correction, He will use whatever tools are at His disposal. In Balaam's case, God used his donkey! Whatever God decides to use to correct us, we should submit to Him knowing that He loves us and only has our ultimate good in mind.

Ending Your Day Right ~ *169*

A More Excellent Way

And this I pray: that your love may abound yet
more and more and extend to its fullest development
in knowledge and all keen insight [that your love
may display itself in greater depth of acquaintance
and more comprehensive discernment].

PHILIPPIANS 1:9

When something abounds, it grows and becomes so big that it chases people down, overtaking and overwhelming them. This is how Paul prayed for the church—that love would abound. Then he said, "So that you may surely learn to sense what is vital, and approve and prize what is excellent and of real value" (Philippians 1:10).

It is very important to be a person of excellence—to do your very best every day in all you believe God is asking you to do . . . to do every job to the best of your ability. You can't be an excellent person and not walk in love, and you can't walk in love and not be an excellent person. To abound in love is the most excellent thing you can do.

Sun, Moon, and Stars

The sun is glorious in one way, the moon is glori-
ous in another way, and the stars are glorious in their
own [distinctive] way; for one star differs from and
surpasses another in its beauty and brilliance.

1 CORINTHIANS 15:41

We are all different. Like the sun, moon, and stars, God has created us to be differ-ent from one another, and He has done it on pur-pose. Each of us fills a need, and we are all part of God's overall plan. When you struggle to be like others, not only do you lose yourself, you also grieve the Holy Spirit. God wants you to fit into His plan, not to feel pressured trying to fit into everyone else's plans.

We are all born with different temperaments, different physical features, different fingerprints, different gifts and abilities, etc. Your goal should be to find out what you individually are supposed to be, and then succeed at being that. Different is good!

Declare the Word

*I have declared from the beginning the former
things [which happened in times past to Israel];
they went forth from My mouth and I made
them known; then suddenly I did them,
and they came to pass [says the Lord].*

ISAIAH 48:3

Notice God's method of operation: first
He declares things, and then He does
them. God wanted Israel to know that it was He
who was doing the great works in their lives, so He
announced them ahead of time. This explains why
God sent the prophets. They came speaking forth
into the earth God-inspired, God-instructed words
that brought forth God's will from the spiritual
realm into the natural. Even Jesus did not come to
the earth until first the prophets had spoken about
Him for hundreds of years.

God operates through spiritual laws that He has
set in place, and you cannot ignore them. You are
created in His image and are expected to follow His
example. Declare the Word of the Lord in your life!
Speak it, believe it, and watch God bring it to pass.

A Faithful Servant

*So then, let us [apostles] be looked upon as
ministering servants of Christ and stewards
(trustees) of the mysteries (the secret purposes)
of God. Moreover, it is [essentially] required of
stewards that a man should be found faithful
[proving himself worthy of trust].*

I CORINTHIANS 4:1-2

A faithful person knows what God has put in their heart, and even though they may feel like quitting, they don't give up. They don't get out of a relationship because it isn't easy anymore. They don't leave a church because there is some "new" thing across town, or a job because it gets too challenging.

One of the most important lessons you can learn is to be faithful with something until God lets you know you are finished with it. Sometimes God will call you out of one place and put you into another one—but God doesn't change the plan very frequently. A faithful person is committed to doing whatever God tells them to do—no matter what!

Don't Be Caught Sleeping

All of you must keep awake (give strict attention,
be cautious and active) and watch and pray,
that you may not come into temptation. The
spirit indeed is willing, but the flesh is weak.

MATTHEW 26:41

Jesus wanted the disciples to pray with Him, but they kept falling asleep. He was trying to prepare them for the trial that was coming. He was saying, "Don't sleep, pray! You're going to be tempted beyond what you can bear if you don't pray." As Jesus prayed, an angel came and strengthened Him in spirit enabling Him to endure the cross. But the disciples didn't pray—they slept—and proved that the flesh truly is weak.

Your spirit is willing to do what is right, but your flesh will not help you. Your flesh will rule you if you don't pray and ask God to strengthen you in spirit and to help you resist temptation. Your flesh may be tired tonight, but spend some time in prayer. You don't know what tests may come tomorrow.

Take a Stand

*Oh, how great is Your goodness, which You have
laid up for those who fear, revere, and worship You,
goodness which You have wrought for those who trust
and take refuge in You before the sons of men!*

PSALM 31:19

The phrase, "before the sons of men" means that if you will not be a closet Christian, but live for Jesus openly before others, God will store up His goodness for you.

Many Christians aren't comfortable talking about their faith. We all have moments where we don't take a stand for God like we should. Maybe we are afraid of being rejected, isolated, or ridiculed. It can feel awkward to say, "I really don't want to hear a dirty joke. I'm a Christian and I'm not interested in going to an inappropriate movie, or hitting the bars after work. That's not what I'm about. My relationship with God is too important to me."

You should not be a lukewarm, wishy-washy Christian. When you take an uncompromising stand for Christ, God will reward you openly.

Waiting on His Goodness

I will make all My goodness pass before you. . . .
Behold, there is a place beside Me, and you shall
stand upon the rock, and while My glory passes by, I
will put you in a cleft of the rock and cover you
with My hand until I have passed by. Then I
will take away My hand and you shall see
My back; but My face shall not be seen.

EXODUS 33:19,21-23

In times of trouble God hides you in Christ. Safe in the cleft of the Rock, there is provision for your needs. It may not be everything you want, but He gives you what you need to get through the situation.

Perhaps you are facing difficulty and have been waiting and waiting to see God's glory. God desires to pour out His goodness upon you. He has covered you with His hand and is continually moving toward you with the answer. You may not see Him coming, but you will certainly know when He has been there!

Wise Choices

Look carefully then how you walk! Live purpose-
fully and worthily and accurately, not as the unwise
and witless, but as wise (sensible, intelligent people).

EPHESIANS 5:15

Many times you ask God to speak to you, but if He doesn't respond with a specific word, you still have to live your daily life. You make decisions every day, and He doesn't dictate every little choice you make. When you don't get a *rhema* (spoken word) from God, you need to use wisdom to make good choices. He expects you to handle some issues on your own. You shouldn't always require a "big word" from God.

For example, if you want to buy something and wonder if you should, the first obvious question you need to ask yourself is, "Can I afford it?" If not, then wisdom would say, "Don't buy it!" The audible voice of God is not needed when wisdom is already shouting the truth. You need to be mature enough to do what you already know is right.

The Work of Patience

I waited patiently and expectantly for the Lord;
and He inclined to me and heard my cry.

PSALM 40:1

Any time you become frustrated and start trying to make things happen on your own, it is a sure sign you are not being patient with God. You need to practice waiting on God and let Him do what He wants to do, in His way and time. The best definition of *patience* I have ever heard is "to be constant or to be the same all the time, no matter what is going on." Patience is not merely waiting; it is how you act while you are waiting.

The hardest thing most of us will ever have to do as Christians is wait on the Lord. You will undoubtedly have to wait on many things during your lifetime. Waiting is not optional. But it is during the waiting periods of life that the most powerful things will happen within you.

Enjoy the Journey

Make a joyful noise to the Lord, all you lands!
Serve the Lord with gladness! Come before
His presence with singing!

PSALM 100:1-2

So many Christians are headed some-where, but not many of us are enjoying the trip. It would be such a tragedy to arrive at the end of your journey only to realize you had not en-joyed life to its fullest. Often, you think you must do something great, and you forget the simple things that bless the Lord. Serving the Lord with gladness is a worthy goal. He rejoices when your heart is filled with joy and your mouth is filled with praise.

You should be determined to finish your course. But like Paul, you should strive to run the race with joy. Whatever your present station in life, whatever you are called to do, wherever you are called to go, enjoy the journey. Don't waste one day of the pre-cious life God has given you. Rejoice in the Lord, and again I say, rejoice!

Love Is Not a Feeling

*Little children, let us not love [merely] in
theory or in speech but in deed and in truth
(in practice and in sincerity).*

1 JOHN 3:18

This Scripture tells you that love is not simply a theory, a feeling, or sweet nothings whispered in the ear—love is deeds. Many people have the mistaken belief that love is a warm, fuzzy feeling. This is why you think you can't love someone who is unpleasant or even hostile. But the truth is that love is an action, doing what needs to be done in every situation. Developing love isn't a horrible struggle—it is simply being good to people.

Take a few minutes tonight to examine your life and seek God more about your love walk. How kind are you to people? What are you doing for others? How are you treating people who aren't treating you very nicely? Change your direction if you haven't been expressing God's love to others through joy, peace, patience, goodness, and kindness. Don't just talk about love, *walk* in love!

Power from Heaven

But you shall receive power (ability, efficiency, and might) when the Holy Spirit has come upon you, and you shall be My witnesses in Jerusalem and all Judea and Samaria and to the ends (the very bounds) of the earth.

ACTS 1:8

It is possible to fill a glass with water without filling it to full capacity. Likewise when you are born again you have the Holy Spirit in you, but you may not yet be totally filled with the Spirit. Many Christians are very busy doing things for God but don't have enough power in their lives to be what God wants us to be.

Going through the motions and following religious formulas is a waste of time. You must have the revelation that Jesus is alive within you and allow Him to change you and make you a new creature in Christ. Don't tuck God away for emergencies and Sunday mornings. Allow Him to work freely in every area of your life through the power of the Holy Spirit.

A Better Blueprint

We are assured and know that [God being a
partner in their labor] all things work together
and are [fitting into a plan] for good to and
for those who love God and are called according
to [His] design and purpose.

ROMANS 8:28

Notice here that Paul does not say that all things are good, but that all things work together for good. Paul also says in Romans 12:16 to "readily adjust yourself to [people, things]." You must learn to become the kind of person who plans things but who doesn't fall apart if that plan doesn't work out.

Perhaps your car doesn't start tomorrow. You can think, "I knew it! My plans always fail." Or you can tell yourself, "Well, I'll go later when the car is fixed. There is probably some reason I need to be at home today, so I'm going to enjoy my time here." Relax and trust God to work out the details of your life—His blueprint is always best.

Be of Good Cheer

In the world you have tribulation and trials and
distress and frustration; but be of good cheer [take
courage; be confident, certain, undaunted]! For I have
overcome the world. [I have deprived it of power to
harm you and have conquered it for you.]

JOHN 16:33

Life in today's world can be stressful and frustrating—but as a Christian you do not have to operate on the world's system. Yes, you will face difficult and trying situations, but you can refuse to be agitated, disturbed, and upset (see John 14:27).

Even in the midst of your problems you can be happy and confident, cheerful and courageous. Now that's good news!

When you come to the end of a tiring and frustrating day, it is good to spend time with God, thanking Him for overcoming the world on your behalf. Reflecting on His goodness will calm your spirit and prepare you for a peaceful night of rest.

Choose Your Words Carefully

*Let no foul or polluting language, nor evil word
nor unwholesome or worthless talk [ever] come out
of your mouth, but only such [speech] as is good
and beneficial to the spiritual progress of others,
as is fitting to the need and the occasion, that
it may be a blessing and give grace (God's
favor) to those who hear it.*

EPHESIANS 4:29

As a Christian, you have an awesome responsibility with regard to the words you speak. The Bible tells us that words are containers for power—either creative or destructive. You can tear down or build up the people around you by what you say.

There is an abundance of discouragement coming from the world, but you have the great privilege of bringing encouragement to others by being positive in a negative world.

It can be difficult however, so I encourage you to ask God to help you choose words that will bring positive changes in the lives of others . . . and in your own life too!

Give Yourself a Break

And I am convinced and sure of this very thing,
that He Who began a good work in you will continue
until the day of Jesus Christ [right up to the time of
His return], developing [that good work] and perfect-
ing and bringing it to full completion in you.

PHILIPPIANS 1:6

If you find it difficult to like yourself, you are not alone. I struggled with self rejection during much of my life and I have discovered many others also struggle with the same thing. But that is not God's plan. He doesn't want you to feel afraid and insecure . . . or to be consumed with achieving perfection in hopes of being considered valuable.

God is the only one who can perfect the good work He has started in your life, but it takes some time. And during the process He wants you to recognize you are making progress. So give yourself a break and say, "I'm okay and I'm on my way!"

Lighten Up

Anxiety in a man's heart weighs it down,
but an encouraging word makes it glad.

PROVERBS 12:25

If you struggle with anxiety you know about the uneasiness, worry, and feeling of heaviness that come with it. Often it is a general feeling of fear that has no specific cause or source.

Many serious things are going on in the world and you need to be aware of them and prepare for them. But you also need to learn to relax and take things as they come without getting all nervous and upset.

You need to learn how to enjoy the good life God has provided for you through the death and resurrection of His Son Jesus Christ (see John 10:10). So the next time you are tempted to become anxious or upset, think about what you are doing, and find something to be happy about. Have a talk with yourself about all the good things God has done in your life.

Let God Build Your House

*Except the Lord builds the house, they labor in
vain who build it; except the Lord keeps the city,
the watchman wakes but in vain. It is vain for
you to rise up early, to take rest late, to eat the
bread of [anxious] toil—for He gives
[blessings] to His beloved in sleep.*

PSALM 127:1-2

As a responsible adult who works hard at
doing things right and trying to build a
good life for yourself and your family, you may
sometimes forget God is the Master Builder.

It is right for you to work and provide the material things you need in life, but only God can build
you into all that you should be. This can only happen
as you fully yield yourself to Him and allow Him to
do the work.

Only the Spirit can cause you to grow into the
perfection of Christ . . . He has started a good work
in you and He will also finish it, so cooperate with
the Master Builder and enjoy the blessings of the
beloved . . . even as you sleep.

Believe in God

*For we have heard of your faith in Christ Jesus
[the leaning of your entire human personality on
Him in absolute trust and confidence in His
power, wisdom, and goodness] and of the love
which you [have and show] for all the saints
(God's consecrated ones).*

COLOSSIANS 1:4

Faith is the leaning of the entire human personality on God in absolute trust. That means you need to lean all of yourself on God, believing that only He can accomplish His will and purpose in your life. Your only job is to abide in Him through faith.

John 6:29 says, "This is the work (service) that God asks of you: that you believe in the One Whom He has sent [that you cleave to, trust, rely on, and have faith in His Messenger]."

As you are quiet before the Lord at the end of your day, believe and lean your entire personality on Him in absolute trust and confidence.

Acknowledge God

*In all your ways know, recognize, and
acknowledge Him, and He will direct and
make straight and plain your paths.*

PROVERBS 3:6

Acknowledging the Lord in all your ways means submitting all your plans to Him and allowing Him to work them out according to His will and desire for you. He wants you to come to know Him in the power of His resurrection (see Philippians 3:10).

It is a sign of maturity to seek God for who He is and not only for what He can do for you. So as you pause at the end of your day, seek God's face (His presence) and get to know your wonderful, loving heavenly Father better. Acknowledge His power and experience the joy of walking in the paths He chooses for you.

A Time for Everything

To everything there is a season, and a time for
every matter or purpose under heaven.

ECCLESIASTES 3:1

If it seems you have been struggling for-ever with negative things in your life, don't despair. There is a time and season for every-thing, and bad things ultimately give way to better things.

Even the good things going on in your life may not stay exactly the same, because things are always changing. Sometimes changes are exciting . . . and sometimes they are difficult. But Jesus never changes—and as long as you keep your eyes on Him, you will make it through the changes in your life and continue growing.

Be careful not to get too attached to people, places, positions, or things, but always be free to move with the Spirit. Let go of what lies behind and press on to what lies ahead (see Philippians 3:13-14). Reach toward the new horizon God has for you. You will be glad you did.

Deposit Yourself with God

*Those who are ill-treated and suffer in accordance
with God's will must do right and commit their souls
[in charge as a deposit] to the One Who created
[them] and will never fail [them].*

I PETER 4:19

The same as you deposit money in the
bank, trusting them to take care of it, you
should also deposit yourself with God, trusting Him
to take care of you. As you pray tonight, release
yourself and all that concerns you to God.

If you are spending so much time trying to take
care of yourself and make sure nobody is taking advantage of you that you have no time left to enjoy
your life, it's time to deposit yourself into God's
care. You can trust Him . . . for He never fails.

Offer a Sacrifice of Praise

*Through Him, therefore, let us constantly and at
all times offer up to God a sacrifice of praise, which is
the fruit of lips that thankfully acknowledge and
confess and glorify His name.*

HEBREWS 13:15

The Bible teaches that you must acknowledge and glorify God and offer up a sacrifice of praise regardless of what you may be going through.

Perhaps you have been experiencing a time of trouble in your life, and you have been praying and trusting God to meet the need . . . but nothing has changed. While you are waiting for the answer is a perfect time to offer a sacrifice of praise.

It is easy to praise God when everything is going well, but when you acknowledge and glorify Him in the midst of a troubling situation, that is a sacrifice—and it does not go unnoticed. So offer a sacrifice of praise as you spend time with God at the end of your day.

You Can Pass the Test

Consider it a sheer gift, friends, when tests and
challenges come at you from all sides. You know that
under pressure, your faith-life is forced into the
open and shows its true colors. So don't try to
get out of anything prematurely. Let it do its
work so you become mature and well-
developed, not deficient in any way.

JAMES 1:2-4 THE MESSAGE

When life is filled with tests and trials, you sometimes feel like throwing in the towel. You are tempted to think God doesn't know where you are and what you're going through . . . or that He doesn't care. But God permits tests in your life so He can bless you. And if you are faithful, you will see good results.

If you want to enjoy your Christian life and be used by God to help others, you must maintain a godly attitude during the time of testing. So cooperate with God and display an attitude of faith, and you will pass the test with flying colors!

Practice the Presence of God

And the Lord said, My Presence shall go
with you, and I will give you rest.

EXODUS 33:14

This was God's reply to Moses when he asked about the particulars of the mission he had been given and how he could get to know God better. God simply assured Moses that His presence would be with him and give him rest. This was considered by God to be a great privilege. To Him, it was all that Moses needed.

What was true for Moses is true for you. As much as you would like to know God's plans and ways for you, all you really need to know is that His presence will be with you wherever He sends you and in whatever He gives you to do.

So when you get concerned that things aren't going the way you think they should, just remember that God's presence is with you and enjoy the rest He promised to give you.

Learn to Wait with Patience

Do not become sluggish, but imitate those who
through faith and patience inherit the promises.
HEBREWS 6:12 NKJV

Experiencing trials while you're waiting to receive something God has promised you can be very difficult. But when you understand how important it is to wait, it makes it worthwhile. This Scripture in Hebrews tells you that you inherit God's promises only through faith and patience.

When you have trials, you grow—or at least you can grow if you learn to develop patience. God does not change, and He says you receive through faith and patience. So you must adapt to His ways—and doing things God's way can bring peace and joy to any situation.

Patience is a fruit of the Spirit . . . and a powerful witness to others. So when you're experiencing a difficult trial, exercise patience. It is like a muscle—the more you use it the stronger it gets.

Be Transformed, Not Conformed

*Do not be conformed to this world . . . but be trans-
formed (changed) by the [entire] renewal of your
mind . . . so that you may prove [for yourselves] what
is the good and acceptable and perfect will of God.*

ROMANS 12:2

God's will for you is transformation,
which takes place from the inside out . . .
not conformation, which is someone's external, superficial idea of what you should be; nor your own
efforts to conform to their ideas, expectations, and
demands.

Often the world wants to draw the borders of a
box and put you in it. But this won't work because
the box is not God's design.

Most people think you should do what they are
doing—that you should be a part of their plan. This
is wonderful if God agrees, but when God says no
we must say no also.

In this quiet moment determine that you will
not be conformed to the wishes of your friends and
relatives, but that you will be transformed and led
by the Spirit of God.

Live in the Now

*But instantly He spoke to them, saying,
Take courage! I AM! Stop being afraid!*

MATTHEW 14:27

This was Jesus' response to the disciples when they encountered a storm while out in a boat. He was saying, "I AM here for you right now, and you must have faith now that everything is going to be all right."

That is how you should be living your life—with a "now" faith. Today you can have faith that yesterday and all of its mistakes can be taken care of by God. You can also have faith today that tomorrow will be taken care of when it arrives. But don't waste today worrying about yesterday or tomorrow. Jesus is the great "I Am" and He is here for you today!

God wants you to live for today. Worrying about yesterday or tomorrow steals today. But the great I AM has given you just enough grace for today. Grace for yesterday is all used up and grace for tomorrow will not come until tomorrow. So use the favor and power of the Holy Spirit to do His will right now.

Love with Your Thoughts

For as he thinks in his heart, so is he.

PROVERBS 23:7

You make a mistake when you have the opinion that your thoughts don't affect other people. You can often feel the thoughts of others, and they can feel your thoughts.

Your thoughts not only affect others, they also affect you in a most amazing way. This verse in Proverbs teaches you that you become what you think.

If you think loving thoughts, you become loving. But often you think things about people that you would never say to them, not realizing that even your thoughts can affect them. It is virtually impossible to treat people in a loving way if you are thinking angry thoughts about them.

This is a good lesson for you. It is possible to sin in thought, word, or deed, so if you want to be a loving person you must choose to think good thoughts about other people. Learn to love with your thoughts—it will be good for you and others.

Follow Wisdom

*I, Wisdom [from God], make prudence my
dwelling, and I find out knowledge and discretion.*

PROVERBS 8:12

There is a lot of powerful information in this small Scripture—information you would do well to explore. In the Scriptures, being prudent means being good stewards or managers of the gifts that God has given you to use. Those gifts include time, energy, strength, and health, as well as material possessions.

Each of us has been given a different set of gifts, and each of us has different abilities to manage those gifts. It is your individual responsibility to develop knowledge and discretion as to how you can best use your gifts. You do this by listening to the Lord and obeying what He tells you to do.

Following Wisdom is an excellent choice—one that will bring you many blessings!

Accept and Share the Love of God

We love Him, because He first loved us.

1 JOHN 4:19

More than anything, you need a revelation of God's love for you personally. God's love for you is the foundation for your faith, your freedom from sin, and your ability to step out in ministry to others without fear in the form of insecurity.

God made you with a longing in your heart to be loved. And the Word assures you that God loves you. Yet many people mistakenly believe they have worn God out with their failures. You can't cause God not to love you. Love isn't something God does—it is who He is (see 1 John 4:8).

As you meditate on God's love at the end of the day, accept it and express your great love for Him. Then as you go about your day tomorrow—and all your tomorrows—share that love with others.

Focus on God Instead
of Your Fear

*Fear not . . . for I am with you; do not look around
you in terror and be dismayed, for I am your
God. I will strengthen and harden you to
difficulties . . . I am the Lord, Who says
to you, Fear not; I will help you!*

ISAIAH 41:10,13

Notice this passage tells you not to look around you in terror and be dismayed. When you look at your circumstances until you become afraid it is always a mistake—yet that's just what many people do.

The more you focus your eyes and your mouth on the problem, the more fearful you become. Instead you should focus on God who is able to handle anything you will ever have to face. He has promised to strengthen you and to harden you to difficulties.

No matter how great and important or small and insignificant your fears may be, God is saying to you, "Fear not; I will help you!"

Trust God, Not Yourself

*Lean on, trust in, and be confident in the Lord
with all your heart and mind and do not rely
on your own insight or understanding.*

PROVERBS 3:5

When you face times of crisis in life you need direction. All of your human reasoning will not provide the answer—it will only add to your confusion. But God will give you direction if you trust Him.

This truth is sometimes difficult for you to deal with because your human nature wants to understand everything. You want things to make sense, but the Holy Spirit can cause you to have peace about things that make no sense at all to your natural mind.

If you are hurting because of a crisis in your life, you must not become angry with God. He is the only one who can help you. Only He can bring the lasting comfort and healing you need. So continue to believe in the goodness of God and lean on, trust in, and be confident in Him.

Give It Up!

Unto You, O Lord, do I bring my life.

PSALM 25:1

This is a very short but powerful verse. In fact it gives you the answer for your whole life: give it to the Lord.

This doesn't mean you should bring Him just your worries and problems. It means bringing Him your entire existence and everything it entails. Grasping that truth will set you free from weariness and a feeling of wanting to give up.

I used to get worn out preparing for my meetings. I would get so intense about it and work so hard at making sure everything was right that I worked myself into exhaustion. Then I learned that all I have to do is give Him my life and everything in it. As we yield to Him, His peace fills us.

As you pray tonight, give your entire life to God and experience the freedom of knowing that whatever you face—good or bad—He has it under control.

Enjoy Everyday Life

*Go your way . . . And be not grieved and de-
pressed, for the joy of the Lord is your strength.*

NEHEMIAH 8:10

I spent a lot of time in years gone by
learning to enjoy my life. The key phrase
is *my life.* I learned not to covet someone else's life,
but to enjoy mine. It has not been easy and I am still
learning. But one thing I do know is that it is God's
will for you to enjoy the life He has provided. The
joy of the Lord is your strength. You must make a
decision to enjoy everyday life.

Enjoying life does not mean you have something
exciting going on all the time; it simply means you
enjoy simple, everyday things. Most of life is rather
ordinary, but you are supernaturally equipped with
the power of God to live ordinary everyday life in an
extraordinary way.

Live life to the fullest and be a witness to the
power of God that is available to everyone.

Keep Looking to Jesus

Let us run with patient endurance and steady and
active persistence the appointed course of the race
that is set before us, looking away [from all that will
distract] to Jesus. . . . Just think of Him . . . so that
you may not grow weary or exhausted, losing heart
and relaxing and fainting in your minds.

HEBREWS 12:1-3

It doesn't take any special talent to give up, lie down on the side of the road of life, and say, "I quit." Any unbeliever can do that.

But once you get hold of Jesus—or, more accurately, He gets hold of you—He begins to pump strength, energy, and courage into you, and something strange and wonderful begins to happen. He won't let you quit!

You may say, "Oh, Lord, I don't want to go on anymore." But He won't let you give up, even if you want to. So keep looking to Jesus and follow His example. When you do, you will keep pressing on no matter what comes your way.

Live in the Liberty of God

Therefore let us not judge one another anymore,
but rather resolve this, not to put a stumbling
block or a cause to fall in our brother's way.

ROMANS 14:13 NKJV

There are many things you cannot do, but there are also numerous things you can do, and do well. You don't have to compare yourself or your abilities and accomplishments with those of others. You are free to follow the God-given plan for your life.

Each of us must have the liberty to be led of God. We even have the right to make our own mistakes and learn from them.

If you allow other people to become a law to you, thinking you must be like them, it steals your freedom, and it's no one's fault but your own. Likewise you must not judge others or expect them to be like you.

Determine now that you will enjoy the liberty of living in God's will . . . and allow others to live in liberty as well.

You Are a New Creation

Therefore if any person is [ingrafted] in Christ (the
Messiah) he is a new creation (a new creature
altogether); the old [previous moral and
spiritual condition] has passed away.
Behold, the fresh and new has come!

2 CORINTHIANS 5:17

When you are born again God conse-
crates or dedicates you to a new and different use, the one for which you were intended in
the first place. You get a fresh new opportunity for
service.

When Christ comes to live inside of you, an im-
perishable seed is planted within you. Everything
you need to be completely healthy and whole is in
Him. And if it is in Him, it is in you. But it is in seed
form, and seeds have to be watered and nourished in
order to grow and produce fruit.

You do this by reading and studying the Word of
God and being a doer of the Word. Don't let the
seed lie dormant inside you. Be the fresh new creation God wants you to be.

Rest for Your Soul

*Come to Me, all you who labor and are heavy-
laden and overburdened, and I will cause you to rest.
[I will ease and relieve and refresh your souls.]*
MATTHEW 11:28

Just as you can be involved in outward activity, you can be involved in inward activity. God wants you not only to enter into His rest in your body, but in your soul as well.

To me, finding rest, relief, ease, refreshment, recreation, and blessed quiet for my soul means finding freedom from mental activity. It means not having to constantly try to figure out what I should do about everything in my life . . . trying to come up with answers I don't have. I don't have to worry; instead I can remain in a place of quiet rest.

At the end of a tiring day, you can experience this peace and rest by going to Christ and allowing Him to relieve and refresh your soul. What a wonderful privilege!

Love One Another

[Let your] love be sincere . . . hate what is evil
[loathe all ungodliness, turn in horror from wicked-
ness], but hold fast to that which is good. Love one
another with brotherly affection, . . . giving prece-
dence and showing honor to one another.

ROMANS 12:9-10

As a Christian, you are to have sincere love—God's kind of love. God doesn't always love the way people act or the things they do, but He always loves them as people.

God calls you to that same kind of love. You don't have to like everything someone does—in fact you are told to turn from wickedness—but it is your Christian responsibility to follow the example of Christ. When you recognize that everyone is God's creation, it is easier to obey His command to love and honor them.

You must have a loving attitude toward people, an attitude that is filled with mercy, kindness, and sincere love. This doesn't always come easy, but God will provide the strength you need to show His kind of love to others.

Prepare for Promotion

> *Dear friends, do not be surprised at the painful*
> *trial you are suffering, as though something strange*
> *were happening to you. But rejoice that you*
> *participate in the sufferings of Christ, so that you*
> *may be overjoyed when his glory is revealed.*
>
> 1 PETER 4:12-13 NIV

Painful trials are a part of life but God loves you and helps you to grow through them. Each challenge you encounter in life is part of your education process—a process that determines when you're ready to be promoted to the next level.

Trials build spiritual muscle, faith, endurance, and longsuffering. They are opportunities to experience firsthand the faithfulness of God and to show your ability to rejoice as you share in the sufferings of Christ.

Trials come and go, but the development of godly character—your personal spiritual maturity—during the process makes you a worthy candidate for the promotion God has planned for you!

Becoming the Righteousness of God

For our sake He made Christ [virtually] to be sin
Who knew no sin, so that in and through Him we
might become . . . the righteousness of God.

2 CORINTHIANS 5:21

This verse gives you cause for great re-joicing, but the enemy tries to undermine your joy by pointing out you don't measure up to God's standard. That's when you must boldly declare that God has done a good work in you and you are in the process of change.

When you accept salvation there is nothing you can do to make God love you any more or less than He already does. This doesn't mean you don't sin anymore or that when you do sin you can just dismiss it. It simply means God loves you even while you are in the process of becoming like Christ. You have not arrived yet, but you are making progress.

God understands that growing and learning is a process, and He wants you to enjoy yourself while you're on the way to reaching the goal.

Sleep in Peace

In peace I will both lie down and sleep, for
You, Lord, alone make me dwell in
safety and confident trust.

PSALM 4:8

In the quiet of the evening after a long day, it's not unusual to think about and evaluate the events of the day. But thoughts can be disturbing, especially if you faced problems that remain unsolved.

Sometimes these thoughts are not easy to turn off and can threaten to rob you of a peaceful night's sleep. But staying awake and worrying will not change or improve the situation at all.

This is a good time to share your concerns with God and ask for His help. He tells us in His Word to cast our cares on Him, so give your thoughts to Him and trust Him to provide a solution. Then lie down and sleep in peace.

Think Good Thoughts on Purpose

And be constantly renewed in the spirit of your mind [having a fresh mental and spiritual attitude].

EPHESIANS 4:23

We know that when God has renewed our mind with a fresh attitude we can choose to make right decisions. For instance, we know that love is not necessarily a feeling but a choice. We must also choose to think good thoughts about other people. Take a moment and think good thoughts about someone you know, and see how much better you feel.

Thinking good thoughts opens the door for God to manifest His good plan in your life. So if you haven't been working with the Holy Spirit to break old thought patterns and form new ones, it's time to get started. Think good thoughts about people on purpose, and as your attitude starts to change toward others, your relationships will also start to change for the better.

An Ant's Life

But [like a boxer] I buffet my body [handle it
roughly, discipline it by hardships] and subdue it,
for fear that after proclaiming to others the Gospel
and things pertaining to it, I myself should become
unfit [not stand the test, be unapproved and
rejected as a counterfeit].

I CORINTHIANS 9:27

Paul is speaking here about self-control, self-denial, restraining the appetite, and subduing the flesh. Self-discipline is keeping yourself going in the right direction without someone making you do so. The problem is that somehow people have gotten the wrong idea that everything in life is supposed to be easy.

Proverbs 6:6-8 talks about the ant, "which having no chief, overseer, or ruler, provides her food in the summer and gathers her supplies in the harvest." You need to be like the ant. You need to be a person who is self-motivated and self-disciplined; who does what is right because it is right, not because someone may be looking or because someone is making you do it.

Be a Friend of God

And [so] the Scripture was fulfilled that says,
Abraham believed in (adhered to, trusted in, and
relied on) God, and this was accounted to him as
righteousness (as conformity to God's will in thought
and deed), and he was called God's friend.

JAMES 2:23

It's obvious some people are closer to God than others. These "close friends" of God speak of talking to Him as if they know Him personally. Their faces shine with enthusiasm as they testify, "And God told me . . ." while skeptical acquaintances grumble to themselves, "Well, God doesn't talk to me like that!"

Why is that? Does God have favorites? No, Scripture teaches that each person determines his or her own level of intimacy with God, depending on their willingness to seek Him and put time into developing a relationship with Him. Everyone has been extended the same open invitation to "fearlessly and confidently and boldly draw near to the throne of grace" (Hebrews 4:16). At this moment, you are as close to God as you choose to be.

Handling Criticism

*And so each of us shall give an account of himself
[give an answer in reference to judgment] to God.*

ROMANS 14:12

We crave acceptance, therefore criticism and judgment are hard on us mentally and emotionally. The fact is—it hurts! But confronting the criticism and judgment of other people becomes easier when you remember that ultimately it is before your own master you stand or fall (see Romans 14:4). In the end you will answer to God alone.

Criticism and judgment are the devil's tools. He uses them to stop people from fulfilling their destiny and to steal their liberty and creativity. Paul did not allow the opinions of others to change his destiny. In Galatians 1:10 he said if he had been seeking popularity with people, he would not have become an apostle of the Lord Jesus Christ. This statement contains important wisdom. How can we succeed at what God has called us to if we are overly concerned about what other people think?

Realistic Expectations

In the world you have tribulation and trials and
distress and frustration; but be of good cheer [take
courage; be confident, certain, undaunted]! For I have
overcome the world. [I have deprived it of power to
harm you and have conquered it for you.]

JOHN 16:33

If you get the idea in your head that everything concerning your life should always be perfect, you are setting yourself up for a fall. This is not to suggest you should be negative. But you do need to be realistic enough to realize ahead of time that very few things in life are ever perfect.

You should not plan for failure, but you do need to remember Jesus said you will have to deal with tribulation and trials and distress and frustration. These things are part of life on this earth—for the believer as well as the unbeliever. But all the mishaps in the world cannot harm you if you will remain in the love of God.

Faith for the Miracle

And there was a woman who had had a flow of blood for twelve years, and who had endured much suffering under [the hands of] many physicians and had spent all that she had, and was no better but instead grew worse. She had heard the reports concerning Jesus, and she came up behind Him in the throng and touched His garment.

MARK 5:25-27

Surely this woman must have been attacked with thoughts of hopelessness. When she considered going to Jesus she must have thought, "What's the use?" But she pressed forward through the thick, suffocating crowd and touched the hem of Jesus' garment. Healing virtue flowed to her and she was made well.

No matter what she felt like, no matter how much others tried to discourage her, even though she had suffered for twelve years, this woman did not give up. Jesus told her it was her faith that had made her whole. Keep pressing forward—and don't give up hope!

The Path of Forgiveness

And whenever you stand praying, if you have anything against anyone, forgive him and let it drop (leave it, let it go), in order that your Father Who is in heaven may also forgive you your [own] failings and shortcomings and let them drop.

MARK 11:25

"Why me, God?" was the cry of my heart for many years. Because of my wounded emotions from a lifetime of suffering, I lived in a wilderness of self-pity and unforgiveness. It was a huge problem that kept me from fulfilling the plan of God for my life.

Many people are hurting terribly and are crying out for help, but they aren't willing to receive the help God has to offer. It is amazing how often we want things our way. When someone hurts you, you may feel they owe you something, yet Jesus wants you to let it go. No matter how much you may want His help, you will receive only when you become willing to do things God's way.

Ask for Help

The Lord says this to you: Be not afraid or
dismayed at this great multitude; for the battle
is not yours, but God's.

2 CHRONICLES 20:15

The twentieth chapter of 2 Chronicles describes a time of crisis in the life of the people of Judah. They were faced with a huge army that was out to destroy them. In verse 12, Jehoshaphat, king of Judah, offered a wise prayer to God: "O our God, will You not exercise judgment upon them? For we have no might to stand against this great company that is coming against us. We do not know what to do, but our eyes are upon You."

Often we spin our wheels trying to do something we are not capable of doing. It is much easier to just say, "I don't know what to do, and even if I did, I couldn't do it without Your help. Holy Spirit, help me!" If you ask for help, God will take care of the battle.

Develop Your Potential

Whatever your hand finds to do,
do it with all your might.
ECCLESIASTES 9:10

Webster's 1828 *American Dictionary of the English Language* defines *potential* as "existing in possibility, not in act." Potential cannot manifest without form. Like concrete it must have something to be poured into, something to give it shape and make it useful. To develop potential properly you must have a plan and pray over that plan, you must have a purpose, and you must be doing something.

Many people are unhappy because they aren't doing anything to develop their potential. In fact, many of them never develop their potential because they don't do anything except complain that they're not doing anything!

If you want to see your potential developed to its fullness, don't wait until everything is perfect. Do something now. Start laying your hand to whatever is in front of you. You cannot start at the finish line. You must start at the beginning like everybody else.

Quick to Love, Slow to Judge

And walk in love, [esteeming and delighting
in one another] as Christ loved us and
gave Himself up for us.

EPHESIANS 5:2

You are instructed to walk in love. To esteem and delight yourself in others, you have to first get to know others, which is an act of love. It takes time and effort to look beyond the surface of any human being. Too often, we are tempted to judge hastily, but the Word says, "Be honest in your judgment and do not decide at a glance (superficially and by appearances); but judge fairly and righteously" (John 7:24).

Before you judge an individual, you must take time to get to know the real person. Everyone has their little quirks, oddball actions, behaviors, and imperfections. God Himself does not judge by appearance—He looks on the heart. You should follow His example. As the saying goes, "never judge a book by its cover"!

Fellowship with the Father

Even when we were dead (slain) by [our own]
shortcomings and trespasses, He made us alive
together in fellowship and in union with Christ.

EPHESIANS 2:5

Fellowship ministers life to you. You are renewed by it. It charges your batteries, so to speak. You are made strong through union and fellowship with God—strong enough to withstand the attacks of the enemy of your soul, who is Satan (see Ephesians 6:10-11).

When you are fellowshipping with God, you are in a secret place where you are protected from the enemy. Psalm 91 talks of this secret place, and the first verse says that those who dwell there will defeat every foe: "He who dwells in the secret place of the Most High shall remain stable and fixed under the shadow of the Almighty [Whose power no foe can withstand]" (Psalm 91:1). This secret place is God's presence. When you are in His presence, you experience His peace. Tonight, as you pray and fellowship with God, enter the holy of holies and rest in the secret place of His Presence.

An Eternal Perspective

*But the day of the Lord will come like a thief, and then the heavens will vanish (pass away) with a thunderous crash, and the [material] elements [of the universe] will be dissolved with fire, and the earth and the works that are upon it will be burned up. Since all these things are thus in the process of being dissolved, what kind of person ought [each of] you to be [in the meanwhile] in consecrated and holy behavior and devout and godly qualities, while you wait and earnestly long for (expect and hasten) the coming of the day of God? . . .
Be eager to be found by Him [at His coming] without spot or blemish and at peace [in serene confidence, free from fears and agitating passions and moral conflicts].*

2 PETER 3:10-12,14

This passage of Scripture should invoke reverential fear and awe within you. It is a waste of time trying to impress people—what matters is what God thinks of you. You must keep an eternal perspective. The world as we know it will one day vanish and Jesus will return. We should spend our time in this world preparing ourselves to enjoy eternity in God's Presence.

At Home in Your Heart

*May Christ through your faith [actually]
dwell (settle down, abide, make His permanent
home) in your hearts!*

EPHESIANS 3:17

If you are born again Jesus dwells on the inside of you. Your inner life—your attitudes, thoughts, and emotions—is holy ground where the Spirit of God wants to make His home. This inner life is of more serious interest to God than your outer life.

If you want to be a comfortable home for God, you must give up grumbling and faultfinding. The Bible says God inhabits the praises of His people (see Psalm 22:3). He is comfortable in the midst of your praises. You need to wake up every morning and say, "Oh, good morning Jesus. I want You to be comfortable in me today." And you need to go to bed every night and say, "Thank You for all the good things You've done today and will be doing tomorrow." Before you do anything else, invite Jesus to make Himself at home in your heart. Then go forward confidently, enjoying the God-kind of life.

Heirs with Christ

*Therefore, you are no longer a slave (bond servant)
but a son; and if a son, then [it follows that you are]
an heir by the aid of God, through Christ.*

GALATIANS 4:7

As a Christian, you believe Jesus died for your sins and that when you die you will go to heaven because you believe in Him. But there is more to our redemption than that. There is a life of victory God wants for you now.

It is impossible to live victoriously in this earth without understanding your rightful authority and dominion over the devil and all his works. Your position "in Christ" is one of being seated at the right hand of the Lord God Omnipotent.

God wants to restore you to the place of authority that is yours. He has already made all the arrangements; you might say He has "sealed the deal." The purchase price has been paid in full. You have been bought by the precious blood of Jesus. Therefore, I encourage you to go forth with confidence and enjoy the life Jesus has provided for you.

Something Good

We have thought of Your steadfast love,
O God, in the midst of Your temple.

PSALM 48:9

David wrote often about the wonderful works of God. When he was feeling depressed he wrote in Psalm 143:4-5, "Therefore is my spirit overwhelmed and faints within me [wrapped in gloom]; my heart within my bosom grows numb. I remember the days of old; I meditate on all Your doings; I ponder the work of Your hands." David's response to his feelings of depression and gloom was to choose to remember the good times of past days—pondering the doings of God and the works of His hands. In other words, he thought on something good, and it helped him overcome depression.

When the enemy comes against you with depression or discouragement, choose to remember the times God has blessed and delivered you in the past. Hope will rise in your heart and your troubles will seem small.

Submit to Suffering

So, since Christ suffered in the flesh for us, for you,
arm yourselves with the same thought and purpose
[patiently to suffer rather than fail to please God].

1 PETER 4:1

It is important to understand the difference between suffering in the flesh and suffering demonic affliction. Giving up the selfish appetites of our flesh does not mean we are to suffer from sickness, disease, and poverty. Jesus died to deliver you from the curse of sin. But unless you are willing to suffer in the flesh you will never walk in the will of God.

When you get up in the morning, set your thoughts on walking in God's will all day long. You might even say to yourself, "Even if I need to suffer in order to do God's will today, I am setting my mind for obedience." Tonight, purpose in your heart that you will face tomorrow with determination to please God no matter the cost.

One Step at a Time

*For our knowledge is fragmentary (incomplete
and imperfect), and our prophecy (our teaching) is
fragmentary (incomplete and imperfect). But when
the complete and perfect (total) comes, the incomplete
and imperfect will vanish away (become
antiquated, void, and superseded).*

1 CORINTHIANS 13:9-10

This scripture says that as long as you are on this earth, until Jesus comes, there will never be a time in your life when you can say, "I have every answer for my life right now, I know everything about everything." God requires us to trust Him and trust requires unanswered questions.

Like I once did, you may think you know it all! But you know in part, and that is why trust is still needed no matter how long you have walked with God. He leads you. He doesn't hand you a map and send you on your way without Him. God wants you to keep your eyes on Him, and follow Him one step at a time.

Comfort for Mourning

You have turned my mourning into dancing for
me; You have put off my sackcloth and
girded me with gladness.

PSALM 30:11

In Isaiah 61:2 it was prophesied that the coming Messiah would "comfort all who mourn." In the Sermon on the Mount, Jesus said those who mourn are blessed for they will be comforted (see Matthew 5:4). The comfort of God that is administered by His Holy Spirit is so awesome it is almost worth having a problem just to be able to experience it. It goes far beyond any kind of ordinary human comfort.

Let God be your source of comfort. In those times when you are hurting, just ask Him to comfort you. Then wait in His presence while He works in your heart and emotions. He will not fail you, if you will only give Him a chance to come to your aid.

Words of Purpose

So shall My word be that goes forth out of My mouth: it shall not return to Me void [without producing any effect, useless], but it shall accomplish that which I please and purpose, and it shall prosper in the thing for which I sent it.

ISAIAH 55:11

The prophets were mouthpieces for God. They were called to speak God's words to people, situations, cities, dry bones, mountains, or whatever God told them to speak to. To fulfill their God-ordained mission they had to be submitted to the Lord—their mouth had to be His.

If you desire the words of your mouth to carry God's power, your mouth must belong to Him. Usually people who have "verbal" gifts also have some glaring weaknesses in the area of their mouth. If you desire to be used by God you need to allow Him to deal with you concerning your mouth and what comes out of it. When you speak His words they will accomplish their purpose and will never return void.

Choose to Forgive

[Now having received the Holy Spirit, and being led and directed by Him] if you forgive the sins of anyone, they are forgiven; if you retain the sins of anyone, they are retained.

JOHN 20:23

The greatest deception Satan has perpetuated in the area of forgiveness is the idea that if your feelings have not changed, you have not truly forgiven. Many people believe this lie. They decide to forgive someone who has harmed them, but the devil convinces them that because they still have the same feelings, they have not really forgiven the person.

You can make the right decision to forgive and not feel any differently. This is where faith is needed to carry you through. You have done your part and now you are waiting on God. His part is to heal your emotions, to make you feel well and whole. Only God has the power to change your feelings toward the person who hurt you.

Always Constant

*Jesus Christ (the Messiah) is [always] the same,
yesterday, today, [yes] and forever (to the ages).*
HEBREWS 13:8

What is the main thing you love so much about Jesus? There are many answers to that question, of course, such as the fact He died for you on the cross so you wouldn't have to be punished for your sins; then He rose again on the third day. But in your daily relationship with Him, one of the things you will appreciate most about Him is the fact you can count on Him not to change.

You love Jesus and are able to trust Him because He is never changing. He has said in His Word, "This is the way I was, and this is the way I'm always going to be." If you can count on anything, you can count on Jesus never changing. He can change anything else that needs to be changed, but He always remains constant.

The Scarlet Cord

*[Prompted] by faith Rahab the prostitute was
not destroyed along with those who refused to
believe and obey, because she had received
the spies in peace [without enmity].*

HEBREWS 11:31

Rahab hid the spies whom Joshua had
sent in to spy out the land. Because of her
they were kept safe from the king who would have
killed them. Before their departure she asked them
to protect her just as she had protected them. These
men told her, "Stay under the scarlet cord, and you
will be safe. Not only you, but all those of your family whom you bring in with you. But if anyone gets
out from under the protection of the scarlet cord,
he will be destroyed" (see Joshua 2). Rahab obeyed
their instructions and was saved from destruction
(see Joshua 6:25).

The scarlet cord represents the blood of Jesus—
which runs throughout the Bible. Use the blood of
Jesus as a marker over you and your family. When
God sees it, He will pass over you.

Stronger by Faith

The Lord is my Strength and my Song, and He has become my Salvation; this is my God, and I will praise Him, my father's God, and I will exalt Him.

EXODUS 15:2

God does not want to just give you strength; He wants to *be* your strength. In 1 Samuel 15:29 God is referred to as the Strength of Israel. There was a time when Israel knew God was their strength. But when they forgot it, they always started to fail and their lives began to be filled with destruction.

How do you receive strength from God? By faith. Hebrews 11:11 says that by faith Sarah received strength to conceive a child when she was well past childbearing age. By faith you can receive strength to stay in a difficult marriage, raise a difficult child, or prosper in a difficult job. Start receiving God as your strength by faith. It will quicken your body as well as your spirit and soul.

A Powerful Compass

And let the peace (soul harmony which comes) from
Christ rule (act as umpire continually) in your hearts
[deciding and settling with finality all questions
that arise in your minds, in that peaceful state]
to which as [members of Christ's] one body
you were also called [to live].

COLOSSIANS 3:15

People who do things they don't have peace about have miserable lives and don't succeed at anything. If you are doing something, like watching television, and you suddenly lose your peace about what you are watching, you have heard from God. He is saying to you, "Turn it off. Go the other way." If you lose your peace when you say something unkind, God is speaking to you. It will save you a lot of trouble if you will stop talking or apologize right away.

God leads His people through peace. Anytime you lose your peace you are hearing from God. There is nothing more powerful than the compass of peace in your heart. Follow after it. Follow peace!

Pray for Blessing

*Invoke blessings upon and pray for the happiness
of those who curse you, implore God's blessing (favor)
upon those who abuse you [who revile, reproach,
disparage, and high-handedly misuse you].*

LUKE 6:28

A common misconception is that all you have to do if you are wronged is make the decision to forgive and your job is finished. But God also says, "Bless those who persecute you [who are cruel in their attitude toward you]; bless and do not curse them" (Romans 12:14).

In this context the word *bless* means "to speak well of." It is extending mercy to people who do not deserve it. Not only are you to extend forgiveness to those who hurt you, you are to pray for them to be blessed spiritually. You are to ask God to bring truth and revelation so they will be willing to repent and be set free from their sins. Don't just forgive—complete the process by asking God to bless them. He will bless you greatly for your obedience.

The Unseen Foe

For we are not wrestling with flesh and blood
[contending only with physical opponents], but
against the despotisms, against the powers, against
[the master spirits who are] the world rulers of
this present darkness, against the spirit forces of
wickedness in the heavenly (supernatural) sphere.

EPHESIANS 6:12

This verse points out that you war not with other human beings, but against the devil and his demons. Your enemy, Satan, attempts to defeat you with strategy and deceit, through well-laid plans and deliberate deception.

The devil is a liar. Jesus called him "the father of lies and of all that is false" (John 8:44). He tells you things about yourself, about other people, and about circumstances that are just not true. He begins by bombarding your mind with little nagging doubts and fears. He moves slowly and cautiously. He knows your insecurities and fears. He has studied you for a long time. But remember the greater One lives in you. You cannot be defeated if you trust God to keep you safe.

Chosen and Adopted

Even as [in His love] He chose us [actually picked us out for Himself as His own] in Christ before the foundation of the world, that we should be holy (consecrated and set apart for Him) and blameless in His sight, even above reproach, before Him in love. For He foreordained us (destined us, planned in love for us) to be adopted (revealed) as His own children through Jesus Christ, in accordance with the purpose of His will [because it pleased Him and was His kind intent].

EPHESIANS 1:4-5

You understand adoption in the natural sense. You know some children without parents are adopted by people who purposely choose them and raise them as their own. In the same way you have been chosen and brought into the family of God even though you were previously an outsider, unrelated to God in any way. God in His great mercy redeemed you and purchased you with the blood of His own Son, and He has provided an inheritance that is wonderful beyond understanding. God has many good things in His plan for you so start expecting blessings!

Ending Your Day Right ~ 239

Be a Peacemaker

Blessed (enjoying enviable happiness, spiritually prosperous—with life-joy and satisfaction in God's favor and salvation, regardless of their outward conditions) are the makers and maintainers of peace, for they shall be called the sons of God!

MATTHEW 5:9

Jesus is the King of Peace. You are called to be a maker and maintainer of peace. If you are going to serve the Lord you cannot live in strife. God did not merely suggest you not be in strife—it is His command: "The servant of the Lord must not strive" (2 Timothy 2:24 KJV).

Being a peacemaker is a decision, but not all are willing because it's not always easy. When you decide to be a peacemaker does that mean you must submit passively to mistreatment from others? Does it mean you can never give your opinion or let someone know how you feel? Not at all! It means you hold your peace in upsetting and frustrating situations, because of your love and devotion to the Lord. Even though it is often challenging, choose to walk in peace and you will be blessed.

The Price of Ishmael

*Now Sarai, Abram's wife, had borne him no
children. She had an Egyptian maid whose name
was Hagar. And Sarai said to Abram, See here, the
Lord has restrained me from bearing [children]. I am
asking you to have intercourse with my maid; it may
be that I can obtain children by her. And Abram
listened to and heeded what Sarai said.*

GENESIS 16:1-2

Abraham and Sarah got tired of waiting
on God. They wondered if there was
something they could do to help move things along.
The result was the birth of a child named Ishmael.
But Ishmael was not the child of promise.

Like all of us, you probably like to do your own
thing, but God is not obligated to take care of those
things you give birth to in the strength of your own
flesh. There are many frustrated people who have
given birth to "Ishmaels." God did not say you should
not build. But He did say, "Except the Lord builds
the house, they labor in vain who build it" (Psalm
127:1). Make sure what you do is led by the Holy
Spirit and not a fleshly desire.

Facing Persecution

Remember that I told you, A servant is not greater than his master [is not superior to him]. If they persecuted Me, they will also persecute you.

JOHN 15:20

People will reject you just as they rejected Jesus and Paul and the other apostles and disciples. It is especially difficult when you are persecuted by people who are living wrong and are saying wrong things about you. Psalm 118:22 says, "The stone which the builders rejected has become the chief cornerstone." This passage is talking about David who was rejected by the Jewish rulers, but later was chosen by the Lord to be the ruler of Israel. In Matthew 21:42 Jesus quoted this verse to the chief priests and the Pharisees, referring to their rejection of Him as the Son of God.

Even though people may reject you, if you will hold steady and continue to do what God is telling you to do with a good attitude, God will promote you and place you where no man can put you.

Think on These Things

Whatever is true, whatever is worthy of reverence
and is honorable and seemly, whatever is just, what-
ever is pure, whatever is lovely and lovable, whatever
is kind and winsome and gracious, if there is any
virtue and excellence, if there is anything worthy
of praise, think on and weigh and take account
of these things [fix your minds on them].

PHILIPPIANS 4:8

Many years ago my philosophy was, "Don't expect anything good to happen, and then you won't be disappointed when it doesn't." Since my thoughts were negative, so was my life.

Perhaps this describes you. You avoid hope to protect yourself against being hurt. Unfortunately this type of behavior sets up a negative lifestyle where everything seems to go wrong.

Maintain a positive outlook and attitude. Speak positive words. Jesus endured tremendous difficulties and yet He remained positive. He always had an uplifting comment, an encouraging word. You have the mind of Christ, so begin to use it. If He wouldn't think it, you shouldn't think it either.

Be a Doer

But be doers of the Word [obey the message], and
not merely listeners to it, betraying yourselves [into
deception by reasoning contrary to the Truth].

JAMES 1:22

Any time you see what the Word says and refuse to do it, reasoning has somehow gotten involved and deceived you into believing something other than the truth. There may be times when you don't understand everything the Word says, but you should move ahead and do it. God wants you to obey him whether or not you feel like it, want to do it, or think it is a good idea. When God speaks, we are not to question His methods. His ways are not our own.

Proverbs 3:5 says, "Lean on, trust in, and be confident in the Lord with all your heart and mind and do not rely on your own insight or understanding." In other words, don't rely on reason or logic. When God speaks, we are to mobilize, not rationalize.

You Have the Mind of Christ

*We have the mind of Christ (the Messiah)
and do hold the thoughts (feelings and
purposes) of His heart.*

1 CORINTHIANS 2:16

The Bible clearly tells you that as a Christian you have the mind of Christ. Why, then, do you experience times when you feel like you're on an emotional roller coaster?

Romans 8 teaches that you also have a mind of the flesh, which causes you to think, say, feel, and do things that make you unproductive.

That's why it's important to recognize your feelings are not reliable. You must choose to go deeper than your feelings and live by what you know deep in your heart.

If you sometimes feel your mind is lost in a maze of confusion, it's time to give up the mind of the flesh and operate in the mind of Christ. It is an exchange that will lead you out of frustration and into victorious Christian living.

Be a Light in a Dark World

By this shall all [men] know that you are My disciples, if you love one another [if you keep on showing love among yourselves].

JOHN 13:35

You have the opportunity every day to show Jesus to the world. You do that by walking in His love—the love of the Father that was first revealed and expressed in His Son Jesus and is now manifested in you.

The world is looking for something real, something tangible. They are looking for love, and God is the source of all love.

According to 2 Corinthians 5:20 you are Christ's ambassador, His personal representative. God is making His appeal to the world through you.

Do people sense you love and care about them? Does the way you live your life make them desire to have a relationship with God? Be a light in the dark places of the world.

Think Before You Speak

Set a guard, O Lord, before my mouth;
keep watch at the door of my lips.

PSALM 141:3

Have you ever said something that hurt someone else . . . or perhaps caused unfavorable consequences for yourself?

I know I have. For years I just said whatever I felt like saying, but thank God I have learned that words are powerful. What you say has the power to impact your life—and the lives of others—for good or bad. So it is wise to think about what you're going to say before you say it.

You should speak only words of encouragement that will build people up and make them feel better. You get many opportunities every day to put this into practice, but it requires real discipline and determination.

You may have been hurt by someone's words . . . or perhaps you have hurt someone with your words. But you can change that, starting now. It will take prayer and discipline, but God will help you develop and exercise control over the words you speak.

Pursue Your Purpose

But seek (aim at and strive after) first of all His kingdom and His righteousness (His way of doing and being right), and then all these things taken together will be given you besides.

MATTHEW 6:33

Have you ever thought, "What is my purpose in life?" Each of us wants to feel we have a purpose . . . that we're making a meaningful difference in the world.

God has a purpose for each of us, and that is to do right and glorify God.

How do you pursue your purpose? By getting up each day and putting God first. There are many other things we may be tempted to chase after—job position, education, relationships, money, material possessions, and so on. But too often when you attain these things your life is just as empty and unfulfilled as when you started.

God knows what you need and is well aware of your heart's desires, and He will grant them if you will just pursue your purpose by seeking Him first.

Enjoy Your Life Now

I came that they may have and enjoy life, and
have it in abundance (to the full, till it overflows).

JOHN 10:10

Life is a journey—a process of advancement and progression. And as you move toward the future, you must be careful not to lose sight of the now and the enjoyment it can bring you.

For many years I was a Christian but not enjoying life. Then God taught me that enjoying life is not based on enjoyable circumstances. It is an attitude of the heart. When I decided to change my approach to some of the circumstances I faced in life, it made a remarkable difference!

As a believer you have available to you the abundant quality of life that comes from God. Don't get so caught up in your busyness that you fail to enjoy the pleasures God provides every day. He has given you abundant life and your goal should be to enjoy it to the fullest.

Let Your Light Shine

*The grace of God . . . has trained us to reject
and renounce all ungodliness (irreligion) and worldly
(passionate) desires, to live discreet (temperate,
self-controlled), upright, devout (spiritually
whole) lives in this present world.*

TITUS 2:11-12

Although you live in the world, you are not to be of the world . . . worldly in your ways. Because it is easy to become worldly without realizing it, you need the godly influence of spiritually mature people in your life. You also need to be a student of God's Word, which can change your ungodly desires and train and establish godly character in you.

As a child of God, you are to be a light to others who dwell in darkness. People should be able to tell by your joy, the light in your eyes, the way you treat people, the way you talk about people—or don't talk about them—that you are a Christian.

Determine now that you will be a light in this present world. Ask God to help you glorify Him through your choices and actions.

Pursue a Life of Excellence

*Don't look for shortcuts to God. The market is
flooded with surefire, easygoing formulas for a
successful life that can be practiced in your spare
time. Don't fall for that stuff, even though crowds
of people do. The way to life—to God!—is
vigorous and requires total attention.*

MATTHEW 7:13-14 THE MESSAGE

Many people are trapped in a mediocre lifestyle. They seem to lack personal motivation, so they are easy targets for those who promise an easy way to success that requires little effort on their part. They do just enough to get by, but they never go the extra mile.

Living that kind of life is a poor substitute for the real rewards in life that can only be found in being a person of excellence, which was God's plan for you from the beginning.

Learn the truth about God's good plan for your life and vigorously pursue it. You will sense a wonderful fulfillment and the fruit of your life will be abundant and bring glory to God.

Face the Truth and Find Freedom

But when He, the Spirit of Truth (the Truth-giving Spirit) comes, He will guide you into all the Truth.

JOHN 16:13

Facing the truth about yourself is a vital key to experiencing a breakthrough to victory. If you want to continually live in new levels of victory, you must remain open and receptive to the truth about yourself. This is not just a superficial acknowledgment of wrong thinking and behavior— it is an open and honest recognition of your sin before God that brings an attitude of repentance, which is a willingness to go in the right direction.

It can be painful, but facing the truth about your mindsets, motives, and methods of doing things enables you to move beyond your despair and experience a wonderful fellowship with God.

The truth about yourself often brings great hurt, but the truth of God's Word brings great healing. As you continue in His Word, the truth will set you free (see John 8:32).

Exercise the Privilege of Prayer

*Pray at all times (on every occasion, in every
season) in the Spirit, with all [manner of] prayer.*

EPHESIANS 6:18

Prayer to many is just a ritual reserved
for church services or special occasions.
To others, it is something they do when they have a
problem or get sick. But prayer is not some ritual or
mechanical function. It is something you should live
out all day long, just like breathing.

Prayer is conversation with God, and effective
prayer includes thanksgiving, praise, and petitions.
And it works for all kinds of situations, from small
to great . . . and at any time of day or night.

Prayer demonstrates humility; it's a symbol of
your dependence upon God. And the humble get
the help.

As you settle down to sleep tonight, pray and let
God know how much you love Him. Thank Him,
praise Him, and offer any petitions you may have,
knowing He hears and answers prayer. Then enjoy a
peaceful night of rest.

Live and Let Live

*Make it your ambition and definitely endeavor
to live quietly and peacefully, to mind your own
affairs, and to work with your hands.*

1 THESSALONIANS 4:11

The phrase *live and let live* means "you mind your business, and I'll mind mine—and vice versa." And the Bible confirms this is a good practice. I have discovered that the application of this principle aids me greatly in enjoying my life.

Many times we get into things that are really none of our business, and sometimes those things make us miserable. I encourage you not to become entangled with the lives of others. Be a good friend, but beware of entanglements. It is possible to lose yourself in someone else's life, but that is not God's plan for you.

Most of us have enough business of our own, without getting involved in the business of others. So make it your ambition to mind your own business and endeavor to live quietly and peacefully. It's a great way to live!

Just Believe

May the God of your hope so fill you with all joy and peace in believing . . . that by the power of the Holy Spirit you may abound and be overflowing (bubbling over) with hope.

ROMANS 15:13

As a believer, your joy and peace are not based on doing and achieving, but on believing. Joy and peace come as a result of building your relationship with the Lord.

Psalm 16:11 tells you that in His presence is fullness of joy. If you have received Jesus as your Savior and Lord, He—the Prince of Peace—lives inside you (see John 14:23; 1 John 4:12-15). You experience peace in the Lord's presence, receiving from Him and acting in response to His direction.

Joy and peace come from knowing, believing, and trusting in the Lord with simple childlike faith. So just believe . . . and be filled with an overflowing hope that cascades into every area of your life.

Experience God's Presence Tonight

My soul yearns for You [O Lord] in the night,
yes, my spirit within me seeks You earnestly.

ISAIAH 26:9

Have you ever noticed that in the quiet darkness of night there seems to be something special about the presence of God?

He is always with you, even during the daytime, and you can talk to Him anytime, even when you're busy. But during the day there are many distractions that keep you from focusing on His presence for an extended period of time. And by the end of the day you've often experienced problems and frustrations that can cause you to feel lonely and needy. It is then that you can finally give time and attention to the one who is the answer to your needs.

When you yearn for God in the night, seek Him earnestly, and you'll find He will minister to you in a special way. He will provide answers to any problems you may have, and He will give you peace and rest.

Speak Words of Wisdom

For out of the fullness (the overflow, the super-abundance) of the heart the mouth speaks.

MATTHEW 12:34

It is challenging to say right things when you feel totally wrong. When your emotions are running high or low, you are tempted to speak emotionally rather than sensibly. But you must allow wisdom to rise above emotion.

God spoke about nonexistent things as if they already existed, and He created the world with faith-filled words. You are created in His image, and you can also call things that are not as though they are. You can speak positive things about yourself into the atmosphere and thereby "prophesy your future."

Think about the words you speak and you will learn a lot about yourself. As a Christian, you are God's representative, and your words should reflect His character. Meditating on the goodness of God will fill your heart with joy, and the words you speak will glorify Him and be a testimony to others.

Learn How to Fly

*Those who wait for the Lord . . . shall change and
renew their strength . . . they shall lift their wings
and mount up [close to God] as eagles . . . they
shall run and not be weary, they shall walk
and not faint or become tired.*

ISAIAH 40:31

God's Word makes several references to eagles, the most powerful winged creature on earth, and I believe you can learn some valuable lessons from them.

Eagles do not fear or run from a storm—they allow the powerful wind currents to lift them above it. Nor do they waste time battling with other birds. When attacked, they simply mount up higher, soaring effortlessly above their enemies.

When you grow weary of the struggles and battles of the "lower life," it's time to learn to fly.

Allow God to teach you how to fly above your problems. Be determined to know Him and the power of His resurrection. You'll discover that when you're soaring close to the heart of God, you can face whatever comes without growing tired and weary.

Take Up the Easy Yoke

Take My yoke upon you and learn of Me, for I am
gentle (meek) and humble (lowly) in heart, and you
will find rest (relief and ease and refreshment and
recreation and blessed quiet) for your souls.

MATTHEW 11:29

There is a life that is so superior to anything the world has to offer that no comparison can be made. But in order to have that kind
of life you must be willing to be yoked to Christ and
learn His ways. This means you must stay close to
Him and learn how He handles every situation that
arises.

His ways and thoughts are far superior to yours,
and you must be willing to abandon yourself to Him
and discover what His will is for your life.

Give up being independent and learn to lean and
depend on God. Give Him full reign of your life. In
return you will find rest, relief, ease, refreshment,
recreation, and blessed quiet.

Pray About Everything

*The earnest (heartfelt, continued) prayer of a
righteous man makes tremendous power available
[dynamic in its working].*

JAMES 5:16

Driving down the road one day, pondering an upcoming change in my life, I found that I was afraid. It really wasn't a major thing, but it felt like it to me.

God spoke to me that day and simply said, "Pray about everything. Fear nothing." He showed me He couldn't work through my fear, but if I would give Him my faith, He would help me in my situation. I needed it that day for something seemingly minor, but I have used it many times since for all types of situations.

Isn't it good to know that God cares about everything that concerns you—even the little things you're afraid of? Your part is to pray and have faith, and God's part is to provide the power to meet your need. What do you need to pray about tonight?

Grace for the Humble

But He gives us more and more grace (power of the Holy Spirit, to meet [our] evil tendency). That is why He says, God sets Himself against the proud and haughty, but gives grace [continually] to the lowly (those who are humble enough to receive it).

JAMES 4:6

All human beings have evil tendencies, but if you are humble enough to ask for and receive God's grace, He will give it to you.

Early in my Christian life I tried to take care of my own evil tendencies, but I was not successful. God opposed all my fleshly "Joyce" plans. I finally learned that the proud try to take care of themselves, but the humble lean on God and get the help.

If you have tried to make things happen in your own strength you are probably frustrated like I once was. But I encourage you to do what I did—trust in the grace and power of the Holy Spirit . . . and receive everything you need from Him.

SEPTEMBER 18

Plant Your Trust in God

*[Most] blessed is the man who believes in, trusts
in, and relies on the Lord, and whose hope and confidence the Lord is. For he shall be like a tree planted
by the waters that spreads out its roots by the
river . . . It shall not be anxious and full of care in
the year of drought, nor shall it cease yielding fruit.*

JEREMIAH 17:7-8

Trust is one of the most powerful facets
of faith because it carries you through
your problems. Faith asks for deliverance, but trust
remains steadfast while we are in God's waiting
room.

We all have trust, and we choose where we place
that trust. If you place your trust in others or in
your own abilities and accomplishments, you will
one day be disappointed. All of these things are subject to change. But God never changes.

So plant your trust in Him and be like the tree
planted by the water—rooted and grounded and
yielding good fruit no matter what comes.

You Are More Than
a Conqueror

Yet amid all these things we are more than
conquerors and gain a surpassing victory
through Him Who loved us.

ROMANS 8:37

Some people believe the only way to victory is to somehow avoid having problems. But I have learned that real victory is not in being problem free. True victory for the child of God comes when there is still peace in the soul right in the midst of the raging storm—when tragedy strikes and one can still say, "It is well with my soul." This can only happen when you are looking at Jesus instead of your circumstances.

The key to having victory is understanding it only comes "through Him who loved us." If you are facing problems that seem insurmountable, remember you are a conqueror through Him. Allow God to strengthen your inner man. When you are strong inside you can defeat anything that comes against you.

Invest in a Pure Heart

Blessed are the pure in heart: for they shall see God.

MATTHEW 5:8 KJV

Purity of heart is not a natural trait—it is something that must be worked in you. I believe purging and purity go together. Purging is a tedious process in which worthless things are removed while the things of value are retained. Removing the worthless without harming the valuable requires an expert—and God is an expert!

He's like the refiner who sits over the fire where gold and silver are being refined. He never leaves you for one second, but watches over you, and when impurities are being extracted He makes sure the valuable things in you are not harmed.

God was willing to pay the price to redeem you. Are you willing to pay the price to have purity in your life—purity of motives, thoughts, attitudes, words, and actions? Think of more than the moment. What feels good now may bring destruction later. But what seems costly now will pay rich rewards.

Hold Fast to Your Dream

A dream comes with much business and
painful effort.
ECCLESIASTES 5:3

In a fast-paced world that is both challenging and demanding it is important to have dreams and visions. Without them it is easy to become complacent and fail to grow beyond where you are right now. However, working toward your dreams and visions requires hard work.

Those who want to do great things without having to work hard will never see it come to pass. Using good business principles and being willing to work are requirements in the kingdom of God.

Walking in kindness and love is a major factor in seeing your dreams fulfilled. No person is an island to himself—we need other people to help us be all we can be. Therefore we must operate with principles that build good relationships.

As you hold fast to the dreams God has placed in your heart, prayerfully seek His guidance, and He will lead you to miraculous victories in your life.

Enjoy Life as You Grow

You, therefore, must be perfect [growing into complete maturity of godliness in mind and character, having reached the proper height of virtue and integrity], as your heavenly Father is perfect.

MATTHEW 5:48

Being perfect sounds good, but it is not reality. Reality is that you are a human being, and no matter how hard you try to be perfect, you still make mistakes. Your heart can be perfect, but your performance will never be perfect as long as you are on earth.

You are legally and positionally perfect in Christ, but experientially, you are in the process of changing every day from glory to glory. It is a growing process, and it takes time.

Struggling for perfection to gain acceptance and approval from God or others only brings frustration and never-ending struggle. And it isn't necessary because Jesus accepts you just as you are. He will never pressure you to perform or demand something of you that you don't know how to give. So just do your best . . . and enjoy life while you're maturing.

Your Weakness Is God's Opportunity

My grace (My favor and loving-kindness and mercy)
is enough for you . . . for My strength and power are
made perfect (fulfilled and completed) and show
themselves most effective in [your] weakness.

2 CORINTHIANS 12:9

Do you ever feel hopelessly weak and down on yourself? God wants you to know that the only power weakness has over you is the power you give it.

Disliking yourself because you have weaknesses opens the door to trouble that can affect many areas of your life. But human weakness is no surprise to God. In fact, it is an opportunity for His strength and power to be made perfect in your weakness.

As you meditate on the truth of this promise tonight, make a decision that you will not get so disturbed about your weaknesses that you fail to recognize them as great opportunities for God. Stop grieving over your weaknesses and start receiving God's grace, strength, and power.

Visit the Still Waters

*He makes me lie down in [fresh, tender] green
pastures; He leads me beside the still and restful waters.*

PSALM 23:2

This particular psalm is familiar to most people, but have you ever given much thought to the "still and restful waters"? I believe this is where you find quiet rest and strength to face the pressures of life.

One might say that the "still waters" are healing waters. The quiet and stillness contain restorative qualities for your soul.

The still waters are available at all times, but we go there far too seldom. Anytime you feel the slightest urge or need you may visit the still waters, if only for a few minutes. Let everything get quiet, and then bask in the beauty of solitude. Silence can teach us more in a moment than all the noise in the world ever could.

So spend more time beside the still waters and find peaceful rest for your soul.

Cooperate with God's Plan

For I know the thoughts and plans that I have
for you, says the Lord, thoughts and plans for
welfare and peace and not for evil, to give
you hope in your final outcome.

JEREMIAH 29:11

God has a plan for every person and His Word clearly says it is a good plan. But Satan starts his dirty work early in your life, attempting to pervert and destroy God's good plan. He arranges for all kinds of disappointing, discouraging, hurtful, and frightening events to take place. And often he does a lot of damage.

But no matter how much you have been hurt, God can restore you. If you experienced a bad beginning, do not despair. God is in the business of repair, and His repairs are better than new. However this restoration will not happen automatically. You must believe the Word of God and fully cooperate with Him during the restoration process. Look to Jesus, the One who loves you unconditionally. He is the Author and Finisher of everything in you and your life.

Learn the Power of Patience

For you have need of steadfast patience and endurance, so that you may perform and fully accomplish the will of God, and thus receive and carry away [and enjoy to the full] what is promised.

HEBREWS 10:36

Patience is powerful because it frees you from the control of the devil and the circumstances he brings to upset us. However, patience—which is a fruit of the Spirit—only grows through trials. It is during these times that you can develop the ability to remain strong and stable.

Patience is required if you are to see the fulfillment of God's promises in your life. So it is important to develop control over your thoughts and what you say when you are faced with challenging circumstances. It isn't easy, but with God's help you can do it.

Actively pursue the patience of Christ and it will lead you into His power. Then you will be able to accomplish God's will and receive His promises.

Enjoy Kingdom Living

*The kingdom of God is not a matter of [getting
the] food and drink [one likes], but instead it is righteousness (that state which makes a person acceptable
to God) and [heart] peace and joy in the Holy Spirit.*

ROMANS 14:17

As a child of God it is your privilege to
live in God's kingdom. But what and
where is His kingdom? Luke 17:21 says the kingdom
of God is within you. And the Scripture for this
evening sheds light on what it is and isn't.

The kingdom of God is not food and drink—
things of this world—but it is righteousness, peace,
and joy in the Holy Spirit. Many people have the
wealth of the world, but they do not have true satisfaction.

Satisfaction in your inner man is what Jesus
wants to give you. When things are right on the inside, the outward things don't matter as much. So
keep your eyes on the true kingdom of God and the
rest will be added in abundance.

Exchange Your Guilt for Freedom

Not that I have now attained [this ideal], or have already been made perfect, but I press on to lay hold of (grasp) and make my own, that for which Christ Jesus (the Messiah) has laid hold of me and made me His own.

PHILIPPIANS 3:12

Satan delights in trying to make us feel guilt and condemnation over our past sins and imperfections. I know because I was plagued with these feelings for many years, until God helped me see that I did not need to be perfect to be forgiven. He let me know I was accomplishing nothing beneficial by feeling guilty.

When you repent and turn away from your sin, God does the rest—and He is more than enough. You don't need to add your guilt to His sacrifice. Complete forgiveness is completely free!

Even though you are not perfect, you can accept the forgiveness Jesus says is yours. Exchange your feelings of guilt and condemnation for His unconditional love and find complete and total freedom.

You Can Be Free!

And all of us . . . are constantly being transfig-
ured into His very own image in ever increasing
splendor and from one degree of glory to another.

2 CORINTHIANS 3:18

Everyone passes through different levels of God's glory and obviously we aren't all at the same level at the same time. Therefore you hinder the maturing process when you compare yourself with someone else and then feel as if you don't measure up. And this is just what the devil wants.

I call this the performance-acceptance syndrome, and if you want to be free you must overcome it. You can do this by seeing yourself through God's eyes. He sees you as valuable, unique, and precious, and He loves you just as you are—imperfections and all.

If you are worn out from trying to be perfect, start enjoying being yourself and trust God to change you. He knows what He's doing and He will get the job done if you will just keep on believing.

Be Confident in Christ

[God] Himself has said, I will not in any way fail you nor give you up nor leave you without support . . . [I will] not in any degree leave you helpless nor forsake nor let [you] down (relax My hold on you)! [Assuredly not!]

HEBREWS 13:5

You are created by a great God for great things. But you will only see the fulfillment of your destiny by placing your confidence in Christ.

Satan works hard attempting to steal your confidence, but you must steadfastly resist him. If you will just remind yourself—and Satan—that it is Jesus who gives you confidence, you can overcome the devil's evil plan.

Don't let insecurities and past failures steal your confidence. God says He will never leave you nor forsake you, so you must believe it and act on it.

Whatever you may be facing right now, remember God is able even when you are not. He loves you and will show himself strong even through your weakness. So just trust and believe.

Stir Up the Gift

That is why I would remind you to stir up (rekindle the embers of, fan the flame of, and keep burning) the [gracious] gift of God, [the inner fire] that is in you.

2 TIMOTHY 1:6

In your spiritual life, you are either aggressively moving forward or slipping backward. Either you grow, or you start to die. There is no such thing as dormant Christianity. It is vital and essential to keep pressing on.

In this passage of Scripture Timothy needed some encouragement. Paul strongly encouraged him to get back on track, remember the call on his life, resist fear, and remember that God had not given him "the spirit of fear; but of power, and of love, and of a sound mind" (2 Timothy 1:7 KJV). If you find you are feeling stagnant or slipping back into old patterns of thought and behavior, stir up the gift that is within you tonight and press forward in Him.

Character Tests

Oh, let the wickedness of the wicked come to an end, but establish the [uncompromisingly] righteous [those upright and in harmony with You]; for You, Who try the hearts and emotions and thinking powers, are a righteous God.

PSALM 7:9

Have you found yourself wondering lately if the condition of this world can get any worse? Life is filled with challenges that test your determination and your faith in God. Whether faced with the impending threat of terrorism or with simple everyday hassles, the quality of your character is sure to be tested on a regular basis.

You must remember that God tests our hearts, our emotions, and our minds. What does it really mean to test something? Pressure is put on it to see if it will do what it says it will do. Will it hold up under stress? Can it perform at the level its maker says it can? Is it genuine when measured against a true standard of quality? God does the same with us. Ask God to give you grace to pass all your tests.

Fight Doubt and Unbelief

[For Abraham, human reason for] hope being gone,
hoped in faith that he should become the father of
many nations, as he had been promised, so [numberless]
shall your descendants be. . . . No unbelief or distrust
made him waver (doubtingly question) concerning the
promise of God, but he grew strong and was empow-
ered by faith as he gave praise and glory to God.

ROMANS 4:18,20

God had promised Abraham an heir from his own body. Despite his advanced years Abraham was still standing in faith, believing what God had said would come to pass. He kept praising and giving glory to God. As he did so, he grew strong in faith.

It would be ridiculous for God to expect you to do something and not give you the ability to do it. Satan knows how dangerous you are with a heart full of faith, so he attacks you with doubt and unbelief. Keep praising God and give Him glory. Faith will rise in your heart and you will overcome.

Saved from Sin

*For we do not have a High Priest Who is unable to
understand and sympathize and have a shared feeling
with our weaknesses and infirmities and liability to
the assaults of temptation, but One Who has been
tempted in every respect as we are, yet without sin-
ning. Let us then fearlessly and confidently and
boldly draw near to the throne of grace (the
throne of God's unmerited favor to us sinners),
that we may receive mercy [for our failures].*

HEBREWS 4:15-16

Sin is a real issue for most people, but sin
does not have to be a big problem. Do
you know God has already made provision in His
Word for your human failures? Most people make a
much bigger deal out of these things than God does.

Jesus understands your human frailty because
He was tempted in every way we are. Because He is
your High Priest, interceding with the Father for
you, you can come boldly to God's throne to receive
all of His grace, favor, and mercy.

A Willing Heart

*And the Lord said to Moses, Speak to the Israelites,
that they take for Me an offering. From every man
who gives it willingly and ungrudgingly with his
heart you shall take My offering.*

EXODUS 25:1-2

When we talk about a willing heart, we are basically talking about "want to." Without it we will never do anything.

"Want to" is a powerful thing. With it you can lose weight, keep your house clean, save money, get out of debt, or reach any other goal in life you may have set for yourself. You don't really like to face the fact that your victory or defeat has a lot to do with your "want to."

We like to blame everything on someone or something else. But you need to sit down and take a good old-fashioned inventory of your "want to." You need to be honest enough to say, "Lord, I didn't win the victory because I really didn't want to." Tonight, ask the Lord to give you plenty of "want to."

Satisfy Your Thirst

*I am the Bread of Life. He who comes to Me will
never be hungry, and he who believes in and cleaves
to and trusts in and relies on Me will never
thirst any more (at any time).*

JOHN 6:35

We all thirst for more of God, but if you
don't know He is what you are craving,
you can be easily misled. Instead, if you set your
mind on seeking God—if you give Him first place in
your desires, thoughts, and choices—your thirst will
truly be quenched and you will not be led astray.

David spoke of this longing for the Lord in
Psalm 42:2, saying, "My inner self thirsts for God,
for the living God." You are to search after God like
a thirsty man in the desert. What does a thirsty man
think about? Nothing but water! He isn't concerned
about anything else but finding what it takes to
quench his thirst. Tonight, God is saying to you,
"Here I am, seek Me, I have everything you need."

The Spirit of Holiness

*And [as to His divine nature] according to
the Spirit of holiness was openly designated
the Son of God in power.*

ROMANS 1:4

The Holy Spirit is the holiness of God
and it is His job to work that holiness in
all those who believe in Jesus Christ as Savior. 1 Peter 1:15-16 says: "But as the One Who called you is
holy, you yourselves also be holy in all your conduct
and manner of living. For it is written, You shall be
holy, for I am holy."

God would never tell you to be holy without
giving you the help you need to make you that way.
An unholy spirit could never make you holy. So God
sends His Holy Spirit into your heart to do a complete and thorough work. Paul tells you that He who
began a good work in you is well able to complete it
(see Philippians 1:6). The Spirit of Holiness will
continue to work in you as long as you are on this
earth; He will continually bring you into new levels
of victory.

It Is Finished!

*Therefore, brethren, since we have full freedom and
confidence to enter into the [Holy of] Holies [by the
power and virtue] in the blood of Jesus, by this fresh
(new) and living way which He initiated and dedicated
and opened for us through the separating curtain (veil
of the Holy of Holies), that is, through His flesh, and
since we have [such] a great and wonderful and noble
Priest [Who rules] over the house of God, let us all
come forward and draw near.*

HEBREWS 10:19-22

Before Jesus died on your behalf, the only
way to receive God's promises was by
living a perfect life or by offering a blood sacrifice.
When Jesus died and paid for the sins of mankind
with His own blood, the curtain of the temple
which separated people from the presence of God
was torn in two.

When Jesus spoke from the cross saying, "It is
finished!" He meant that the system of the law was
finished, and now all people can enter freely into the
presence of God. Through the blood of Jesus you
can draw near to God! Ponder this important truth.

Grow in Grace

But grow in grace (undeserved favor, spiritual strength) and recognition and knowledge and understanding of our Lord and Savior Jesus Christ (the Messiah). To Him [be] glory (honor, majesty, and splendor) both now and to the day of eternity. Amen (so be it)!

2 PETER 3:18

Grace is God's power coming into your situation to do for you what you cannot do for yourself. Once you understand grace, you must grow in learning how to receive it in every situation. Trusting God fully is something you grow into—the more you trust Him, the stronger you are spiritually. You only learn to trust God by doing it. You grow in grace by continually putting forth your faith in God and receiving His grace in situations that are difficult or impossible for you.

If you are struggling with something right now in your life, ask yourself honestly if you are putting your faith in God that His grace will meet the need. Tonight, decide to walk in His grace!

Signs of Success

And these attesting signs will accompany those who believe: in My name they will drive out demons; they will speak in new languages; they will pick up serpents; and [even] if they drink anything deadly, it will not hurt them; they will lay their hands on the sick, and they will get well.

MARK 16:17-18

Salvation is in the name of Jesus. You are baptized in that name, both in water and the Holy Spirit. You pray and expect your prayers to be heard and answered in that name. The sick are healed and demons are cast out in that wonderful name.

The early disciples used the name of Jesus, and Satan came against them fiercely. The devil does not want you to start anything of value—and if you do manage to get started, he does not want you to finish. He knows well his time on this earth is quickly running out. Accomplish great things in the name of Jesus and finish strong!

Find Your Backbone

*And as for you, brethren, do not become weary or
lose heart in doing right [but continue in
well-doing without weakening].*

2 THESSALONIANS 3:13

Passivity is the opposite of activity. The Word of God clearly teaches that you must be alert, cautious, and active (1 Peter 5:8). The devil knows inactivity will spell the believer's ultimate defeat. As long as you are moving against the devil by using your will to resist him, the enemy will not win the war. However if you enter into a state of passivity, you are in serious trouble.

Passivity can best be described as a lack of desire, general apathy, and laziness. Many believers want the good life but they are passively sitting around "wishing" something good would happen to them. If you desire victory over your problems this evening, if you truly want to live the resurrection life, resolve to have a strong backbone (determination) and not just a wishbone!

The Favorable Time

He who observes the wind [and waits for all con-
ditions to be favorable] will not sow, and he who
regards the clouds will not reap.

ECCLESIASTES 11:4

When the Lord asks His people to do something, there is a temptation to wait for "a convenient season" (Acts 24:25 KJV). There is always the tendency to hold back until it won't be so difficult. The problem is that in order to accomplish something for God, you have to be willing to leave your comfort zone and take on new responsibility.

God expects you to do something that will produce good fruit. If you do not use the gifts and talents that He has given you, then you are not being responsible over what He has entrusted to you. You need to be a person who is unafraid of responsibility and change. It is in times of challenge that you build your strength. If you only do what is easy, you will always remain weak and ineffective. The time to move forward is now!

The Trust Test

Trust in, lean on, rely on, and have confidence in
Him at all times, you people; pour out your hearts
before Him. God is a refuge for us (a fortress and a
high tower). Selah [pause, and calmly think of that]!

PSALM 62:8

One thing you can expect to encounter in your journey with God is the trust test. How many times do you say to God, "What is going on in my life? What are You doing? What is happening? I don't understand." If you are in a place right now where nothing in your life makes any sense, trust God anyway.

You are not just to have faith and trust in God once in a while or from time to time, but at all times. You must learn to live from faith to faith, trusting the Lord when things are good and when things are bad. There is no such thing as trusting God without unanswered questions. There are always going to be things you just don't understand.

He Yearns for You

*Or do you suppose that the Scripture is speaking
to no purpose that says, The Spirit Whom He has
caused to dwell in us yearns over us and He yearns for
the Spirit [to be welcome] with a jealous love?*

According to James 4:4, when you pay more attention to the things of the world than you do to God, He looks upon you as an unfaithful wife who is having an illicit love affair with the world and breaking her marriage vow to Him. To keep you faithful to Him and in close fellowship and communion with Him, sometimes He must remove things from your life that are keeping you from Him.

The Holy Spirit wants to be made welcome; He yearns for fellowship with you. Don't allow jobs, friends, family, money, or success to take His rightful place in your life. Open up your entire life and say with all your heart, "Welcome, Holy Spirit; I am glad You have made Your home in me!"

Holy Ground

And Moses said, I will now turn aside and see this great sight, why the bush is not burned. And when the Lord saw that he turned aside to see, God called to him out of the midst of the bush and said, Moses, Moses! And he said, Here am I. God said, Do not come near; put your shoes off your feet, for the place on which you stand is holy ground.

EXODUS 3:3-5

Moses removed his sandals because he was standing on holy ground. Just moments before, it was ordinary ground—now it was holy. God's presence made it holy!

You are God's tabernacle. Your body is the temple of the Holy Spirit. He lives in you! Wherever you go, He goes. If you go to the grocery store; if you go play golf; if you go to work—He goes. Ordinary things and places are not holy in themselves, but when we go and do them God has promised to be with us. And any place God is becomes holy.

Be of Good Cheer!

Be strong (confident) and of good courage, for you shall cause this people to inherit the land which I swore to their fathers to give them.

JOSHUA 1:6

In John 16:33, Jesus said, "Be of good cheer!" One definition of the word *cheer* in this verse is, "to be of good courage." When the Lord was giving Joshua direction, He repeatedly told him to be of good courage. Without the cheerful attitude that God encouraged Joshua to walk in, he would have given up when the enemy repeatedly came against him, and the children of Israel would never have reached the promised land.

The same is true of you in your daily walk. Joy and cheer give you the strength to carry on toward the goal the Lord has set before you. Lack of joy is why many times you give up when you should endure. The presence of courage and a cheerful attitude gives you the endurance to outlast the devil, overcome your negative circumstances, and "inherit the land."

The Road of Relationship

If anyone thinks himself to be religious (piously observant of the external duties of his faith) and does not bridle his tongue but deludes his own heart, this person's religious service is worthless (futile, barren).

JAMES 1:26

Sometimes it seems that religion is killing people. There are many who are seeking a relationship with God, but the religious community tells them what they need to "do" in order to be acceptable to Him. This religious spirit was alive in Jesus' day, and even though He died to put an end to it and bring people into close personal relationship with Himself, the Holy Spirit, and the Father, that same spirit still torments people to this day—if they don't know the truth.

Religion says, "You must find a way, no matter how impossible it may seem. You had better follow the rules or suffer punishment." But relationship says, "Do your best because you love Me. I know your heart. Admit your faults, repent of your mistakes, and just keep loving Me."

A Step of Faith

A man's mind plans his way, but the Lord directs
his steps and makes them sure.

PROVERBS 16:9

There are times in life when you must take a step in order to find out, one way or the other, what you should do. Some doors will never open unless you move toward them. At other times you may take a step and find that God will not open the door. If you trust Him for guidance and the door opens easily, you can trust that He is leading you to enter into the opportunity before you.

Sometimes the only way to discover God's will is to practice "stepping out and finding out." If you have prayed about a situation and still don't know what you should do, take a step of faith. We can stand before an automatic door at a supermarket and look at it all day, but it won't open until we step forward to trigger the mechanism. Trust God, take a step, and see if the door opens!

Faint Not

When you go forth to battle against your enemies
and see horses and chariots and an army greater than
your own, do not be afraid of them, for the Lord your
God, Who brought you out of the land of Egypt, is
with you. . . . Let not your [minds and] hearts faint;
fear not, and do not tremble or be terrified [and
in dread] because of them. For the Lord your
God is He Who goes with you to fight for
you against your enemies to save you.

DEUTERONOMY 20:1,3-4

A fainthearted person cannot take much. He has to have everything a certain way or he gives up and quits. He gets discouraged and depressed quickly.

What happens when your heart faints? It just gives up. In your heart you say, "I can't do this. It's just too hard." If that describes you, know that you don't have to stay that way. The power of God is available to you to break that fainthearted spirit off your life. Instead of thinking and saying, "It is too hard," say, "I can do whatever I need to do because God is with me."

Prisoners of Hope

Return to the stronghold [of security and prosperity], you prisoners of hope; even today do I declare that I will restore double your former prosperity to you.

ZECHARIAH 9:12

As a "prisoner of hope," you must be filled with hope, you must think hope, and you must speak hope. Hope is the foundation on which faith stands. Some people try to have faith after having lost all hope. It won't work. Refuse to stop hoping no matter how dry the bones may seem, how dead the situation may appear, or how long the problem has been around.

Psalm 42:5 says, "Why are you cast down, O my inner self? And why should you moan over me and be disquieted within me? Hope in God and wait expectantly for Him, for I shall yet praise Him, my Help and my God." God is still God, and if you will remain positive and become a "prisoner of hope," He will restore to you double everything you have lost.

A Word in Season

[The Servant of God says] The Lord God has given Me the tongue of a disciple and of one who is taught, that I should know how to speak a word in season to him who is weary. He wakens Me morning by morning, He wakens My ear to hear as a disciple [as one who is taught].

ISAIAH 50:4

You can bless people with the words of your mouth. The power of life and death is in the tongue (see Proverbs 18:21), therefore you can speak life to others. Proverbs 15:23 says, "A man has joy in making an apt answer, and a word spoken at the right moment—how good it is!" When you edify or exhort, you are urging people forward in Christ. You can actually hold people back or encourage them forward just by your words.

What a tremendous honor to be used by God to lift up another. Ask Him to teach you; to give you words in season that will heal and encourage, bless and edify.

No Fear

> *For God did not give us a spirit of timidity (of
> cowardice, of craven and cringing and fawning
> fear), but [He has given us a spirit] of power
> and of love and of calm and well-balanced
> mind and discipline and self-control.*
>
> 2 TIMOTHY 1:7

In this passage of Scripture, Paul was encouraging Timothy and saying, "You may
feel like giving up, but you have everything you need
to succeed. The Holy Spirit gives you peace and the
power to face anything. Press on without fear!"

You may not understand what is going on in the
world around you, but you must trust God through
it all. You can pray and ask God for answers, but
when heaven is silent you need to keep doing what
God has told us to do and just trust Him. God will
make all the pieces work together for His purpose,
even when you don't see tomorrow clearly. Tomorrow's answers usually don't come until tomorrow.

Not of This World

*Do not be conformed to this world (this age),
[fashioned after and adapted to its external, superficial customs], but be transformed (changed) by the
[entire] renewal of your mind [by its new ideals and
its new attitude], so that you may prove [for your-
selves] what is the good and acceptable and perfect
will of God, even the thing which is good and
acceptable and perfect [in His sight for you].*

ROMANS 12:2

Constant vigilance is required to avoid becoming like the world. You are ex-posed to so much violence today that you hardly no-tice it or pay any attention to it. Many people are desensitized to the agonies real people suffer due to the wealth of violence that is seen in movies and on television.

You may reach the point where you have no em-pathy for people that are suffering. This is under-standable, but not acceptable. You must fight apathy. As a Christian, you may not be able to solve all the world's problems, but you can care—and to truly end this day right, you can pray.

Crowned with Favor

*You have made him but a little lower than God [or
heavenly beings], and You have crowned him with
glory and honor. You made him to have dominion
over the works of Your hands; You have put
all things under his feet.*

PSALM 8:5-6

In this Scripture, honor and favor have the
same meaning. According to this promise
you can have favor with God and with other people.
But just because something is available to you does
not mean you will partake of it. The Lord offers
many gifts that you never receive and enjoy because
you don't activate your faith in that area.

For example, if you go to a job interview confessing fear and failure, you will be almost certain
not to get the job. On the other hand, even if you
apply for a job you aren't fully qualified for, you can
still go in confidence, knowing God will give you favor in every situation that is His will.

In His Time

Nevertheless, do not let this one fact escape you,
beloved, that with the Lord one day is as a thousand
years and a thousand years as one day.

2 PETER 3:8

God moves in His timing, not yours. He is never late, but He is usually not early either. He is often the God of the midnight hour. He sometimes waits until the last second before He gives you what you need. Before He intervenes on your behalf, He has to be sure you are not going to take matters into your own hands and do something out of His perfect timing.

You must learn to trust God's timing. But first your self-will and your spirit of independence must be broken so that God is free to work His will in your life and circumstances. If you are waiting for something, set aside your own timetable tonight. Trust God and believe that while you are waiting for your breakthrough, He is doing a good work in you for His purpose.

Submit to Authority

Be submissive to every human institution and
authority for the sake of the Lord, whether it be to
the emperor as supreme, or to governors as sent by him
to bring vengeance (punishment, justice) to those who
do wrong and to encourage those who do good service.

1 PETER 2:13-14

A godly response to those in authority over you provides you with spiritual safety. If you submit to authority for the sake of honoring God and His Word, you will enjoy a free flow of His anointing in your life. If you rebel and refuse to submit, you will block the anointing. Submission protects you from demonic attack, while rebellion opens the door for the enemy.

Live by the anointing. God has given it to you to help you in all that you do. You must remember that things are accomplished by the Spirit of God and not by might nor by power (see Zechariah 4:6). Tonight, stay peaceful and calm; be quick to forgive, slow to anger, patient, and kind. You'll find that your anointing will be stronger.

The Apple of His Eye

The Lord makes poor and makes rich;
He brings low and He lifts up.

1 SAMUEL 2:7

A perfect example of this Scripture is found in the life of Esther. God raised her up out of obscurity to become the queen of the entire land. He gave her favor with everyone she met, including the king. Esther drew upon that favor to save herself and her people from being murdered by the evil Haman. Despite great personal risk, she was not afraid to go to the king and ask him to intervene, because she had favor with God.

Regardless what circumstances come into your life, believe God for supernatural favor. Despite how hopeless things may seem, God can lift you up. If your life is in His hands, the light of the Lord shines upon you. It is time you believe the words of your Father: "You are the apple of My eye. You are My child." Think about that as you end your day right!

A Kind Reward

*But love your enemies and be kind and do good
[doing favors so that someone derives benefit from
them] and lend, expecting and hoping for nothing in
return but considering nothing as lost and despairing
of no one; and then your recompense (your reward)
will be great (rich, strong, intense, and abundant).*

LUKE 6:35

Has God ever asked you to do something really special for somebody who hurt you? If so, I am sure that like me you found it very difficult to do. Perhaps you have spent a lot of time in your life blessing someone who never blesses you in return. In that case, don't become bitter but trust God to reward you.

Some of us are a little more naturally disposed toward kindness than others. Many of us find we can be kind to those who are kind to us, but we run into trouble with those we don't think deserve kindness. God delights in being kind to those of us who don't deserve it. Actually, kindness isn't even kindness unless it is extended toward the undeserving.

End your day by being kind to someone.

Once and For All

He went once for all into the [Holy of] Holies [of heaven], not by virtue of the blood of goats and calves [by which to make reconciliation between God and man], but His own blood, having found and secured a complete redemption (an everlasting release for us).

HEBERWS 9:12

Under the Old Covenant, the sins of the people were covered, but they were never rid of the consciousness of sin. The blood of bulls and goats could be used for the purification of the body, but it could never reach the inner man and purify his conscience (see Hebrews 10:1-3).

Everything until that time was done to "tide us over," until the fullness of God's time. But when the time came to put into action the plan God had announced in the Garden of Eden, He sent His Son to do the job right. Jesus offered His blood once and for all. This means two things—first, He never has to do it again, and second, it has been done for everyone. You can go to sleep tonight knowing your sins are completely forgiven.

Freedom and Liberty

Now the Lord is the Spirit, and where the Spirit
of the Lord is, there is liberty (emancipation
from bondage, freedom).

2 CORINTHIANS 3:17

Jesus came to set the captives free. You are not free to do whatever you feel like doing, but you have been set free from legalism and are now free to follow the leadership of the Holy Spirit. A legalistic mentality says that everybody has to do exactly the same thing, the same way, all the time. But realize tonight the Spirit of God leads us individually, and often in unique, creative ways.

Jesus wants you to have liberty and not legalism. If the Son has set you free, you are free indeed (see John 8:36). You are free from sin. Free from manipulation and control. Free from competition with others. Free from addiction. Free from fear. Free from selfishness. Free to be who you are. Free! Free! Free!

Turn Away from Evil

Turn not to those [mediums] who have familiar
spirits or to wizards; do not seek them out to be
defiled by them. I am the Lord your God.

LEVITICUS 19:31

This is a serious command! Spiritualism, divination, and witchcraft are all forbidden in the Word of God. Many people, including some who consider themselves to be Christians, participate in practices that God considers vile and evil. God says He will set His face against anyone who turns to mediums and spiritists to prostitute themselves by following them (see Leviticus 20:6). Yet Christians still read horoscopes and consult psychics and wonder why they don't have peace.

God wants you to seek Him and it offends Him if you seek these other sources. No one who does so will ever have a peaceful, joy-filled, and prosperous life. If you have been involved in any activity of this sort, I strongly encourage you to thoroughly repent, ask God to forgive you, and turn away completely from such practices.

Give Thanks Every Day

In everything give thanks; for this is the will of
God in Christ Jesus for you.

1 THESSALONIANS 5:18 NKJV

During this Thanksgiving month, I encourage you to take time each day to thank God for something He has done for you. You are to thank Him always for everything—great or small—but being specific about something each day that is especially meaningful to you will be a blessing to you . . . and to God.

There is so much in life to be thankful for, and that's where you need to keep your focus—not just on Thanksgiving Day but every day.

Fill your mind with memories that are true, pure, lovely, excellent, and worthy of praise. Then express your thanks to God. As the psalmist says in Psalm 100:4, "Be thankful and say so to Him, bless and affectionately praise His name!" End this day right by being thankful.

Cherish the Anointing

But as for you, the anointing (the sacred appoint-
ment, the unction) which you received from Him
abides [permanently] in you; [so] then . . . you must
abide in (live in, never depart from) Him.

1 JOHN 2:27

You have a precious treasure within you as a believer in Christ. The presence and power of the Holy Spirit dwells in you through the anointing. You can depend on it to lead and instruct you.

The anointing makes such a difference in your daily living. Without it everything is a struggle. But with the anointing, all things are possible. Only as you understand the anointing can you know how to release it and increase it in your life.

You are empowered by the anointing for service and fruitfulness. So learn to respect it, be thankful for it, and put it to good use. Let it flow first to you to minister to your needs. Then let it flow through you to make a meaningful difference in the lives of those around you.

Seek to Be Humble

Do nothing from factional motives [through contentiousness, strife, selfishness, or for unworthy ends] or prompted by conceit and empty arrogance. Instead, in the true spirit of humility (lowliness of mind) let each regard the others as better than and superior to himself.

PHILIPPIANS 2:3

Having pure motives and humility are required if you are to fulfill the command to think more highly of others than yourself. In fact it cannot happen without a willingness to be obedient to the Holy Spirit.

To live in harmony you must recognize and respect the right of others to disagree with you, and you must do so with a good attitude. Humility requires that you forgive quickly and frequently . . . and that you not be easily offended. You cannot be self seeking, but instead you must be generous in mercy and patience.

Humble yourself and follow God's instructions and you will enjoy the wonderful benefits of obedience: peace, joy, and a powerful, victorious life.

Pray with Boldness and Confidence

*Let us then fearlessly and confidently and boldly
draw near to the throne of grace . . . that we may
receive mercy . . . and find grace to help in good
time for every need [appropriate help and well-
timed help, coming just when we need it].*

HEBREWS 4:16

Prayer opens the windows of heaven and touches the heart of God. It is a beautiful and powerful privilege that brings many changes in both circumstances and people. Prayer is often the difference between confusion and clarity, hurt and healing, defeat and victory, and even between life and death.

There are many ways to pray, but the best way is to pray boldly and effectually. God loves you and He doesn't want your communication with Him to be vague and unclear. He wants you to come to Him fearlessly and confidently, being specific in your prayers.

Exercise the liberty and privilege of prayer tonight, fully expecting to receive the promised help just when you need it.

The Son Has Set You Free

So if the Son liberates you [makes you free men],
then you are really and unquestionably free.

JOHN 8:36

Are you "really and unquestionably free"? If you allow yourself to be controlled by other people, thoughts, feelings, and habits, you are not free.

People who are free are spontaneous and unconfined, not bound, fastened, or attached. They are not limited by past mistakes because they serve a God to whom nothing is impossible.

The psalmist made this bold statement in Psalm 119:45: "I will walk at liberty and at ease." By saying "I will," he indicates he has made a decision to be free and refuses to be in bondage.

I believe this is what God wants you to do. He wants you to have enough holy boldness to declare that the Son has liberated you from all bondage and that you are determined to walk in the glorious freedom He has provided for you.

Experience God's Peace and Rest

The Lord . . . has given peace and
rest to His people.

1 CHRONICLES 23:25

This declaration of David speaks of a God who has faithfully given peace and rest to His people—down through the ages, and still today.

In your busy world, your days are often filled to overflowing with all kinds of work and activities that can drain you of your physical energy and leave your mind reeling from the sheer volume.

I'm sure it was the same in David's day. The pace may have been slower but the responsibilities were just as demanding and draining. But David knew the secret to receiving the goodness of God was thanking and praising the Lord both morning and evening.

If you feel drained from a trying day, spend some quiet time with the Lord before you go to bed. Tell Him how much you thank Him and praise Him for being with you today . . . and for the peace and rest you are about to experience as you lie down to sleep.

Abide in the Vine

I am the Vine; you are the branches. Whoever
lives in Me and I in him bears much (abundant)
fruit. However, apart from Me [cut off from
vital union with Me] you can do nothing.

JOHN 15:5

In God's order of things, right thinking comes first and right actions follow. I believe that correct behavior is a "fruit" of right thinking. Many believers struggle, trying to do right, but fruit is not the product of struggling. Fruit comes as a result of abiding in the Vine.

As a Spirit-filled Christian, you are to manifest the fruit of His Spirit, things like kindness, gentleness, meekness, and humility. You are created in His image and you can have the same soothing countenance Jesus displayed. Your words can bring encouragement, edification, and exhortation, which are produced by a pure and positive mind.

As you abide in the Vine, seek to bear much good fruit and exhibit His image and nature. Your own life will be richly blessed and you will be a blessing to others.

Speak a Blessing into Your Life

*He who invokes a blessing on himself . . . shall do
so by saying, May the God of truth and fidelity . . .
bless me; and he . . . shall swear by the God of truth
and faithfulness to His promises . . . because the
former troubles are forgotten and because
they are hidden from My eyes.*

ISAIAH 65:16

You can bless or curse yourself with your
mouth. You can bring a blessing by speaking positive truths from God's Word . . . or you can
bring a curse by speaking negatively.

Satan is a deceiver and He tries to bring you
trouble and then influence you to prophesy that
same kind of trouble for your future. But you can
choose to bless yourself. If you mentally stop living
in the past you can begin to think and speak in agreement with God.

Take notice of the things you say, because what
you say does matter—to you and to your well-being.
Say what you believe Jesus would say in your situation, and you will open the door for the miracle-
working power of God.

Live the Good Life

For we are . . . recreated in Christ Jesus, [born anew] that we may do those good works which God predestined (planned beforehand) for us [taking paths which He prepared ahead of time], that we should walk in them [living the good life which He prearranged and made ready for us to live].

EPHESIANS 2:10

The heart of God is a father's heart and He wants you to take full advantage of the good life that He prearranged for you. Yet many Christians settle for less than God's best for their lives because they listen to the devil's lies.

The devil tries to convince you that you've made too many serious mistakes in the past and disobeyed God too many times to live the good life. But this is not true.

We all make mistakes, but God still loves us, and when you repent He is quick to forgive you and lead you back to the right path.

God has provided the best . . . and you might as well have it!

Bend Before You Break

Readily adjust yourself to [people, things]
and . . . if possible, as far as it depends
on you, live at peace with everyone.

ROMANS 12:16,18

You live in a fast-paced world that seems to be placing more demands on you with each passing year. People are hurrying everywhere, and often they are rude and short-tempered. It seems the very atmosphere of the world is charged with stress and pressure.

But the good news is that as a Christian, you don't have to operate on the world's system, reacting like the world. The world responds to difficulties by getting upset, but Jesus said in John 14:27 that you should stop allowing yourself to be agitated, disturbed, and upset.

You do this by learning to be adaptable. It's not always easy on the flesh to give in and do things differently, but it is easier than being upset and miserable.

Learn to bend so you won't break. Allow God's Spirit to lead you out of a stressful lifestyle into one of peace and joy.

Practical Ways for Your Days

*Oh, that they had such a [mind and] heart in
them always [reverently] to fear Me and keep all
My commandments, that it might go well with
them and with their children forever!*

DEUTERONOMY 5:29

God's Word offers wise instructions about
how to make the practice of peace a part
of your everyday life.

First of all, you need to hush. Be still and stop all
the rushing around. "Be still, and know that I am
God" (Psalm 46:10 KJV). The creator of the uni-
verse wants a word with you, but how can He really
talk to you if you're always on the go? Chill . . . and
listen!

Second, you must prepare your heart to receive
Him and to hear His voice on a regular basis. This
requires a reverent fear of God and obedience to His
commandments.

Finally, you must acknowledge Him in every-
thing you do. Make it a lifestyle to be identified with
Jesus Christ and faithfully be a doer of the Word.
The rewards are great!

Be Fruitful for God

*We . . . have not ceased to pray and make [special]
request for you, [asking] that you may . . . walk (live
and conduct yourselves) in a manner worthy
of the Lord, fully pleasing to Him . . .
bearing fruit in every good work.*

COLOSSIANS 1:9-10

We live in a busy world . . . and most of us are far too busy. God never told you to be busy, but He says a lot in His Word about being fruitful. One of His first instructions to Adam and Eve was to be fruitful and multiply. And Genesis 8:17 records the same commandment to Noah. To multiply means to "increase."

God wants you to increase by working with what you have. He supplies you with many seeds—gifts and talents—but you must cultivate and use them.

God has planted some great things in you, and as you water and nourish what He has planted, He will give the increase. So work with Him. You are a special person, uniquely called to bear fruit as only you can do.

Overcome Evil with Good

Do not let yourself be overcome by evil, but
overcome (master) evil with good.

ROMANS 12:21

As a Christian, you can resist the enemy and overcome evil by having an aggressive, power-packed attitude. You can release positive spiritual power that will always conquer negative power. But it doesn't happen automatically. You must take a spiritually aggressive position and stand your ground.

Dealing with people requires a different approach, however. You are to treat people with dignity, respect, and love. For myself, I had to learn how to be a "lion-hearted lamb"—spiritually strong in dealing with the enemy and meek and gentle in dealing with people.

Being good to people will require that you walk in love, which is an effort that always costs you something. But people who are spiritually powerful always walk in love. It is God's way of overcoming evil with good. And it is well worth the effort.

Be a Good Example

Teach what is fitting and becoming to sound (wholesome) doctrine [the character and right living that identify true Christians].

TITUS 2:1

Being a Christian is not so much a matter of doing as it is of being. When you're willing to get out there and shine, you'll eventually swallow up the darkness in your realm of influence.

God anoints normal, everyday people to live supernaturally in a frustrating world. He wants you to be a doer of the Word and not a hearer only. He wants you to stop just telling people Jesus loves them and start letting Jesus flow through you to meet their needs.

The best way to show the love of Christ is by example. People in the world want to see Christians who live what they preach and teach.

You can be a shining *example* of a victorious Christian, and that's the best way to "teach what it fitting."

Enjoy Life Like a Child

*Unless you repent (change, turn about) and
become like little children [trusting, lowly,
loving, forgiving], you can never enter
the kingdom of heaven.*

MATTHEW 18:3

As a believer you can have the abundant quality of life that comes from God. He is not impatient or in a hurry. He takes time to enjoy His creation, the works of His hands. And He wants you to do the same.

Joy is available to you if you know how to tap into it. I have learned that simplicity brings joy and complication blocks it. Instead of getting entangled with the complications of religion, you must return to the simplicity of believing and maintaining a Father/child relationship.

God wants you to approach life with childlike faith. He wants you to grow up in your behavior but remain childlike in your attitude of trust and dependence on Him.

Living your life with the simplicity of a child will change your whole outlook in a most amazing way.

You Can Be Molded into His Image

*For those whom He foreknew . . . He also destined
from the beginning . . . to be molded into the image
of His Son [and share inwardly His likeness].*

Your goal as a Christian is to become Christlike. The Bible says you are an ambassador of Christ and that He personally makes His appeal to the world through you. The only way you can ever properly represent Jesus to the world is to let His character show through your attitudes and actions. This can only happen through divine transformation, and that's exactly what God had in mind from the beginning of time.

God predestined you to be molded into His image. He said, "Behold, as the clay is in the potter's hand, so are you in My hand" (Jeremiah 18:6). In your relationship with God, you are the clay and He is the potter, and you must never forget that. Become pliable in the Master Potter's hands as He molds you into a vessel He can use to change many lives.

Let Go of All Anger

*When angry, do not sin; do not ever let your wrath
(your exasperation, your fury or indignation) last
until the sun goes down. Leave no [such] room or
foothold for the devil [give no opportunity to him].*

EPHESIANS 4:26-27

Everyone has anger from time to time, and understanding it and knowing how to handle it properly is important.

Anger begins as a feeling and then manifests itself in words and actions. You feel something, and it causes you to do or say something. Anger is not necessarily always sin—however, what you choose to do with anger directly determines your quality of life.

All anger has the same effect on your life. It upsets you, causing you to feel pressure. Keeping anger locked inside can even be dangerous to your health. So you must take responsibility for your anger and learn to deal with it.

If you struggle with anger, ask God to help you process it and bring it to closure. You can be bitter or better—the choice is yours!

Discover the Cure for the Insecure

May Christ through your faith [actually] dwell
(settle down, abide, make His permanent home)
in your hearts! May you be rooted deep in
love and founded securely on love.

EPHESIANS 3:17

The world is full of insecure people. In fact an article I once read described insecurity as a psychological disturbance of epidemic proportions. So is there a cure for the insecure?

The answer is yes. The Word of God says that you can be secure through Jesus Christ. As a believer, you will find our Lord Jesus Christ is the only lasting cure for insecurity. He took all of your insecurities upon himself at Calvary. His death and resurrection purchased your freedom from the pain and behavior patterns produced by a lifetime of insecurity.

All the areas of your life that are out of order can be reconciled through Jesus and the work He accomplished on the cross. Start believing it—and remember: "The Lord your God is with you wherever you go" (Joshua 1:9).

Receive the Goodness of God

Whatever is good and perfect comes to us from
God above, who created all heaven's lights. Unlike
them, he never changes or casts shifting shadows.

JAMES 1:17 NLT

There was a time when I believed God was good—but I wasn't sure He would be good to *me*. I was afraid I hadn't been good enough to receive His goodness. But He taught me that our inability to do everything right doesn't cancel out His goodness. Thankfully, receiving God's goodness is based on His righteousness, not ours.

I now keep a journal to list all the good things God does for me. This gives me a greater appreciation for His provisions and confirms His constant flow of blessings in my life.

God is good, and His goodness radiates from Him like heat radiates from the sun. And those rays of goodness reach out to you every day. Make a list of all His blessings, and you'll have no doubt about the good and perfect gifts that come from Him.

Exercise Moderation

*I discipline my body . . . training it
to do what it should.*

1 CORINTHIANS 9:27 NLT

The holidays are upon us again! From the traditional American observation of Thanksgiving and the celebration of our Savior's birth to the first day of the brand-new year, the holidays present us with ample opportunities to celebrate . . . and to eat.

For many who tend to overeat and gain weight, it can be a challenging time. But it doesn't have to be that way. With God's help you can discipline yourself instead of giving in to all your food desires.

I'm not suggesting you stay away from the Thanksgiving dinner, the Christmas Brunch, or the New Year's gathering. It's not necessary to sacrifice all your seasonal favorites, but it is important to exercise moderation. Pray and ask God to help you focus on the season instead of the food . . . and receive a double blessing.

Give Thanks with a Grateful Heart

Bless (affectionately, gratefully praise) the Lord, O my soul, and forget not [one of] all His benefits.

PSALM 103:2

In a few days you will be celebrating a day set aside to give thanks to God for all His blessings. You are probably already making plans and preparations for this special day. As you prepare, begin to think about all the wonderful things God has given you this year.

It might be a good idea to make a list. You won't be able to think of all your blessings, but you will remember enough to humble you and fill you with gratitude.

Then on Thanksgiving Day don't allow the activities that are attached to the traditions of Thanksgiving to crowd out the real purpose of the day. Talk about the goodness of God and share about one or two special blessings.

Don't forget to thank God for life, family, friends, and provisions. Most important, express your special thanks to Him.

Get Ready for the Joy

*Weeping may endure for a night, but joy
comes in the morning.*

PSALM 30:5

Does your happiness depend on everything in your life being just right? If you
think you can't be happy until all your circumstances are right, you will never be happy. We all experience times in life when we feel down for various
reasons, but you can't allow your circumstances to
control your emotions.

Satan seeks to fill your mind with negative
thoughts and emotions that cause you to feel down
because He is a discourager. But Jesus is your encour-
ager and He came to lift you up. He came to give you
righteousness, joy, and all the things that cause you to
feel "up"!

We all experience times of frustration and distress over unfulfilled hopes and dreams. When things
don't go according to your plans, it's normal to feel
disappointment. Things may make you feel sad tem-
porarily, but when you know that weeping only lasts
for a time and then comes joy, it makes everything
better.

Be Happy

Blessed (happy, fortunate, to be envied) is he who has forgiveness of his transgression continually exercised upon him, whose sin is covered. Blessed (happy, fortunate, to be envied) is the man to whom the Lord imputes no iniquity and in whose spirit there is no deceit.

PSALM 32:1-2

God created you to live the abundant life He died to provide for you—and knowing your sins are completely forgiven should be enough to keep you happy.

But many Christians operate in the works of the flesh trying to serve God. They spend so much time trying to be good they miss the blessing of simple prayer and fellowship with God.

God is not seeking your "works." He wants you! You must remind yourself that you have been made righteous through the death and resurrection of Jesus . . . and you can add nothing to that.

As a Christian, you are no longer your own—you were purchased by the blood of Jesus. He paid the ultimate price for your happiness, so enjoy it.

Trust the Unchanging Rock

Jesus Christ (the Messiah) is [always] the same,
yesterday, today, [yes] and forever.

HEBREWS 13:8

Feelings are emotions that are always changing, so you cannot depend on them. As a follower of Christ, you must learn to live by truth and wisdom, not by feelings and emotions.

1 Corinthians 10:4 refers to Jesus as the Rock. An important part of His nature is His emotional maturity, which includes unchanging stability. During His time on earth, Jesus did not allow himself to be led around by His emotions. He was led by the Spirit even though He was subject to all the same feelings we experience in our daily lives. Jesus was always the same.

And He is still the same . . . and will be forever. You can safely put your trust in Him tonight, knowing He will not change, but will help you develop the same kind of emotional maturity and stability that marked His own life.

Make Excellence a Habit

The righteous man walks in his integrity.

PROVERBS 20:7

Integrity is defined as "a firm adherence to a code or standard of values; soundness." As a Christian, your standards should be much higher than those of the world. What would an integrity check reveal about you? It's something to think about.

People of integrity are committed to a life of excellence—seeking to be better or to go beyond what is normally expected of them. Having integrity means you do the right thing even when nobody is looking . . . and you keep your word even if it costs you something.

I encourage you to make excellence a habit, by following the example of Jesus, our standard of integrity. As God's representative, you are called to show the world what He is like—and you may be the only Bible some people read.

Seek God's Wisdom

If any of you is deficient in wisdom, let him ask of the giving God [Who gives] to everyone liberally and ungrudgingly, without reproaching or faultfinding, and it will be given him.

JAMES 1:5

If things seem so complicated that you're no longer able to enjoy life as God intended, it's time to seek God's wisdom. In all things, God wants you to acknowledge and seek Him, use wisdom, and make the best decisions you know how to make.

Through a simple prayer from wherever you are, you can ask God for wisdom about any situation you face. Before you commit to participating in certain activities, buying things, or being involved with other people, check with God. If you have peace about it, then proceed. But if you don't feel right about it, wait.

Seek God's wisdom and make decisions based on what you sense in your spirit. Then move forward, believing that God will bless you because you acknowledge Him in your decisions.

Listen for God's Voice

My sheep hear My voice, and I know
them, and they follow me.

JOHN 10:27 NKJV

One of the questions that people most frequently ask me is "How can I know specifically what God wants me to do?"

Of all the ways God speaks to you, He most frequently uses peace, wisdom, and the voice of our conscience—that still, small voice inside your spirit that tells you what is right and wrong. The Holy Spirit, who dwells in believers, speaks to your spirit what He wants you to do. Your spirit then communicates the message to your mind, and your mind is then enlightened on what action to take.

God is speaking to you! And He wants to direct you in every area of your life. So delight yourself in Him, follow after peace, and obey the voice of your conscience.

You Reap What You Sow

Whatsoever a man soweth, that shall he also reap.

GALATIANS 6:7 KJV

As God's representative here on earth, your purpose is to do right and glorify God. When you do right, you bring God glory by manifesting His excellence in a tangible way.

One way you can bring Him glory is in the way you treat people. There are many practical ways you can be a blessing to others. You can build others up by giving them a compliment. You can express your appreciation and acknowledge people by giving them a pat on the back or writing them a note of encouragement.

You can also take advantage of opportunities to listen to people and lend a helping hand when they need it. You can believe the best of others and offer forgiveness to those who have offended you.

I encourage you to treat everybody with love and respect. You will not only glorify God, you will also receive blessings by reaping what you sow.

Develop the Mind of the Spirit

The mind of the flesh . . . [is sense and reason
without the Holy Spirit] . . . but the mind of the
[Holy] Spirit is life and [soul] peace.

ROMANS 8:6

As a young Christian I was always trying to figure out the "why" behind everything and planning excessively for what was ahead. But one day God required me to give it up. He showed me that reasoning is the opposite of trust.

The Bible tells us that the mind of the flesh is sense and reason without the Holy Spirit. It is being hostile to God and refusing to submit to His ways. But the mind of the Spirit is life and soul peace.

If you want to be free of trying to figure everything out, you can develop the mind of the Spirit by constantly renewing your mind with the Word. Little by little, the Word will wash away the wrong thinking and replace it with truth . . . follow that truth instead of your own ability to reason things out and you'll have new life and peace.

Get Away with God

*Are you tired? Worn out? Burned out on religion?
Come to me. Get away with me and you'll recover
your life. I'll show you how to take a real rest. Walk
with me and work with me—watch how I do it.
Learn the unforced rhythms of grace. I won't lay
anything heavy or ill-fitting on you. Keep company
with me and you'll learn to live freely and lightly.*

MATTHEW 11:28-30 THE MESSAGE

That sounds good, doesn't it? I've had enough "heavy stuff" in my life, and I want to enjoy freedom. When you are overloaded with the cares of life you need some help. Your mind needs rest from worrying, your emotions need rest from being upset, and your will needs a rest from stubbornness and rebellion. So you need to be humble enough to call out to God and say, "I need help!"

Your beginning doesn't have to dictate your ending. Get God involved in every area of your life and allow Him to lead you into "real rest."

Still the Storm

And He arose and rebuked the wind and said to the sea, Hush now! Be still (muzzled)! And the wind ceased (sank to rest as if exhausted by its beating) and there was [immediately] a great calm (a perfect peacefulness).

MARK 4:39

When Jesus and the disciples were crossing the lake and a storm arose, the disciples panicked. They were as stormy inside as the tempest around them. But when Jesus spoke "Peace, be still" out of that well of peace within Him, immediately the wind and the waves became calm.

You cannot rebuke the storms in your life if you have a storm raging on the inside of you. We maintain peace by trusting God. Don't be mad at God because you didn't get what you prayed for. Don't be mad at God because your friend got a promotion at work and you didn't. Don't be mad at God because your friend got married and you're still single. Trusting God in every situation is the only way to still the storm within.

Dreams and Visions

Where there is no vision [no redemptive revelation of God], the people perish.

PROVERBS 29:18

The Israelites had no positive vision for their lives—no dreams. They knew where they came from, but they did not know where they were going. Everything was based on what they had already seen and could see. They did not know how to see with "the eye of faith."

Jesus came to open the prison doors and set the captives free. You will only begin to progress when you start to believe you can experience freedom. You must have a positive vision for your life—a vision for a future that is not determined by your past or even your present circumstances.

Exercise your faith tonight and take a positive look at the possibilities God has planned for you. Begin to "call those things that be not as though they are" (see Romans 4:17). Think and speak about your future in a positive way, according to what God has placed in your heart.

An Inheritance of Peace

Peace I leave with you; My [own] peace I now
give and bequeath to you. Not as the world gives
do I give to you. Do not let your hearts be
troubled, neither let them be afraid.

JOHN 14:27

The word *bequeath* in this verse is a term used in the execution of wills. In preparation for death, people usually bequeath their possessions, especially those things of value, as a blessing to those they love who are left behind.

Jesus knew He was about to pass from this world and He wanted to leave us something. He could have left any number of good things, like His power and His name, and He did. But He also left us His peace.

You don't leave junk for people you love—you leave them the best you have. Jesus had a special kind of peace that surpassed anything mankind had ever known. He knew it was one of the most precious things He could give. Ask for and receive your inheritance tonight!

A Calm Delight

You will show me the path of life; in
Your presence is fullness of joy.

PSALM 16:11

When you consider joy, you may immediately think about one of those bubbly people you know who is "up" all of the time, and perhaps you are not like that. I'm not like that either. But for those of us who tend to be more serious, it is important that we also learn how to have fun, to cut loose, and lighten up a little.

What is joy and what is joy based on? *Joy* is defined as "a shout; a proclamation that can manifest in singing; a calm delight." Your joy is not to be based on your circumstances. Happiness may be based on what is happening to you, but not joy. Joy—a fruit of the Spirit—is like a deep well on the inside of you. It is not the fruit of your circumstance. No matter what you are facing in life, you can have joy in the midst of it. Learn to abide in the midst of a calm delight.

His Words

But the Lord said to me, Say not, I am only a
youth; for you shall go to all to whom I shall send
you, and whatever I command you, you shall speak.
Be not afraid of them [their faces], for I am with you
to deliver you, says the Lord. Then the Lord put forth
His hand and touched my mouth. And the Lord said
to me, Behold, I have put My words in your mouth.

JEREMIAH 1:7-9

God called Jeremiah as "a prophet to the nations," and He had to straighten out Jeremiah's mouth before He could use him.

It is no different with you. You must understand that when God calls you to do something, you should not say you cannot do it. If God says you can, then you can! So often we speak out of our insecurities, or we verbalize what others have said about us, or what the devil has told us. Make a decision tonight that from now on you will say about yourself what God says about you.

A Deeper Walk

When He had stopped speaking, He said to Simon
(Peter), Put out into the deep [water], and
lower your nets for a haul.

LUKE 5:4

Faith is deposited in the spirit. Romans 12:3 says that every man is given a measure of faith. Faith is a force that comes out of the spirit, and it can accomplish great things, but faith must be released to be of value.

If you have faith in your heart to step out and do something but begin to take counsel with your mind, negative, doubtful, and unbelieving thoughts can talk you right out of what faith is telling you. If your head believes the opposite of what your spirit is telling you, you must go deeper.

Do you want a haul of blessings in your life? If the answer is yes, then like the disciples, you have to leave the shallow places of your own soul—what you think and feel—for the deeper life in God . . . what you know down deep inside.

By His Spirit

Not by might, nor by power, but by My Spirit [of Whom the oil is a symbol], says the Lord of hosts.

ZECHARIAH 4:6

It is only by the power of the Holy Spirit living inside you that you can have true success in life. In your own strength you simply become tired and frustrated. But allowing the Holy Spirit to work through you brings contentment and deep joy to your life. You need to give your problems to God and spend your time doing something for those around you who are hurting. Through the anointing of the Holy Spirit, you can do anything.

Real joy comes from being an empty vessel for God's use and glory. At the close of this day, let Him choose where He's going to take you, what He's going to do with you, and when He's going to do it—without arguing about it. It's one thing to be willing to do *everything* for the glory of God (1 Corinthians 10:31); it's another thing entirely to be willing to do *anything* for Him.

Exercise Self-Control

And in [exercising] knowledge [develop] self-control, and in [exercising] self-control [develop] steadfastness (patience, endurance), and in [exercising] steadfastness [develop] godliness [piety].

2 PETER 1:6

Jesus not only commanded you to not allow your heart to be troubled and afraid, He also said, "[Stop allowing yourselves to be agitated and disturbed; and do not permit yourselves to be fearful and intimidated and cowardly and unsettled]" (John 14:27).

You can choose not to get upset. If you are around someone whose good opinion you value, it's amazing how much easier it can be to control yourself. It's much harder to stay calm when you're around people you don't have a need to impress.

When you start to get upset, remember only one thing will put an end to it. *You* have to stop it, you must exercise self-control. You have to get hold of yourself and say, "No, I'm not getting upset." You need to remember that everywhere you go, you are a witness for the One you serve and love.

But for the Grace . . .

*Though I formerly blasphemed and persecuted and
was shamefully and outrageously and aggressively
insulting [to Him], nevertheless, I obtained mercy
because I had acted out of ignorance in unbelief.*

1 TIMOTHY 1:13

In this Scripture Paul speaks of his past
when he aggressively and vehemently persecuted Christians and had them stoned, beaten, and
jailed. His ignorance was so great he actually believed
God was pleased. But when Jesus appeared to him on
the Damascus road, the scales fell from his eyes and
he saw Truth (see Acts 9). Paul realized at that moment that he was a sinner and God's grace became a
living reality in his life.

On the cross, Jesus said, "Father, forgive them,
for they know not what they do" (Luke 23:34).
Stephen, while being stoned, said, "Lord, fix not this
sin upon them!" (Acts 7:60). What did Jesus, Paul,
and Stephen have in common? They proclaimed
God's grace to people who were deceived and ignorant. Recall how much mercy and grace God has
given you; surely you can extend His grace to others.

The Blame Game

*And the man said, The woman whom You gave to
be with me—she gave me [fruit] from the tree, and I
ate. . . . And the woman said, The serpent beguiled
(cheated, outwitted, and deceived) me, and I ate.*

The problem has been manifesting since the beginning of time. When confronted with their sin in the Garden of Eden, Adam and Eve blamed each other, God, and the devil. This unwillingness to take personal responsibility by trying to blame anyone and anything that might be convenient, is a major cause for not living triumphantly. While in the wilderness, the Israelites complained that all of their problems were the fault of God and Moses. This was one of the major factors that kept them wandering in the wilderness for forty years, when they could have been living in the promised land.

There is nothing more emotionally painful than facing the truth about yourself and your actions. Because it is painful, most people run from it. Admitting your own mistakes and failures is difficult, but it is the only way to freedom.

Be a God Pleaser

> *Servants, obey in everything those who are your*
> *earthly masters, not only when their eyes are on you*
> *as pleasers of men, but in simplicity of purpose [with*
> *all your heart] because of your reverence for the Lord*
> *and as a sincere expression of your devotion to Him.*
>
> COLOSSIANS 3:22

This Scripture tells you to be a good, faithful, loyal, profitable, and hardworking employee. You are to do your job well and with a good attitude. You are not to be two-faced, showing your employer what you think he wants to see and then doing differently when he is not around. You need to be real, sincere, honest, and trustworthy.

Do you know what happens when you do your work with all your heart and soul, and do it not unto men but unto God? You receive your reward from Him, not your boss. You can look to the Lord for the reward you truly deserve. Tomorrow, decide to please God and His blessings will follow.

Enter His Rest

*And He raised us up together with Him and
made us sit down together [giving us joint
seating with Him] in the heavenly sphere
[by virtue of our being] in Christ Jesus.*

EPHESIANS 2:6

There are many places in the Bible where
Jesus, after the Resurrection, is described
as being seated. We might think standing would be
more powerful. But being seated has special signifi-
cance.

Under the Law, when a priest entered the Holy
of Holies to make sacrifices for the people's sins, he
could not sit. He had to keep moving and working
the entire time. If the bells on his robe stopped ring-
ing, that meant that he had done something wrong
and had fallen over dead.

That is why it is so awesome that Jesus ascended
into heaven and sat down as our high priest. He entered the rest of God. As joint heirs with Christ, we
can sit too. We no longer have to work and strive to
atone for our sins. Choose to rest in His presence
tonight.

A Big Dose of Humility

*For in posing as judge and passing sentence on
another, you condemn yourself, because you who judge
are habitually practicing the very same things [that
you censure and denounce].*

ROMANS 2:1

Humility is defined as "freedom from pride
and arrogance . . . a modest estimate of
one's own worth." In theology, it means having a
consciousness of your own defects. We often judge
other people because we don't really have a conscious awareness of our own flaws. We look at everybody else through a magnifying glass, but we look at
ourselves through rose-colored glasses. For others
who make mistakes, "there is no excuse," but it seems
for us, there is always a reason why our behavior is
acceptable.

The Bible says to "humble yourselves . . . under
the mighty hand of God" (1 Peter 5:6). Examine
your own heart and actions and humble yourself before Him. God gives us an opportunity to humble
ourselves, but if we refuse, He will do it for us. So
pray for God to make you aware of areas that need
attention and refuse to sit in judgment on others.

The Standby

But the Comforter (Counselor, Helper, Intercessor,
Advocate, Strengthener, Standby), the Holy Spirit,
Whom the Father will send in My name [in My
place, to represent Me and act on My behalf],
He will teach you all things.

JOHN 14:26

As the third person of the Trinity, the Holy Spirit has a personality. He can be offended and grieved and He must be treated with great respect. Once you have the understanding that He lives inside those who believe, you should do everything you can to make him feel welcome. The Holy Spirit is a Gentleman. He will not push His way into your daily affairs. If given an invitation, He is quick to respond, but He must be invited.

The Holy Spirit is always available. The *Amplified Bible* calls Him the Standby. That is a wonderful description! Think of Him ready and waiting at all times in case you need anything at all. Every single day, no matter what you may face the Holy Spirit is standing by you. Invite him to get involved in everything you do.

Finish the Journey

> *And Terah took Abram his son, Lot the son of*
> *Haran, his grandson, and Sarai his daughter-in-law,*
> *his son Abram's wife, and they went forth together to*
> *go from Ur of the Chaldees into the land of Canaan;*
> *but when they came to Haran, they settled there.*
>
> GENESIS 11:31

God gave Abram's father an opportunity to go to the place of His blessing—Canaan. But instead of going all the way with the Lord, he chose to stop and settle in Haran. Many believers do what Terah did. They start out for one place and settle somewhere else along the way.

It is easy to get excited when God first directs you to do something. But many times you never finish what you start because the road gets difficult. It would be nice to reap the benefits of the journey without actually having to leave your comfort zone, but it doesn't work that way. To receive your blessing, you must be willing to push on through to the finish.

Don't Look Back

Weeping may endure for a night,
but joy comes in the morning.
PSALM 30:5

Ecclesiastes 3 tells us there is a time for everything—a time to weep and a time to mourn; a time to laugh and a time to play. You'd be coldhearted and lacking compassion if you experienced loss and felt nothing. But after a while you must let go of what lies behind and press forward. If you don't, the past will destroy your future.

God said, "Moses My servant is dead. So now arise [take his place], go over this Jordan, you and all this people, into the land which I am giving to them, the Israelites. Every place upon which the sole of your foot shall tread, that have I given to you, as I promised Moses" (Joshua 1:2-3). Like the children of Israel, God wants you to let go of the past and take new ground. Don't spend the rest of your life mourning something you have lost. Go forward and don't look back.

Avoid Selective Hearing

Whatever He says to you, do it.

JOHN 2:5

An interesting truth about your ability to hear God's voice is that when you are unwilling to hear in one area of your life, it may render you unable to hear in other areas. Sometimes you turn a deaf ear to what you know the Lord is clearly saying to you—it's called "selective hearing." After a while people think they can't hear from God anymore, but in reality there are lots of things they already know He wants them to respond to and they haven't done so.

If you really want to hear from God you can't approach Him with selective hearing, hoping to narrow the topics down to only what you want to hear. Don't just go to God and talk to Him when you want or need something; also spend time just listening. He will speak to you about many issues if you will be still before Him and simply listen. Then, be sure to obey His direction.

Not Too Hard

*For this commandment which I command you this
day is not too difficult for you, nor is it far off.*

Have you ever caught yourself telling
God, "I know You want me to do this, but
it's just too hard!" The enemy tries to inject this
phrase into your mind so you will give up. But this
Scripture assures you that even when things seem
impossible, nothing God expects from you is too
difficult to accomplish.

The reason the Lord's commands are not too
hard is because He gives you His Spirit to work in
you powerfully and to help you in all He has asked.
Things get hard when you are trying to do them on
your own without leaning and relying on God's
grace. If you know God has asked you to do something, don't back down just because it seems hard.
When things get difficult, spend more time with
Him, lean more on Him, and receive more grace
from Him (Hebrews 4:16).

Words of Life

*Death and life are in the power of the tongue,
and they who indulge in it shall eat the fruit
of it [for death or life].*

PROVERBS 18:21

Think about it for a moment—death and life are in the power of the tongue. Do you have any idea what that really means? It means you and I go through life with an awesome power—not unlike fire or electricity or nuclear energy—right under our noses. It is an energy source that can produce death or life, depending on how it is used.

With this power you have the capacity for great good or great evil, for great benefit or great harm. You can use it to create death and destruction, or you can use it to create life and health. You can speak forth sickness, disease, dissention, and disaster, or you can speak forth healing, harmony, exhortation, and edification. Tonight, choose to speak life into every situation.

Love Is Selfless

*Love endures long and is patient and kind; love
never is envious nor boils over with jealousy, is not
boastful or vainglorious, does not display itself
haughtily. It is not conceited (arrogant and inflated
with pride); it is not rude (unmannerly) and does
not act unbecomingly. Love (God's love in us)
does not insist on its own rights or its own way.*

I CORINTHIANS 13:4-5

Why do we start wars over petty things?
Usually because we want to be right and
we want our way, which is selfishness. The solution
is love. You simply must learn to love peace and harmony, and to love them with all your being. You
need to love them more than you love being right or
having your own way.

This is what Paul meant when he said, "I die
daily" (1 Corinthians 15:31). Dying to self is something you and I are going to have to do on a daily basis if we are to maintain peace and harmony with
one another. It may hurt our flesh to adapt or adjust
to someone else instead of fighting to get our own
way, but in the end we will reap a life of peace and
joy that is a great reward.

Peace in the House

*Fill up and complete my joy by living in harmony
and being of the same mind and one in purpose,
having the same love, being in full accord and
of one harmonious mind and intention.*

PHILIPPIANS 2:2

When Jesus sent the disciples out two by
two to do miracles, signs, and wonders,
in essence He said to them, "Go and find a house and
say, 'Peace be unto you.' And if your peace settles on
that house, you can stay there. If it doesn't, shake the
dust off your feet and go on" (see Mark 6:7-11).

One day God showed me what Jesus was really
saying to them: "I want you to go out with the
anointing, but to do that you need to have peace in
the house." You need to do whatever you can to
maintain peace in your home because it dramatically
affects the anointing and power of God that rests on
your life. Keep the strife out of your life! No peace,
no power! Know peace, know power!

Encourage and Edify

Let each of you esteem and look upon and be
concerned for not [merely] his own interests,
but also each for the interests of others.

PHILIPPIANS 2:4

The minute someone hurts you . . . the moment you experience disappointment—the devil begins to whisper lies about how unjustly you have been treated. All you need to do is listen to the thoughts rushing into your mind during such times and you will quickly realize how the enemy uses self-pity to keep you in bondage. However, God's Word gives you no liberty to feel sorry for yourself. Instead, we are to encourage and edify one another in the Lord.

There is a gift of compassion, which is having godly pity toward others who are hurting. But self-pity is perverted, because it is taking something God intended to be given to others and turning it in on yourself. You should live your life as 1 Thessalonians 5:11 says, "Therefore encourage (admonish, exhort) one another and edify (strengthen and build up) one another."

He Who Laughs Lasts

> *The kings of the earth take their places; the rulers
> take counsel together against the Lord and His
> Anointed One (the Messiah, the Christ). They say, let
> us break Their bands [of restraint] asunder and cast
> Their cords [of control] from us. He Who sits in the
> heavens laughs; the Lord has them in derision [and in
> supreme contempt He mocks them].*
>
> PSALM 2:2-4

When God's enemies gather against Him, He sits in the heavens and laughs. He is the Alpha and Omega, the Beginning and the Ending, so He already knows how things are going to turn out.

We spend too much time looking at what is taking place now instead of looking at the finish line. Like Abraham, you can laugh the laugh of faith. When God told him He would do the impossible—that even though he was too old, God would give him a child—Abraham laughed! (see Genesis 17:17) Tonight, laugh with confidence in the face of the enemy. God has already won!

Uncommon and Extraordinary

*Now to Him Who, by (in consequence of) the
[action of His] power that is at work within us, is
able to [carry out His purpose and] do superabundantly, far over and above all that we [dare]
ask or think [infinitely beyond our highest prayers,
desires, thoughts, hopes, or dreams].*

EPHESIANS 3:20

God uses common, ordinary people who have uncommon goals and visions. You should not be content to be average. Average is basically okay. It is not bad, but it is also not excellent. It is just good enough to get by, and that isn't what God wants for you. You don't serve an average God. Therefore you don't have to settle for an average life.

Every single person can be mightily used by God. You can do great and mighty things if you believe God can use you and if you will be daring enough to have an uncommon goal and vision. These things won't make sense to the mind—you have to believe God for them.

A Holy Thing

*The angel Gabriel was sent from God to a town of
Galilee named Nazareth, to a girl never having been
married and a virgin engaged to be married to a man
whose name was Joseph, a descendant of the house of
David; and the virgin's name was Mary. And he came
to her and said, Hail, O favored one [endued with
grace]! The Lord is with you! . . . And listen! You
will become pregnant and will give birth to a Son,
and you shall call His name Jesus.*

LUKE 1:26-28,31

When Gabriel appeared to Mary, the
Holy Spirit came upon her and planted in
her womb a "Holy Thing." This Seed was the Son of
God sent to deliver mankind from sin.

When you are born again, a "Holy Thing," the
Holy Spirit, is planted in you. As you water that
Seed with God's Word, it will grow into a giant tree
of righteousness, "the planting of the Lord, that He
may be glorified" (Isaiah 61:3).

Roll Away the Reproach

And the Lord said to Joshua, This day have I rolled away the reproach of Egypt from you. So the name of the place is called Gilgal [rolling] to this day.

JOSHUA 5:9

The Lord ordered that all the Israelite males be circumcised, since this had not been done during the entire forty years they had wandered in the Wilderness. After this was done, the Lord told Joshua He had "rolled away" the reproach (blame, disgrace, and shame) of Egypt from His people. When God said this, He was making a point. Egypt represents the world. After a few years of being in the world, we all need the reproach of it rolled away.

For God to roll away the reproach from you means you must receive for yourself the forgiveness He is offering for all your past sins. It is impossible to deserve God's blessings—you can only humbly accept and appreciate them, and be in awe of how good He is and how much He loves you.

Minding Our Own Business

When Peter saw him [John], he said to Jesus, Lord, what about this man? Jesus said to him, If I want him to stay (survive, live) until I come, what is that to you? [What concern is it of yours?] You follow Me!

JOHN 21:21,22

Jesus was talking with Peter about the hardships he would have to endure in order to serve and glorify Him. As soon as Jesus finished speaking, Peter turned, spotted John and immediately asked Jesus what His will was for him. Peter wanted to make sure that if he was going to go through rough times, so would John. Jesus politely told Peter to mind his own business.

You should be encouraged and take hope in the fact that Jesus' disciples struggled with many of the same things you do. Jealousy, envy, and comparing yourself with others is childish. As with the disciples, Jesus has great patience with you. But it helps to remember that minding our own business is more than enough for us to handle.

Learn to Enjoy Him

*But You are a God ready to pardon, gracious and
merciful, slow to anger, and of great steadfast love.*

NEHEMIAH 9:17

The highest call on your life is to enjoy God. But you can't enjoy Him if you are convinced He is upset with you. Jesus came to deliver you from the wrong kind of fear in your relationship with your heavenly Father. You should be relaxed in His presence. You need to have reverential fear—the kind that provokes respect, honor, and obedience. But you must refuse to believe any thoughts that the Lord is angry with you.

You are no surprise to God. Jeremiah 1:5 states that before He formed you in the womb, God knew you! He knew what He was getting when He drew you into relationship with Himself. He already knows the things you will do wrong in the future. God is not nearly as hard to get along with as you think He is. It is not your sin that hinders you—it is unbelief!

Dwell in Unity

Behold, how good and how pleasant it is for
brethren to dwell together in unity!

PSALM 133:1

Great power was manifested in the lives of the early believers. Acts 2:46 tells us why: "And day after day they regularly assembled in the temple with united purpose." They had the same vision, the same goal, and they were all pressing toward the same mark. They prayed in agreement (see Acts 4:24), lived in harmony (see Acts 2:44), cared for one another (see Acts 2:46), met each other's needs (see Acts 4:34), and lived a life of faith (see Acts 4:31). The early church lived in unity—and operated in great power.

Now the church is divided into countless factions with different opinions about everything. Even individual congregations are split by the most trivial differences. When we finally see Jesus face-to-face, we will surely discover that not one of us was 100 percent right. Only love holds people together. Make a strong commitment to do whatever is necessary to live in unity—you will discover how good it is!

He Is Strong

We are weak, but you are [so very] strong!
1 CORINTHIANS 4:10

We need help—and a lot of it. Jeremiah 10:23 says, "the way of a man is not in himself; it is not in man [even in a strong man or in a man at his best] to direct his [own] steps." It really is impossible for man to properly run his own life. Admitting that fact is not a sign of weakness, it is a sign of spiritual maturity. You are weak unless you find your strength in God, and the sooner you face that fact, the better.

Many people have position, wealth, and power, but they may not have what really matters—good relationships, right standing with God, peace, joy, contentment, satisfaction, good health, and the ability to enjoy life. Not everything that appears well is well! You may be trying hard to make things work out right and always failing. Your problem is not that you are a failure. Your problem is simply that you have not gone to the right source for help.

A New Thing

*Behold, I am doing a new thing! Now it
springs forth; do you not perceive and know it
and will you not give heed to it?*

ISAIAH 43:19

Do you ever get really tired of doing the
same old thing all the time? You want to
do something different but you either don't know
what to do, or you are afraid to do the new thing you
are thinking about doing?

You often get into ruts. You do the same thing all
the time even though you are bored with it because
you are afraid to step out and do something different. You would rather be safe and bored than excited
and living on the edge. There is a certain amount of
comfort in sameness—you may not like it, but you
are familiar with it.

God has created you to need and crave diversity
and variety. You require freshness and newness in
your life. As this year and this day come to an end,
make a quality decision to step out into the new thing
God has for you. And don't forget to enjoy yourself!

About the Author

JOYCE MEYER has been teaching the Word of God since 1976 and in full-time ministry since 1980. She is the bestselling author of more than sixty inspirational books, including *In Pursuit of Peace*, *How to Hear from God*, *Knowing God Intimately*, and *Battlefield of the Mind*. She has also released thousands of teaching cassettes and a complete video library. Joyce's *Enjoying Everyday Life* radio and television programs are broadcast around the world, and she travels extensively conducting conferences. Joyce and her husband, Dave, are the parents of four grown children and make their home in St. Louis, Missouri.

To Contact the Author Write:

Joyce Meyer Ministries

P O. Box 655

Fenton, Missouri 63026

or call: (636) 349-0303

Internet Address: www.joycemeyer.org

Your prayer requests are welcome.

To contact the author

in Canada, please write:

Joyce Meyer Ministries Canada, Inc.

Lambeth Box 1300

London, ON N6P IT5

or call: (636) 349-0303

In Australia, please write:

Joyce Meyer Ministries-Australia

Locked Bag 77

Queensland 4122
or call: 07 3349 1200

In England, please write:
Joyce Meyer Ministries
PO Box 1549
Windsor
SL4 1 GT
or call: (0) 1753-831102

In South Africa, please write:
Joyce Meyer Ministries
PO Box 5
SOUTH AFRICA
(27) 21-701-1056

Books by Joyce Meyer

Battlefield of the Mind

Battlefield of the Mind Study Guide

Approval Addiction

Ending Your Day Right

In Pursuit of Peace

The Secret Power of Speaking God's Word

Seven Things That Steal Your Joy

Starting Your Day Right

Beauty for Ashes Revised Edition

How to Hear from God

How to Hear from God Study Guide

Knowing God Intimately

The Power of Forgiveness

The Power of Determination

The Power of Being Positive

The Secrets of Spiritual Power

The Battle Belongs to the Lord

Secrets to Exceptional Living

Eight Ways to Keep the Devil Under Your Feet

Teenagers Are People Too!

Filled with the Spirit

Celebration of Simplicity

The Joy of Believing Prayer

Never Lose Heart

Healing the Brokenhearted

Me and My Big Mouth!

Me and My Big Mouth! Study Guide

Prepare to Prosper

Do It Afraid!

Expect a Move of God in Your Life . . . Suddenly!

Enjoying Where You Are on the Way to Where You Are Going

The Most Important Decision You Will Ever Make

When, God, When?

Why, God, Why?

The Word, the Name, the Blood

Tell Them I Love Them

Peace

The Root of Rejection

If Not for the Grace of God

If Not for the Grace of God Study Guide

JOYCE MEYER SPANISH TITLES

Las Siete Cosas Que Te Roban el Gozo (Seven Things That Steal Your Joy)

Empezando Tu Día Bien (Starting Your Day Right)

BY DAVE MEYER

Life Lines

Notes

Notes

Starting
Your Day
Right

Starting Your Day Right

DEVOTIONS FOR
EACH MORNING OF THE YEAR

Joyce Meyer

NEW YORK   BOSTON   NASHVILLE

FaithWords
Hachette Book Group
1290 Avenue of the Americas
New York, NY 10104

Visit our Web site at www.faithwords.com

Book design by Fearn Cutler de Vicq
Printed in China
First International Edition: October 2007

10   9   8   7   6   5

FaithWords is a division of Hachette Book Group, Inc.
The FaithWords name and logo is a trademark of
Hachette Book Group, Inc.

ISBN 978-0-446-50044-9

My soul, wait only upon God *and* silently submit to
Him; for my hope *and* expectation are from Him.

PSALM 62:5

Introduction

God wants you to enjoy your life. Jesus said, "I came that they may have *and* enjoy life, and have it in abundance (to the full, till it overflows)" (John 10:10). Your days can be filled with an overflowing joy that will spill into the lives of others. You can experience this joy all day if you learn to start your day right—by spending time with God, reading His Word, praying, and listening for His direction.

Listening to God each morning fills you with expectancy and favor for a better day, and those days add up to a better life. The Lord wants you to have Him clearly in sight in order to follow Him. He is willing to wake you in the morning and make your ear alert to His instruction. If you will seek Him with all your heart, He will renew your strength and make clear your path (see Isaiah 40:31; Proverbs 3:6).

I have written this book to remind you of the benefits of starting your day with God. It is not written to replace your personal time with Him, but

simply to enhance it and to point you to your own daily encounter with Him so that you will enjoy every day of your life. He will teach you to balance out your extremes, gain self-control, and live in a way that has a positive impact on others. I encourage you to seek God early each morning and to wait on Him to write in your spirit direction for the day. God will fill your heart with knowledge that will enlighten you at the right time. Once you experience the empowerment of beginning your day with God, you will never want to start your day without Him.

Starting
Your Day
Right

Start Your Day Right

When I said, My foot is slipping, Your mercy and
loving-kindness, O Lord, held me up.

PSALM 94:18

Some people seem to start their day on the "wrong foot." They feel all right when they wake up, but as soon as something goes wrong, they lose their footing and walk with a "loser's limp" the rest of the day. Once they are off to a bad start, it seems they never catch up.

If someone offends us early in the morning, our anger can keep us defensive all day. If we start the day rushing, it seems we never slow down. But to-day our feet can be firmly planted in God's Word. There will be no "bad day" when God's Word sup-ports, strengthens, and directs us.

Get Up and Get Going

I am weary with my groaning; all night I soak my
pillow with tears, I drench my couch with my
weeping . . . Depart from me, all you workers
of iniquity, for the Lord has heard the
voice of my weeping *(emphasis mine).*

PSALM 6:6, 8

Even before we are totally awake, Satan is bidding to deceive us and is ready to plant defeating thoughts in our mind. He wants us to be hopeless, faithless, and negative. He definitely doesn't want us to *be* positive when we get up. He wants us to have a bad attitude and be selfish and self-centered, full of hatred, bitterness, resentment, doubt, unbelief, and fear — to be mad at everybody.

But thank God, through Jesus Christ, we have been redeemed from all of those negative patterns. We can resist the devil and trust God's power in order to live victoriously today.

Keep in Touch with God

*Blessed (happy, fortunate, prosperous, and
enviable) is the man who walks and lives not in the
counsel of the ungodly [following their advice,
their plans and purposes] . . . But his delight and
desire are in the law of the Lord, and on His law
(the precepts, the instructions, the teachings
of God) he habitually meditates (ponders
and studies) by day and by night.*

PSALM 1:1—2

Keep in touch with God today; stay tuned
to His voice. You may have a plan for the
day, but God may lead you in a totally different direction if you are sensitive to the Holy Ghost. Be
brave enough to flow with what you feel in your
heart God wants you to do.

Today is going to be a good day. Listen for the
voice of God to lead you. Be determined to walk in
the Spirit and stay in the flow of God's leading today.

Avoid the Slingers

O God, You are my God, earnestly will I seek You;
my inner self thirsts for You . . . in a dry and weary
land where no water is . . . I have looked upon You
in the sanctuary to see Your power and Your glory.
Because Your loving-kindness is better than life,
my lips shall praise You.

PSALM 63:1–3

There were people in the Bible called slingers who defeated their enemies by slinging stones and throwing dirt into their wells, contaminating their life source of water (see 2 Kings 3:25). We all know people who sling accusation, judgment, criticism, and faultfinding at others. We certainly don't want slingers in our life, and we don't want to become slingers either.

Don't be a slinger who contaminates your own faith or the faith of those around you. Spending time with God will fill you with "living water" (see John 7:38). You will be edified and become a source of encouragement for others all day long.

Get in the Flow

*You cause them to drink of the stream of Your
pleasures. For with You is the fountain of life; in Your
light do we see light. O continue Your loving-kindness
to those who know You, Your righteousness (salvation)
to the upright in heart.*

PSALM 36:8—10

I have never been much of a swimmer. I
may not be the best at fighting the cur-
rent, but I can float. It is wonderful just to trust the
water to keep us up and go with the flow. We can
trust God to keep us afloat through the rapids and
lead us to still waters.

The Bible says God's mercy and loving-kindness
are "new *every* morning" (see Lamentations 3:22–
23). His mercy isn't just there waiting for us; it is
new, fresh, flowing, and powerful every new day.
We need to get in the flow of God's river of life
early each day and learn to float on the power of His
presence.

Get Rest

As for me, I will continue beholding Your face in
righteousness (rightness, justice, and right standing
with You); I shall be fully satisfied, when I awake
[to find myself] beholding Your form [and
having sweet communion with You].

PSALM 17:15

Each evening the sun sets on all of our
problems and on all of the mistakes we
made that day. But something marvelous happens to
us as we sleep — the Lord gives us rest physically,
mentally, and emotionally. We are renewed and re-
juvenated to face the next day.

Today we may wake up with the same problems
we had when we went to bed, problems that yesterday we felt we just couldn't take anymore. But somehow today, after proper rest and sleep, we think, *I
can do it; I can face it again.* God promises to renew
our strength when we rest in Him.

Rejoice Today

Let the hearts of those rejoice who seek the Lord!
Seek the Lord and His strength; yearn for and seek
His face and to be in His presence continually!
[Earnestly] remember the marvelous deeds which He
has done, His miracles, and the judgments He uttered.

1 CHRONICLES 16:10–12

Many people don't realize how important the morning is, especially those first moments of time that we are awake. God calls the sun to rise for us. He is eager for us to wake up and talk to Him again.

David the psalmist talked a lot about mornings, saying "This is the day that the Lord has made; I *will* rejoice and be glad in it" (see Psalm 118:24). David didn't always *feel* like rejoicing, but he *decided* to rejoice in God's new day.

As soon as you get up, look at yourself in the mirror, smile, and say, "I am going to have a good day because Jesus loves me."

Start Out Joyfully

You try the heart and delight in uprightness. In the uprightness of my heart I have freely offered all these things. And now I have seen with joy Your people who are present here offer voluntarily and freely to You. O Lord . . . keep forever such purposes and thoughts in the minds of Your people, and direct and establish their hearts toward You.

1 CHRONICLES 29:17–18

My husband always seems happy. Within five minutes of waking, Dave is humming, singing, or listening to music as he gets ready for the day. Years ago I didn't want music on in the morning. I didn't want singing or humming or noise of any kind. I wanted silence so I could think.

Today I still need a little more quiet than Dave does in the morning. But we have both found the way to start our day out right. We set our hearts and minds to follow God. And it works.

Listen for His Purpose

Who is the man who reverently fears and *worships
the Lord? Him shall He teach in the way that he
should choose. He himself shall dwell at ease . . . The
secret [of the sweet, satisfying companionship] of the
Lord have they who fear (revere and worship) Him.*

PSALM 25:12–14

It is God who wakes us each morning.
If He didn't keep us alive overnight, it
wouldn't matter what kind of an alarm clock we
had! The prophet said, "God wakens me morning by
morning, and He wakens me for a purpose so that
I can hear; I am like a disciple who is taught" (see
Isaiah 50:4).

Before you even get out of bed, listen to hear
what God has to say to you. It will be a good day if
you start it with a ready ear, taking time to listen to
Him. God is eager to reveal today's plan to you.

Expect Something New

In the morning, O LORD, you hear my voice;
in the morning I lay my requests before you
and wait in expectation.

PSALM 5:3 NIV

If you get up and do the exact same thing every morning, you may get pretty bored after a month or so. But seeking God when you first wake up is never boring. He will always have a new revelation ready for you to hear.

Keep your expectation fresh by changing what you do in your time with God. You might worship the Lord with singing one morning, listen to Christian music another morning, read God's Word the third morning, sit in His presence or confess His Word the following morning. Let the Holy Spirit lead you as you learn to enjoy starting your day with God.

Form Godly Habits

Fix these words of mine in your hearts and minds . . . talking about them when you sit at home and when you walk along the road, when you lie down and when you get up. Write them on the doorframes of your houses and on your gates, so that your days . . . may be . . . as many as the days that the heavens are above the earth.

DEUTERONOMY 11:18–21 NIV

Waiting for God's direction each day is something you may have to *make* yourself do at first, but through practice, it will become natural to begin your day this way. New habits are formed by being consistent. Seeking God first in the morning will soon be something you can't do without.

When God wanted His people to remember something, He told them to write it down. You may have to post reminders to seek the Lord around your house in order to follow through with your new intention. But be consistent to seek God first every day, and He will make your ways successful (see Joshua 1:7–9).

Crave God's Presence

My soul yearns for You [O Lord] in the night, yes,
my spirit within me seeks You earnestly; for [only]
when Your judgments are in the earth will the
inhabitants of the world learn righteousness
(uprightness and right standing with God).

ISAIAH 26:9

If we are hungry enough, we will get something to eat. And if we can't eat before we leave home, we will go to a drive-thru at a fast-food restaurant. Or we will call a place that delivers food to bring us something to eat.

If we are hungry enough for God, we will find a way into His presence. We should be *so hungry* for the presence of God that we absolutely will not go out of our house or tackle any kind of project until we have spent some time with Him.

Don't Be Too Busy

It is because of the Lord's mercy and loving-
kindness that we are not consumed, because His
[tender] compassions fail not. They are new
every morning; great and abundant is
Your stability and faithfulness.

LAMENTATIONS 3:22—23

If we are too busy to spend time with God, then we are just too busy, and we are asking for a disaster in our life. We need to ask God to show us things we can get rid of in our life that aren't bearing any fruit.

In His Word God says, "Awake, O sleeper, and arise from the dead, and Christ shall shine (make day dawn) upon you *and* give you light . . . Live purposefully . . . making the very most of the time [buying up each opportunity], because the days are evil" (Ephesians 5:14—16). God wants us to be strong in the power of His might and to be ever filled with the Holy Spirit.

Pray and Listen

*Cause me to hear Your loving-kindness in the
morning, for on You do I lean* and *in You do I trust.
Cause me to know the way wherein I should walk,
for I lift up my inner self to You.*

PSALM 143:8

We need to pray and then stop and listen.
Sometimes we can hear God as a still,
small voice from deep within our heart. Many times
God will speak through our inner witness so that we
"just know" the truth and it sets us free. Suddenly
we know what we should or shouldn't do.

King David had a lot to say about seeking God in
the morning. He prayed in the morning and then
watched and waited for God to speak to his heart. I
like knowing that God is listening for our prayers.
He likes it when we listen to His answers too.

Go with What You Know

Satisfy us in the morning with your unfailing
love, that we may sing for joy and
be glad all our days.

PSALM 90:14 NIV

This morning pray, "Lord, I am waiting for You to direct me." While you honor the Lord by listening for His response, you may hear Him speak something specific to you right away. It may seem as though He inscribes direction in your spirit for the day. The devil may tell you that it wasn't really God who spoke to you. Or while you are waiting to hear from God, Satan may tell you that you are wasting your time.

It is important to know the truth of God's Word so that the direction God sows in your heart will not be snatched away from you through doubt. God may not lay out a blueprint for your day, but He *will* direct your path, if you acknowledge Him in all of your ways (see Proverbs 3:6).

Be Happy

The Lord is my Strength and Song; and He has become my Salvation. The voice of rejoicing and salvation is in the tents and private dwellings of the [uncompromisingly] righteous: the right hand of the Lord does valiantly and achieves strength!

PSALM 118:14–15

Happiness is the result of a radical, outrageous relationship with God. If we want to walk in victory, we have to put some time into our relationship with the Lord. There is much to discover about His plans for us.

Our contentment won't last if we are not obeying God by seeking Him with our whole heart. God wants us to really talk to Him and pay attention to His answers. Spend enough time with Him this morning to walk in victory all day.

Give Personal Time

But I say, walk and live [habitually] in the
[Holy] Spirit [responsive to and controlled and
guided by the Spirit]; then you will certainly not
gratify the cravings and desires of the flesh
(of human nature without God).

GALATIANS 5:16

Many believers serve God with their time, but still miss spending personal time in His presence. God wants us to *abide* in Him, not just visit Him occasionally. Jesus said, "If you abide in My word [hold fast to My teachings and live in accordance with them], you are truly My disciples" (John 8:31).

Jesus will actually dwell, settle down, abide, and make His permanent home in your heart! His presence will cause you to be rooted deep in love so that you may experience His love and be filled through all your being with the fullness of God (see Ephesians 3:17–19).

Receive By Faith

I pray You, if I have found favor in Your sight,
show me now Your way, that I may know You
[progressively become more deeply and intimately
acquainted with You, perceiving and recognizing
and understanding more strongly and clearly] and
that I may find favor in Your sight . . . And the
Lord said, My Presence shall go with you,
and I will give you rest.

EXODUS 33:13–14

Everything that we receive from God comes by faith. When you are waiting for Him to speak to your heart, just believe that He *will* speak to you, even if you don't hear anything right that minute.

Believe that because you have acknowledged Him, you can expect to see His hand moving in your life all day long. Then step forward, knowing that He will keep you on the right path because you have asked Him to do so. Watching God's hand of favor move on our behalf is one of life's greatest delights.

Don't Chase Blessings

Blessed (happy, fortunate, to be envied) is the man whom You choose and cause to come near, that he may dwell in Your courts! We shall be satisfied with the goodness of Your house, Your holy temple.

PSALM 65:4

Instead of chasing after blessings, we need to chase after God. If we chase God, He will chase us with blessings. That is why the kingdom of God is sometimes called "the upside-down kingdom."

God's economy doesn't work the way we think it would. First is last, and last is first. If we want more, we are to give away some of what we have. To be great in God's kingdom, we must serve the needs of others. And if we want blessings, we must get our mind off of them. God knows what we want and what we need. He wants to give us blessings that we haven't even verbally asked for.

Don't Fall Apart

But He said to me, My grace (My favor and loving-kindness and mercy) is enough for you [suffi-cient against any danger and enables you to bear the trouble manfully]; for My strength and power are made perfect (fulfilled and completed) and show themselves most effective in [your] weakness.

2 CORINTHIANS 12:9

Come apart and spend some time with God before *you* come apart. No matter how strong and healthy you are, no matter what your age is, no matter what you think you know, without God, you are going to get weary and tired.

God doesn't get tired, and the Word says He gives power to the faint *and* weary, and increases strength to those who have no might. But those who wait for the Lord, who expect, look for, and hope in Him, will be renewed (see Isaiah 40:29–31). God is willing to increase your strength. Get alone with Him anytime you need to be strengthened.

Wait for the Lord

Keep the charge of the Lord your God, walk in
His ways, keep His statutes, His commandments, His
precepts, and His testimonies, as it is written in the
Law of Moses, that you may do wisely and *prosper in*
all that you do and wherever you turn.

1 KINGS 2:3

When you pray, wait for the Lord. This means to look for, to expect, and to hope in God. This isn't a passive state of mind, but one of expectancy.

Tell Him, "God, I have my hope in You. I believe that You are working on my problems. I believe that You are making arrangements for my day. You are posting angels all throughout my walk, everywhere along my path where You already know I am going to walk today. Thank you, Lord, that You are a pioneer who has already gone before me and made a way for me to have a blessed day."

Lord, What's Next?

Show me Your ways, O Lord; teach me Your paths.
Guide me in Your truth and faithfulness and teach
me, for You are the God of my salvation; for You
[You only and altogether] do I wait
[expectantly] all the day long.

PSALM 25:4–5

Start your day saying, "I am excited about this day, God. I can hardly wait to see what You are going to do. I believe You are going to keep me, help me, bless me, and give me favor. I love You, Father. I am waiting on You, Lord, and I am listening to You."

Ask God to put into your spirit everything He wants you to know. Ask Him to show you things to come and what you are supposed to do (see John 16:13). He will give you direction, and you will have much to praise Him for today.

Be Renewed

*God selected . . . what the world calls weak to
put the strong to shame. And God also selected
(deliberately chose) what in the world is lowborn* and
insignificant and branded and *treated with contempt,
even the things that are nothing, that He might
depose* and *bring to nothing the things that are,
so that no mortal man should [have pretense for
glorying and] boast in the presence of God.*

I CORINTHIANS 1:27–29

If you are weak in faith, in mind, in body,
in discipline, in self-control, or in determination, simply wait on God. He will be strong
through your weakness.

Isaiah 40:31 teaches that if you expect God, look
for Him, and hope in Him, you will change *and* renew your strength *and* power; you will run, and not
faint *or* become tired. The Bible doesn't say "hope
so, it could be, or it may be"; it declares that you *will*
be renewed.

He Will Reward You

*So repent (change your mind and purpose);
turn around and return [to God], that your sins may
be erased (blotted out, wiped clean), that times of
refreshing (of recovering from the effects of heat,
of reviving with fresh air) may come from
the presence of the Lord.*

ACTS 3:19

Success principles alone will not work in your life if you don't spend time with God, allowing His Holy Spirit to be your Counselor and to give you revelation and understanding of what to do each day. But if you flow in God's plan, you will learn to stop trying to figure out how everything will work together for your good.

Learn to seek God's face and not His hand all the time. Then keep your hands open and be ready to receive from Him. God is good; you can trust what He speaks to your heart to do.

Invest in Someone

*The wicked borrow and pay not again [for they
may be unable], but the [uncompromisingly]
righteous deal kindly and give [for they are able].*

PSALM 37:21

Take chances today and invest in someone else's life, especially if God tells you
to do so. You may give them something of value only
to learn they waste it as they have always done in the
past. But remember that God made an investment in
you, and He wants you to be willing to make an investment in somebody else.

Jesus died to give *everybody* a chance. Not everyone takes advantage of His provision, but we all have
an equal opportunity to enjoy the abundant life. If
you help someone, and they end up not doing what
is right with it, that is between them and God. Give
thanks that you are able to give, and then do whatever God tells you to do.

God Will Keep You

[As for me] I am poor and needy, yet the Lord
takes thought and *plans for me. You are my Help*
and my Deliverer. O my God, do not tarry!

PSALM 40:17

God has a plan for each of us, and the good things that happen to us are not just a coincidence. All good and perfect gifts come from God (see James 1:17). It is exciting to have a relationship with God when we are aware that He is carefully leading and guiding us to His blessings.

If you don't understand something the first time God speaks to you, He will give you another chance and will continue to teach you until you know clearly the way you should go. Jesus came to seek and to save those who are lost (see Luke 19:10). This means that He will find you if you go astray.

Love God First

Come and see what God has done, how
awesome his works in man's behalf!

PSALM 66:5 NIV

We give attention to whatever we love the most. God wants to be first in our life (see Exodus 20:3). Jesus said, "'Love the Lord your God with all your heart and with all your soul and with all your mind.' This is the first and greatest commandment" (Matthew 22:37–38 NIV).

What might happen in your life if you became so intent on seeking God that you hired a babysitter to watch your children, or used a vacation day, in order to spend time with the Lord? You can't afford *not* to spend time with God. Give Him your full attention, and make a point to observe all He is doing for you.

Confess God's Provision

In conclusion, be strong in the Lord [be empowered through your union with Him]; draw your strength from Him [that strength which His boundless might provides].

EPHESIANS 6:10

When your faith feels weak, ask God to show you how to pray. The Bible says plainly in Jude 1:20–21 and 1 Corinthians 14:2–4 that when you pray in the Holy Spirit, you edify yourself, which means you build yourself up on your most holy faith. Praying in the Holy Spirit causes you to make progress, and His leading will guard *and* keep you full of expectancy and patience for God's mercy to bless your day.

There is no excuse for anybody to drown in doubt and unbelief, when God has given us His Spirit to fill us with faith through prayer and time spent in His presence. Today, start confessing what you have in God. Declare that your needs are met because the Word says so (see Philippians 4:19).

Keep Your Peace

Only fear the Lord and serve Him faithfully
with all your heart; for consider how great are
the things He has done for you.

1 SAMUEL 12:24

To have peace, keep your eyes on God. Get alone to fellowship with Him. If you have to get in a closet and sit in the middle of all your shoes and hang clothes over your head to hide in order to find solitude, do it! Then focus on all that God has done for you.

Jesus said to go to your most private room when you pray to the Father, and He will reward you openly for the time you spend with Him (see Matthew 6:6). Don't miss out on God's abundant blessings for your life.

Prepare to Love Others

The night is far gone and the day is almost here.
Let us then drop (fling away) the works and deeds
of darkness and put on the [full] armor of light.

ROMANS 13:12

Before your feet touch the floor in the morning, put on the full armor of God with which you can quench all the fiery darts of the enemy (see Ephesians 6:13–17). Put on the belt of truth, the breastplate of righteousness, and the readiness of the gospel of peace.

Don't let the devil steal your peace in the morning. Start talking to God before you even get out of bed. Tell Him, "I love You, Lord, and I need Your help today. Please strengthen me to walk in the fruit of the Spirit. Help me walk in love all day long. Help me to keep my thoughts on You, Lord."

Enjoy Confident Trust

In peace I will both lie down and sleep,
for You, Lord, alone make me dwell in
safety and *confident trust.*

PSALM 4:8

Some people feel their lives are an emotional mess, but they have a right to stability. There is stability, peace, and power in the presence of God. People don't have to let their emotions control them; they can learn to dwell in the secret place of the Most High.

The Word says, "HE WHO dwells in the secret place of the Most High shall remain stable *and* fixed under the shadow of the Almighty [Whose power no foe can withstand]. I will say of the Lord, He is my Refuge and my Fortress, my God; on Him I lean *and* rely, *and* in Him I [confidently] trust!" (Psalm 91:1–2).

That is why we should dwell in that place where we experience the presence of the Almighty.

Wait with Purpose

*My [inner] self [as well as my body] is also
exceedingly disturbed and troubled. But You, O Lord,
how long [until You return and speak peace to me]?
Return [to my relief], O Lord, deliver my life; save me
for the sake of Your steadfast love and mercy.*

PSALM 6:3–4

Avoid getting negative when you look at
your circumstances. Actively wait on God
to give you strength to walk in the fruit of the Spirit
(Galatians 5:22–23). Wait with purpose, silently listening for Him to speak, eagerly watching for Him
to act.

Tell Him, "Lord, I receive strength to be Your
ambassador and witness. Your Word tells me to love
people who mistreat me. Though it is hard to do in
the natural, I receive strength from You to be loving
today."

Then watch for the opportunity to act godly as
He gives you strength to do so.

Be Proactive

Have mercy and *be gracious to me; grant*
strength (might and inflexibility to
temptation) to Your servant.

PSALM 86:16

Jesus warned His disciples about all that He was to go through, because He knew it would be difficult for them too. He said, "Pray that you won't be tempted" (see Matthew 6:13; 26:41). He didn't say, "Wait to pray until you have *been* tempted, or until you have *given in* to temptation, or until you are up to your neck in sin and perversion!" Jesus teaches us to be proactive, which Webster defines as "acting in anticipation of future problems, needs, or changes."

Many Israelites had already died from snake bites before the rest of them finally said, "Pray for us, Moses, for we have sinned" (see Numbers 21:4–9). They should have recognized their need for God's help much sooner than they did! Don't wait until you are in trouble to seek God. Ask Him to keep you from being tempted to sin today.

Let God Strengthen You

My life dissolves and *weeps itself away for heaviness; raise me up* and *strengthen me according to [the promises of] Your word. Remove from me the way of falsehood* and *unfaithfulness [to You], and graciously impart Your law to me.*

PSALM 119:28–29

We need to be strengthened and renewed on a daily basis. We need to be strengthened physically, mentally, and emotionally. We need to be strong so we do not fall apart every time we have to face some situation we had not planned on.

Jesus is the same yesterday, today, and forever, and He expects us to develop stability in our lives. We can be strengthened and renewed by drawing strength from God, by exercising our faith, and by doing what He tells us to do.

Be Secure

I love You fervently and devotedly, O Lord, my Strength. The Lord is my Rock, my Fortress, and my Deliverer; my God, my keen and firm Strength in Whom I will trust and take refuge, my Shield, and the Horn of my salvation, my High Tower.

PSALM 18:1—2

God can strengthen us to the point that we can make progress even *during* trouble. The psalmist said of God, "He makes my feet like hinds' feet [able to stand firmly *or make progress* on the dangerous heights of testing and trouble] . . . You have girded me with strength for the battle" (Psalm 18:33, 39 emphasis mine).

Trials and testing do not come to cause us to lose stability. They are opportunities to prove the strength of God. We don't have to waver in our confidence. Nothing will keep us from making progress today because God is our strength.

Be Strong

The Lord is my Strength and my [impenetrable]
Shield; my heart trusts in, relies on, and confidently
leans on Him, and I am helped; therefore my heart
greatly rejoices, and with my song will I praise Him.
The Lord is their [unyielding] Strength, and He is the
Stronghold of salvation to [me] His anointed.

PSALM 28:7–8

We can plan to be worn out before we
ever feel tired. I used to expect to be totally wiped out physically and emotionally after my
conferences. Then I prayed that as I poured energy
and strength into obeying God, He would pour energy and strength back into me.

The Bible says that giving is sowing a seed that
will reap a harvest (Galatians 6:7–10). If we give our
strength, we will reap God's strength. We should
expect a harvest of strength in our life, as we serve
the Lord. He will anoint us with strength today, if
we call on Him to do so.

Make Adjustments

*Adding your diligence [to the divine promises],
employ every effort in exercising your faith to
develop virtue (excellence, resolution, Christian
energy), and in [exercising] virtue [develop]
knowledge (intelligence).*

2 PETER 1:5

Sometimes we have to make a few adjustments in our lifestyle to follow wisdom.
We may have to say no to too much activity. Hebrews 11:1 teaches that faith is the assurance of
things we do not see now. But, like God, we can call
"those things that be not, as though they are" (see
Romans 4:17). This spiritual principle applies in the
negative realm as well as in the positive realm. So we
may need to make some adjustments to the things
we say.

If you feel that it is hard to get up in the morning,
don't say, "I am too tired." Get all of that weak, tired,
wimpy, quitter, give-up talk out of your vocabulary.
Instead, say, "Because the Lord is my strength, I can
do whatever I need to do today."

God Will Help You

The Lord will give [unyielding and impenetrable]
strength to His people; the Lord will bless
His people with peace.

PSALM 29:11

God has been showing me that we need to be aware of His present provisions now, and not in the future. In Psalm 28:7 David said of God, "I am helped; therefore my heart greatly rejoices, and with my song will I praise Him." He did not say, "I *will be* helped."

Wait on God, because God's help will strengthen you to behave in a godly way all day long, if you trust in Him. Even while you wait on God to manifest His plan, your heart can greatly rejoice in His presence. Tell someone something good that God has done for you, and then watch Him move in the presence of your praise.

Offer Yourself Freely

We are the sweet fragrance of Christ
[which exhales] unto God.

2 CORINTHIANS 2:15

The Bible says that every morning God's people brought freewill offerings to Him. They all had various sacrifices such as animals, grains, and cereals (see Exodus 35). God wants us to offer our lives in dedicated service to him.

The Bible says that God is pleased with our sacrifice of praise (see Hebrews 13:15), and that our prayers go up before God as a sweet-smelling sacrifice. He wants us to bring ourselves to Him every morning and say, "God, here I am; I want to be a living sacrifice."

Sacrifice Yourself to Serve

"Give, and it will be given to you. A good
measure, pressed down, shaken together and running
over, will be poured into your lap. For with the
measure you use, it will be measured to you."

LUKE 6:38 NIV

Do you know what Romans 12:1 means when it says that we are to offer ourselves as a living sacrifice? It means that we are to be alive with the power, zeal, and enthusiasm that any born-again person ought to have. It means we are to be excited about Jesus. We are to offer our mouths, our thoughts, our words, our attitudes, our bodies, our hands, and our feet to Him to use to continue His ministry.

This may mean that we do not get everything we want in life, but anything we give up for the sake of the Gospel, Jesus has said we will receive back a hundred times in this lifetime (see Mark 10:29–30). Enjoy God's blessings now. Offer yourself for service and watch the blessings return.

Sacrifice Praise

Know, recognize, and understand therefore this
day and turn your [mind and] heart to it that the
Lord is God in the heavens above and upon the
earth beneath; there is no other.

DEUTERONOMY 4:39

Praising God starts your day right. Start thanking God as soon as you get out of bed in the morning. Hebrews 13:15 says, "Let us constantly *and* at all times offer up to God a sacrifice of praise, which is the fruit of lips that thankfully acknowledge *and* confess *and* glorify His name."

Jesus said, "Whoever believes in me, as the Scripture has said, streams of living water will flow from within him" (John 7:38 NIV). Acknowledge the Lord, and drink that living water.

Enter His Gates

*You shall [reverently] fear the Lord your God; you
shall serve Him and cling to Him, and by His name
and presence you shall swear. He is your praise; He is
your God, Who has done for you these great and
terrible things which your eyes have seen.*

DEUTERONOMY 10:20–21

It is not good to feel grumpy when we
wake up. Complaining won't bring us
into the presence of God. Psalm 100:4 says that we
are to enter His gates with thanksgiving and His
courts with praise. Without thanksgiving we won't
even get into the gate! If we want to enter into
God's presence, we must lay aside all murmuring
and complaining.

An irritable attitude may be keeping you from
enjoying God's presence. Each morning look at all
you have to thank God for, and then enter into your
day with praise for all He has done for you.

Give Something Away

*Yes, the Lord will give what is good, and our land
will yield its increase. Righteousness shall go
before Him and shall make His footsteps
a way in which to walk.*

PSALM 85:12–13

God is the ultimate Giver. He expects
nothing less than for us to follow His example. I challenge you to give away something every
day of your life. You may think you won't have anything left if you do that, but if you give as the Lord
leads you to do, soon you will receive so much that
you will have to figure out where to put it all.

God gives you bread to eat and seed to sow (see
2 Corinthians 9:10). Some things that God sends
your way are given as seed for you to sow into the
lives of others. Ask God to show you what He wants
you to give away.

Live Unselfishly

*The people curse him who holds back grain
[when the public needs it], but a blessing [from God
and man] is upon the head of him who sells it.
He who diligently seeks good seeks [God's] favor.*

PROVERBS 11:26—27

I believe strongly in living a "giving life-style." I was selfish for years before I finally realized that joy comes in giving and reaching out to other people. We don't need to be afraid of losing our goods or ending up with nothing, because the Word of God is true.

You will get joyful when you begin to think about how you can bless somebody else. Consecrate your gift to God, saying, "Lord, I give myself to You. I renew my vow, and my commitment to obey You. I want to stay strong in You, so I seek Your face. Bless me, and make me to be a blessing to others."

Bless Somebody

And let us not lose heart and *grow weary* and
faint in acting nobly and *doing right, for in due time*
and *at the appointed season we shall reap, if we do
not loosen* and *relax our courage* and *faint.*

GALATIANS 6:9

The Word says, "Let each one of us make it a practice to please (make happy) his neighbor for his good *and* for his true welfare, to edify him [to strengthen him and build him up spiritually]" (Romans 15:2).

This tells me that we need to have our mind *full* of ways to bless people. Early in the day, think up something you want to do to bless someone. Think up something you can do to surprise somebody or to make somebody happy. You will be amazed at how quickly the Lord leads you to something good you can do for someone. Joy comes from giving on His behalf.

Be Honest with God

I will wash my hands in innocence, and go about
Your altar, O Lord, that I may make the voice
of thanksgiving heard and may tell of all
Your wondrous works.

PSALM 26:6—7

Each morning we need to come clean with God. If there is anything between us and God, when we try to pray and get into His presence, it will bother us until we deal honestly with it. God wants us to confess our faults. I have found over the years in a ministry of dealing with other people, and also in dealing with my own flesh, that we don't really like to confront wrongdoing as we should.

Most of us like to make excuses, but excuses keep us deceived. An excuse is a reason stuffed with a lie. The Bible says that the truth will set us free (John 8:32). Honesty with God will free us to enjoy our whole day.

Receive Mercy

All the paths of the Lord are mercy and *steadfast love, even truth* and *faithfulness are they for those who keep His covenant and His testimonies.*

PSALM 25:10

The Israelites were lost in the wilderness because they didn't believe that their problems were their own fault. They blamed Moses, God, and everybody else for their sorrows. They refused to take responsibility for their sins, and their unwillingness to repent kept them from entering the promised land.

When you talk with God, be sure to ask for forgiveness. "If we [freely] admit that we have sinned *and* confess our sins, He is faithful and just (true to His own nature and promises) and will forgive our sins [dismiss our lawlessness] and [continuously] cleanse us from all unrighteousness [everything not in conformity to His will in purpose, thought, and action]" (1 John 1:9). Repent in the morning to enjoy God's mercy, forgiveness, and love all day.

Receive God's Gifts

If you are willing and obedient,
you shall eat the good of the land.

ISAIAH 1:19

What good is it to have a glass of water, if we won't drink it? Our thirst will not be quenched until we do. Jesus said, "If any man is thirsty, let him come to Me and drink!" (John 7:37). He said that if we have any kind of need, we are to ask Him for what we want, and then *receive* it. The good things of God are available to those who simply surrender themselves to Him and accept His blessings and mercy.

People beg God for forgiveness but forget to say, "I *receive* that forgiveness right now; I believe I am forgiven." Mercy is a free gift. You can't earn it, you can't deserve it, and you can't buy it. The only thing you can do is *receive* it. Just humble yourself, and accept God's forgiveness.

Abound in Grace

And God is able to make all grace abound to you,
so that in all things at all times, having all that you
need, you will abound in every good work.

2 CORINTHIANS 9:8 NIV

My definition of *get* is to obtain by struggle and effort, and *receive* is to act like a receptacle and simply take in what is offered. We can *receive* mercy, grace, strength, forgiveness, and love from the Lord. It is a new day — and God's mercy is new every morning (see Lamentations 3:22–23).

You can have a brand new start today. Allow God's mercy to strengthen and heal you before starting your routine activities. Receive His healing power, and let its grace work in you. Today can be effortless as you depend on God's grace to do what He has called you to do.

Approach God's Throne

*Let us then fearlessly and confidently and boldly
draw near to the throne of grace (the throne of God's
unmerited favor to us sinners), that we may receive
mercy [for our failures] and find grace to help
in good time for every need [appropriate help and
well-timed help, coming just when we need it].*

HEBREWS 4:16

What a great High Priest we have in Jesus. He understands our experiences, and He knows what it is like to live in a human body. He positioned Himself to go through the same kind of temptations we do, but He didn't give in to them.

He knows that the tempter lies in wait for us, and He knows we need His mercy and strength. We still fall short even when we have the best intentions to do good. God tells us to receive, not strive to get, but just to *receive* new mercy for each day.

Be Transformed

But now put away and rid yourselves [completely]
of all these things: anger, rage, bad feeling toward
others, curses and slander, and foulmouthed abuse
and shameful utterances from your lips! . . . And . . .
clothe . . . yourselves with the new [spiritual self],
which is [ever in the process of being] renewed
and remolded into [fuller and more perfect
knowledge upon] knowledge after the image
(the likeness) of Him Who created it.

COLOSSIANS 3:8,10

If you want your life to be different, pray to receive God's transforming power. Simply say:

"God, please forgive my sins and change me into the person You want me to be. I know You are working in me, right now, because I have come to You. You have said that if I abide in Your Word and come into Your presence, I will be changed from glory to glory into Your image. Thank You, Lord, for changing me today."

Believing that God is at work to change you will bring its manifestation.

Simply Believe

*We who first hoped in Christ [who first put our
confidence in Him have been destined and appointed
to] live for the praise of His glory!*

EPHESIANS 1:12

In the world, you don't believe anything
until you see it. When you pray, believe
that you receive, and you will get the manifestation
of it. In God's kingdom, you have to believe it first,
and then you see it.

Jesus said, "If you believe, you will receive whatever you ask for in prayer" (Matthew 21:22 NIV).
God's ear is turned toward those who pray to Him
in faith. Peter was the only one who walked on water besides Jesus, but he was also the only one who
got out of the boat. Until you make a decision to believe, and then act on it, nothing will happen.

Throw Away Excuses

I will call upon the Lord, Who is to be praised;
so shall I be saved from my enemies.

PSALM 18:3

In Deuteronomy 7:1–2, God instructed His people to utterly destroy their enemies. They were to show no mercy. When God tells us it is time to deal with our negative, faithless attitudes, it is time to throw away our excuses. No more rationalizing, "Well, everybody else is negative; why should I be any different?"

Get some things over with in your life today. Get rid of bad habits and negative attitudes and move on with the future God has for you. Pray: "Lord, please help me to change. Show me the root of my problem and how to get over it. I want positive changes in my life."

Enjoy Forgiveness

Blessed (happy, fortunate, to be envied) is the man
to whom the Lord imputes no iniquity and in
whose spirit there is no deceit.

PSALM 32:2

If we aren't living the way God has instructed us to live, we will be miserable until we confess our sins. Once we thoroughly get everything out in the open before the Lord, He gives us the power to be set free *from* our sins: "BLESSED (HAPPY, fortunate, to be envied) is he who has forgiveness of his transgression continually exercised upon him, whose sin is covered" (Psalm 32:1).

The Word says that God desires truth in our inner being (see Psalm 51:6). So we need to be honest with ourselves and with God, if we want to enjoy the blessing of God's forgiveness. Ask God to show you what needs to be changed in your life, and trust His forgiving power to continually bring about those changes in you.

Seek God Early

And in the morning, long before daylight,
He got up and went out to a deserted place,
and there He prayed.

MARK 1:35

When Jesus told us to *abide* in Him and in His Word, He used the Greek word *meno,* which is translated in Strong's concordance as "continue, dwell, endure, be present, remain, stand, tarry." We are to spend time with God — continually. When we do, we get in the flow of His plan for our day.

We are not told just to *wish* for everything to work together; we are told to *seek God* for a fresh word each day. If we seek Him early in the day, we will have "a word in due season" to share with others (see Proverbs 15:23). We can succeed at what God calls us to do, if we listen for His instructions. He has said, "If you seek Me early and diligently, you will find Me" (see Proverbs 8:17).

Get Alone with God

*But when you pray, go into your [most] private
room, and, closing the door, pray to your Father, Who
is in secret; and your Father, Who sees in secret,
will reward you in the open.*

MATTHEW 6:6

Jesus rose early to be alone with God,
but Peter pursued Him to let Him know
that everyone was looking for Him (see Mark 1:35–
36). When you get alone to pray, it may seem that
everybody tries to hunt you down. But Jesus sought
time alone with God so He could focus on His
purpose.

We see the scenario of Jesus praying alone and
then meeting the needs of others again and again.
Jesus went throughout Galilee preaching and driving out demons. When a leper begged to be clean,
Jesus touched him, and the leprosy completely left
him (see Mark 1:39–42). If Jesus needed to be alone
with the Father before He ministered to others, so
do we.

Speak God's Mind

Hear, for I will speak excellent and *princely*
things; and the opening of my lips
shall be for right things.

PROVERBS 8:6

One of our biggest mistakes we make is that we sometimes answer people too quickly, just giving them something off the top of our head. Only a fool utters his whole mind (see Proverbs 29:11 KJV). Those who speak frequently and hastily are always in trouble, as the Bible says, "There are those who speak rashly, like the piercing of a sword, but the tongue of the wise brings healing" (Proverbs 12:18).

Jesus operated in wisdom. He always knew just the right thing to say, at just the right moment, to astound everybody. If we don't spend enough time with God, we will say the wrong thing at the wrong time. Decide to wait on God before speaking your mind today.

Be Filled with Truth

*Because he has set his love upon Me, therefore will
I deliver him; I will set him on high, because he knows
and understands My name [has a personal knowledge
of My mercy, love, and kindness — trusts and relies
on Me, knowing I will never forsake him, no, never].*

PSALM 91:14

Don't let the devil have your thoughts first thing in the morning. Begin early to get your day started right. As soon as you wake up, tell the Lord you love Him. Tell Him you need Him and are depending on Him. Read His Word and confess His promises as you prepare for the day.

Listen to teaching tapes while you are driving to work. Fill yourself with knowledge of God's truth. Don't talk yourself into a disaster before the day even begins. Instead say, "I am the righteousness of God in Christ; because He is with me today, I will rejoice in all things."

Stay in Agreement

Know the God of your father [have personal knowl-
edge of Him, be acquainted with, and understand
Him; appreciate, heed, and cherish Him] and serve
Him with a blameless heart and a willing mind. For
the Lord searches all hearts and minds and under-
stands all the wanderings of the thoughts. If you seek
Him [inquiring for and of Him and requiring Him
as your first and vital necessity] you will find Him.

1 CHRONICLES 28:9

God's Word reveals a wonderful plan for your life. It shows how God sees you, and what He has for you through Jesus Christ. Keep your thoughts and words in agreement with God's Word.

Say, "Everything I lay my hand to prospers and succeeds. I am the head and not the tail, above and not beneath. I am blessed going in and going out. The blessings of God chase me down and overtake me. God is on my side. I am blessed to be a blessing to everyone I meet today."

Obey Quickly

*Jesus then said to them, I assure you, most
solemnly I tell you, Moses did not give you the Bread
from heaven [what Moses gave you was not the
Bread from heaven], but it is My Father Who
gives you the true heavenly Bread.*

JOHN 6:32

Jesus said to ask God for *daily* bread (see
Matthew 6:11). He also called Himself
the "Bread of Life" (see John 6:35). Seek God's direction in the morning to gather His daily words for
you. You will feel well nourished all day long. Obey
quickly if God tells you to do something.

Even if God gives you a difficult task, don't put
it off and dread it all day. Abraham rose early to
offer Isaac on the altar; God blessed his obedience
and provided an acceptable sacrifice in place of Isaac
(see Genesis 22:1–14). David rose up early on the
morning that he was to kill Goliath, and through
him, God delivered the Israelites from their enemies
(see 1 Samuel 17:20–53). He will bless and deliver
you too.

Break Free from Bondages

The humble shall see it and be glad; you who seek
God, inquiring for and requiring Him [as your first
need], let your hearts revive and live!

PSALM 69:32

If it is still hard to start your day right, pray this prayer:

"Lord, I struggle in taking time to fellowship with You and read Your Word. I know that spending time with You is not a law, it is a privilege. It is something that benefits my life. I pray that the bondages, the lies of Satan that keep me out of the prayer closet and away from time with You, will be broken off of me.

"Help me to see clearly that this is something I must do to live in victory. I pray for an anointing that will draw me into Your presence and cause me to run after You. Help me to get every morning started right."

Wake Up with Praise

My mouth shall praise You with joyful lips when I remember You upon my bed and meditate on You in the night watches. For You have been my help.

PSALM 63:5—7

Many people never have a decent finish to their day because they let the enemy keep them from starting it right. Satan tries to capture our thoughts early in the morning. He wants to get us thinking about all the wrong things as soon as we wake up. His intent is to steal our peace by upsetting us as soon as our alarm goes off. He is always working to set us up to get us upset.

That is why it is important to learn how to defeat the devil early each day. Every morning is a new opportunity to start your day right. Praise God as soon as your eyes open to a new day.

Cling to God

My whole being follows hard after You and *clings
closely to You; Your right hand upholds me.*

PSALM 63:8

The Word of God has much to say about
morning. David started his day praying
and listening to God. He instructed the priests to
stand every morning to thank and praise the Lord,
and likewise at evening. He said "The Lord has
given peace *and* rest to His people" (see 1 Chronicles
23:25–30).

Many times we pray and pray, but, like Lot, we
don't listen. For example, angels prompted Lot early
in the morning to flee from Sodom and avoid its
coming destruction (see Genesis 19:15). We can
avoid disasters when we wait on God's instructions
before acting.

A great beginning leads to a great finish. Begin
your day with thanksgiving and praise, and in the
evening before you rest, thank the Lord again for a
great day.

Answers Will Come

Wait and *hope for* and *expect the Lord;*
be brave and *of good courage and let your*
heart be stout and *enduring.*

PSALM 27:14

I used to wake up wishing it was night, and at night I wished it was morning; I was not enjoying my life. Now I look forward to each day. God arranged life in twenty-four-hour periods; we sleep for a while, and then wake up refreshed to start all over again. God intended every morning to be a brand new start, a fresh opportunity.

We can go to bed feeling hopeless and worn out, thinking, *I just don't believe I can go on.* But somehow a good night's rest renews us, and we wake up with faith again, thinking, *Maybe today my breakthrough will come, and I will get an answer; I can make it one more day.* So thank God for mornings.

Speak Life

*Death and life are in the power of the tongue,
and they who indulge in it shall eat the
fruit of it [for death or life].*

PROVERBS 18:21

If we ride to work with somebody and gossip about our boss and talk about how we hate our job and what a stupid place it is, we will have a bad day. The Bible says, "A man's [moral] self shall be filled with the fruit of his mouth; and with the consequence of his words he must be satisfied [whether good or evil]" (Proverbs 18:20).

Clearly, we will have to eat our words, so we need to talk about the right things to be happy. If we murmur and gossip, we will eat the fruit of death. But if we speak life, we will eat the fruit of the Spirit (see Matthew 12:37). Choose to eat good fruit today.

Be Prepared

*What does the Lord your God require of you but
[reverently] to fear the Lord your God, [that is] to
walk in all His ways, and to love Him, and to serve
the Lord your God with all your [mind and]
heart and with your entire being.*

DEUTERONOMY 10:12

Complaining is death, and thanksgiving is life. Yet there are people who complain on their way to church while hoping to receive blessings. They don't understand that complaining keeps them from getting what they want. They don't come prepared to receive blessings in the Lord's presence.

Prepare yourself for blessings by offering thanksgiving for what God has already done for you. The Word says, "For by your words you will be justified *and* acquitted, and by your words you will be condemned *and* sentenced" (Matthew 12:37). Choose your words wisely today, and prepare yourself for God's blessings.

Worship with Your Whole Heart

I will cry to God Most High, Who performs on my behalf and rewards me [Who brings to pass His purposes for me and surely completes them]!

PSALM 57:2

Great worship leaders know to come into the presence of God with their entire being, prepared to give thanks and praise (see Deuteronomy 10:12). They don't just roll out of bed, throw water on their face, and run a comb through their hair before church. They know that the anointing comes from a sincere pursuit of loving God with their whole heart.

Likewise, as you approach God in the morning, come to Him with a heart full of worship, expressing your awe of Him for His faithfulness toward you. He promises that He will never forsake you, but will be with you all day long (see Joshua 1:5).

Find Quiet Time

The [reverent] fear of the Lord is clean, enduring
forever; the ordinances of the Lord are true and righ-
teous altogether. More to be desired are they than
gold, even than much fine gold; they are sweeter also
than honey and drippings from the honeycomb.

PSALM 19:9–10

Sometimes I set aside the entire day just to be with God. I stop everything and seek Him. I know I am not going to hear from God if I don't get quiet on purpose by that time set aside for Him.

It is so important to have some "down time" to be alone and just sit quietly. You may think you don't have time, but if somebody was giving out thousand-dollar bills at the mall, you would find time to get there. Don't use the time to try to figure out something; just be still and available to the Lord's attention.

Increase Your Days

Behold, the Lord's eye is upon those who fear
Him [who revere and worship Him with awe],
who wait for Him and *hope in His mercy*
and *loving-kindness, to deliver them from*
death and keep them alive in famine.

PSALM 33:18–19

When I talk about seeking God early, many people think they will have to get up at three o'clock in the morning! I am not trying to tell you *how* to do it. I am not even suggesting that you pray for an hour. I am just saying that some way, somehow, if you want to start your whole day right, you must find time to seek God's wisdom in the morning.

Time with God adds years to your life! God is eager to give us insight and understanding. His Word says, "For by me [Wisdom from God] your days shall be multiplied, and the years of your life shall be increased" (Proverbs 9:11).

Refill Your Peace

It is the Lord Who goes before you; He will
[march] with you; He will not fail you or let you go
or forsake you; [let there be no cowardice or flinching,
but] fear not, neither become broken [in spirit]
(depressed, dismayed, and unnerved with alarm).

DEUTERONOMY 31:8

Many times, believers with Christian bumper stickers on their cars are seen driving around like crazy people, yelling at their kids, throwing their hands in the air, and looking mad at the world. If there isn't any peace in our heart when we leave home, our bumper stickers are not going to impress anybody. We need to get our-selves straightened out before we go out.

Pray, "My [inner] self [as well as my body] is also exceedingly disturbed *and* troubled. But You, O Lord, how long [until You return and speak peace to me]?" (Psalm 6:3). Let God refill you with peace.

Put God First

But seek (aim at and strive after) first of all His kingdom and His righteousness (His way of doing and being right), and then all these things taken together will be given you besides.

MATTHEW 6:33

I have learned that spending time with God is a vital necessity in my life. I cannot do what I am called to do if I don't seek the presence of God every day. If I don't have time for God first, nothing else in my life works out.

God isn't happy with second place or third place in our lives.

When we are desperate enough, we find time to seek God. We turn the telephone off, we say no to our friends, and we turn our face away from all distractions and seek Him. That is when we get our breakthrough.

Go to Your Room!

*And I have filled him with the Spirit of God,
in wisdom and ability, in understanding and
intelligence, and in knowledge, and
in all kinds of craftsmanship.*

EXODUS 31:3

My children didn't like it when I started spending time alone to seek God. They said, "You're always in that room."

One day I told them, "You'd better be glad I am in that room, because it is making your life a whole lot better. If you were smart, you would beg me to go to my room, instead of calling me to come out."

Next time you find yourself screaming, ranting, raving, and carrying on at your children (or anyone else), excuse yourself and say, "I am going to my room." Take time to ask God what He thinks of everything that is going on. You will quickly get your day started over right.

Slow Down

*Peace I leave with you; My [own] peace I now give
and bequeath to you. Not as the world gives do
I give to you. Do not let your hearts be troubled,
neither let them be afraid. [Stop allowing yourselves
to be agitated and disturbed; and do not permit
yourselves to be fearful and intimidated and
cowardly and unsettled.]*

JOHN 14:27

Hurrying affects our spiritual life. Jesus wasn't in a hurry. We can't even picture Him jumping up and saying to His disciples, "Come on, boys, get up. Up, up, up, up! Get this camp meeting cleaned up. Come on, we have to get to the next town. We have some preaching to do. Get the camels packed up, boys. Let's go, let's go!"

When we think about Jesus, we picture peace. He went slow enough to hear from God all day long. We should set our pace with His today.

Turn Down the Noise

Take My yoke upon you and learn of Me, for I am gentle (meek) and humble (lowly) in heart, and you will find rest (relief and ease and refreshment and recreation and blessed quiet) for your souls.

MATTHEW 11:29

Noisy people don't hear from God. And we don't hear from Him when we are making noise, or when everything around us is noisy. The only kind of noise you should have in the morning is my television program; that's all (I am teasing). But don't turn on the radio or television just for noise.

Learn how to get comfortable being quiet. The Bible says, "But whoso hearkens to me [Wisdom] shall dwell securely *and* in confident trust and shall be quiet, without fear *or* dread of evil" (Proverbs 1:33).

Linger in God's Presence

Be still and *rest in the Lord; wait for Him* and
patiently lean yourself upon Him.

PSALM 37:7

Sometimes in our conferences, we just
"hang out" in God's presence. We sing
and worship Him, and soon we enjoy the freshness
of His marvelous wonder.

When we sense God is working in people's
hearts, we don't worry about our meeting schedule
or agenda. We set everything aside to just enjoy His
awesome power working among His people. Many
who came feeling bad are refreshed, and the sick are
healed during this time of worship and waiting on
the Lord. It happens all the time — there is healing
in God's presence.

If you feel discouraged, He will cheer you up. If
you feel tired, He will strengthen you. Just sit in His
presence and wait for Him to move in your life.

Focus on God's Promises

For I the Lord your God hold your right hand;
I am the Lord, Who says to you, Fear not;
I will help you!

ISAIAH 41:13

The Lord says to you this morning the same thing He told Jacob in a dream: "I am with you and will keep (watch over you with care, take notice of) you wherever you may go, and I will bring you back to this land; for I will not leave you until I have done all of which I have told you." (Genesis 28:15). Keep your mind on this promise in spite of any news you may hear that tempts you to be afraid today.

God promises to be with you, watch over you with care, take notice of you wherever you may go, and bring you back again. He says He will not leave you, and He will complete all the promises He has made to you. This means that no weapon formed against you will prosper (see Isaiah 54:17).

Rededicate Yourself

*O Lord, [earnestly] remember now how I have
walked before You in faithfulness and truth and with
a whole heart [entirely devoted to You] and have
done what is good in Your sight.*

2 KINGS 20:3

"And Jacob awoke from his sleep and he said, Surely the Lord is in this place and I did not know it" (Genesis 28:16). Many times the Lord is with us, and we don't even know it. God is there with you even when circumstances seem out of control. He is already working everything together for your good.

"And Jacob rose early in the morning and took the stone he had put under his head, and he set it up for a pillar (a monument to the vision in his dream), and he poured oil on its top [in dedication]" (v. 18). Likewise, we should rededicate ourselves to God every morning.

Give Your All to God

Before I formed you in the womb I knew [and]
approved of you [as My chosen instrument], and
before you were born I separated and set you apart,
consecrating you; [and] I appointed you as a
prophet to the nations.

JEREMIAH 1:5

Every day you need to give yourself entirely to God. Say, "Lord, I am Yours. I want to be a vessel fit for Your use. I dedicate myself to You: I give You my hands, my mouth, my mind, my body, my money, and my time. Father, here I am. I am Yours; do with me whatever You want to do today."

Once you dedicate yourself to God, then go on about your business. But expect His leading all day long. Listen for His voice to direct you in the way you should go. Accept the challenge to be an instrument for the Lord's use today.

Grasp Every Chance

*I will keep Your law continually, forever and ever
[hearing, receiving, loving, and obeying it].*

PSALM 119:44

You can meet with God while lying in bed. You don't have to be in a private room, with the door closed, bowed down on your knees to meet God. You can meet Him in the shower, while driving to work, or when stuck in a traffic jam.

I am not suggesting that you shouldn't set apart time for God. But you should also take advantage of any time you do have that you could be talking and listening to the Lord. Don't wait to talk to Him until you have a full hour to spend with Him. Grasp every minute you can find to open your ears to His voice. Take advantage of the idle moments already available to you and spend them with God.

Make a Fresh Commitment

Honor the Lord with your capital and *sufficiency*
[from righteous labors] and with the firstfruits of
all your income; so shall your storage places be
filled with plenty, and your vats shall be
overflowing with new wine.

PROVERBS 3:9–10

The parable of the talents (see Matthew
25:14–30) instructs us to use what God
gives to us to expand the Master's kingdom. Invest
yourself, your time, and your money in the Lord's
work. Rededicate your finances to God today.

Make a fresh commitment to be a giver. Don't
let the devil talk you out of giving just because you
have bills to pay and obligations that cause you to
worry. In Matthew 6:25–34 Jesus said not to be
anxious about anything, for God knows your needs
and promises to care for you.

Consecrate Your Money

And God is able to make all grace (every favor and earthly blessing) come to you in abundance, so that you may always and under all circumstances and whatever the need be self-sufficient [possessing enough to require no aid or support and furnished in abundance for every good work and charitable donation].

2 CORINTHIANS 9:8

The apostle Paul said that the believers in Macedonia not only gave their money to God, but they also gave themselves to the Lord's service (see 2 Corinthians 8:1–5). Paul too gave his life in service to God's people.

Many people want to receive all they can from God, but they are not willing to give all of themselves to Him. If you have never dedicated yourself to the Lord's service, you are missing a great adventure. Dedicate this day to Him; He will lead you on a path to victory.

Consecrate Your Life

He who brings an offering of praise and *thanks-giving honors* and *glorifies Me; and he who orders his way aright [who prepares the way that I may show him], to him I will demonstrate the salvation of God.*

PSALM 50:23

When I minister to people, I share with them my life and my family. We tell about our victories and our failures. We tell about our mistakes, the stupid things we do, and the wise things we do. We give the testimony of our lives to help others live victoriously too.

Someone needs your life today. Give your life to God, and let Him show you who needs ministry on His behalf. Give Him everything that you are, every-thing you hope to be, all your dreams, all your visions, all your hopes, and desires. Make everything His, and He will demonstrate His power through your life.

Consecrate Your Mouth

*I have proclaimed glad tidings of righteousness
in the great assembly [tidings of uprightness and
right standing with God]. Behold, I have not
restrained my lips, as You know, O Lord.*

PSALM 40:9

What would happen if every morning we gave our mouth to God so that only godly things came out of our lips? Psalm 34:13 says, "Keep your tongue from evil and your lips from speaking deceit."

Dedicate your mouth to God and use it only for what pleases Him: praise and worship and edification and exhortation and giving thanks. Put your lips on the altar each morning. Give your mouth to God through praying His Word: "O Lord, open my lips, and my mouth shall show forth Your praise" (Psalm 51:15).

Know God Intimately

Rejoice in the Lord always [delight, gladden
yourselves in Him]; again I say, Rejoice!
PHILIPPIANS 4:4

In Philippians 3:10 the apostle Paul wrote, "[For my determined purpose is] that I may know Him [that I may progressively become more deeply and intimately acquainted with Him, perceiving and recognizing and understanding the wonders of His Person more strongly and more clearly], and that I may in that same way come to know the power outflowing from His resurrection [which it exerts over believers]."

As you grow in the knowledge of God, you will get so happy you will run the devil right out of your life. Decide that today will be dedicated to recognizing God's power at work in your life. Keep your mind on whatever is right and true and lovely and pure and of a good report (see Philippians 4:8).

Start with Praise

*Through Him, therefore, let us constantly and at
all times offer up to God a sacrifice of praise, which is
the fruit of lips that thankfully acknowledge and
confess and glorify His name.*

HEBREWS 13:15

Moses rose early in the morning, built an altar, and offered burnt offerings and peace offerings to God. Then he prayed and read the Book of the Covenant (see Exodus 24:1–7). Thankfully, God no longer asks us to build an altar out of rocks, slaughter a bull, drain its blood, and build a fire in order to honor Him with a burnt sacrifice.

God doesn't want a dead sacrifice anymore. He wants us, living sacrifices, full of zeal to serve Him each day. All we have to do is wake up and say, "Thank You, Lord. I give You the sacrifice of praise. I give You myself, a living sacrifice, ready to live for You today."

Be God's Ambassador

And [pray] also for me, that [freedom of]
utterance may be given me, that I may open my
mouth to proclaim boldly the mystery of the good
news (the Gospel), for which I am an ambassador
in a coupling chain [in prison. Pray] that I may
declare it boldly and *courageously, as I ought to do.*

EPHESIANS 6:19–20

If you start your day right, you will have a better day, and you will be a better witness for the Lord. Dedicate yourself to God afresh each morning.

Tell Him, "Lord, I give You the gifts and talents that You put in me. I want to use them for Your glory. I want to lead somebody to You. Put in my path someone to whom I can minister, someone I can encourage. Help me to be a blessing to someone today. Lord, I want to be Your ambassador and represent You today."

Petition with Thanksgiving

*And God's peace [shall be yours, that tranquil
state of a soul assured of its salvation through Christ,
and so fearing nothing from God and being content
with its earthly lot of whatever sort that is, that
peace] which transcends all understanding shall
garrison and mount guard over your hearts
and minds in Christ Jesus.*

PHILIPPIANS 4:7

We can petition the Lord for things we need every morning. God's Word tells us to lay our requests before Him: "Do not fret *or* have any anxiety about anything, but in every circumstance *and* in everything, by prayer and petition (definite requests), with thanksgiving, continue to make your wants known to God" (Philippians 4:6).

But don't spend all your time with God petitioning for things. You are out of balance if your petitions outweigh your praise and thanksgiving. A heart full of thankfulness will make any day better.

God Will Brighten Your Day

He set himself to seek God . . . and as long as
he sought (inquired of, yearned for) the Lord,
God made him prosper.

2 CHRONICLES 26:5

Jesus got up early in the morning, long before daylight, and went out to a deserted place, and prayed — He got alone (see Mark 1:35). There were so many people who followed Jesus everywhere He went that He probably wouldn't have had any time alone if He hadn't gotten up really early.

If you aren't a morning person, the thought of getting up early may make you nervous. But you can decipher for yourself what "early" means for you. Nine o'clock is early if you are used to staying in bed until noon. Even if you only get up fifteen minutes earlier than usual to have some time alone with God, you will still honor Him, and that time with Him, will make your whole day brighter.

Enjoy the Pursuit

*Blessed (happy, fortunate, to be envied) is he who
considers the weak and the poor; the Lord will deliver
him in the time of evil and trouble.*

PSALM 41:1

Do you ever feel that no matter where
you go, somebody pursues you and hunts
you down? Does someone seem to need something
every time you start doing what you set out to do?
Someone needs a ride to school, or somebody forgets their lunch, and before you know it, half your
day is wasted.

Jesus knows what it is like to be pursued, but He
was never upset by it. As soon as He ministered to
everyone in one place, He went to the next town to
find more people who needed Him. He never said,
"Leave Me alone." Ask God to show you the needs of
people through the eyes of Jesus today, and your
days will never be wasted.

Prepare for Ministry

*You prepare a table before me in the presence of
my enemies. You anoint my head with oil; my
[brimming] cup runs over. Surely or only goodness,
mercy, and unfailing love shall follow me all the
days of my life, and through the length of my days
the house of the Lord [and His presence]
shall be my dwelling place.*

Every day offers opportunities to "be in ministry." Someone will always need a helping hand, but you won't minister well if you don't prepare yourself by spending time with God. People can tell when you have had intimate moments with God recently, and also when you haven't.

The Lord anoints us to meet the needs of others, but if we are not being filled by Him, we will hinder the flow of His healing oil in our lives. Seek God early, before someone calls and needs your help.

Operate in Wisdom

Oh, the depth of the riches and wisdom and
knowledge of God! How unfathomable (inscrutable,
unsearchable) are His judgments (His decisions)!
And how untraceable (mysterious, undiscoverable)
are His ways (His methods, His paths)!

ROMANS 11:33

Without wisdom we can make poor decisions and later wonder why we didn't pray first. It is wise to seek God early each day before we start making decisions in order to know ahead of time what we ought to do, and then to receive the grace to do it. Wisdom keeps us from a life of regret.

Jesus operated in wisdom. When others went home to rest, Jesus went to the Mount of Olives to spend time with God. And early in the morning (at dawn), He came back into the temple and taught people (see John 7:53–8:2). Jesus always spent time with the Father before facing the crowds. If Jesus needed time with God, we need even more time with Him. Walk in wisdom today.

Realize God's Continual Presence

Though a sinner does evil a hundred times and his
days [seemingly] are prolonged [in his wickedness],
yet surely I know that it will be well with those who
[reverently] fear God, who revere and *worship*
Him, realizing His continual presence.

ECCLESIASTES 8:12

You can form such a habit of prayer that you will wake up in the morning talking to God. You can fall asleep at night talking to God, and wake up in the middle of the night still talking to Him. The Word calls it "prayer without ceasing" (see 2 Timothy 1:3).

I have learned to start my day with prayer and just keep praying all day. I pray when I see somebody hurting. I pray if I don't feel good. I pray when I feel hurried.

Prayer is conversation with God. It is simply being aware of His continual presence and acknowledging Him in all of our ways. If we do, He promises to direct our path to a place of peace and victory (see Proverbs 3:6).

Quit Complaining

*Whoso is wise [if there be any truly wise] will
observe and heed these things; and they will
diligently consider the mercy and loving-
kindness of the Lord.*

PSALM 107:43

Today thank God and decide not to complain about anything. Ask Him to show
you anytime you are getting ready to complain, and
to help you hold your tongue. Today, give thanks for
what you have without looking at what you don't
have. Some people have the same problems you
have, but they don't know God. At least you can
give thanks that God is in your life.

The Word says, "Let there be no filthiness (ob-
scenity, indecency) nor foolish *and* sinful (silly and
corrupt) talk, nor coarse jesting, which are not fitting *or* becoming; but instead voice your thankfulness
[to God]" (Ephesians 5:4). Guard your tongue today.

Pray before Answering

For [of course] I will not venture (presume) to
speak thus of any work except what Christ has
actually done through me [as an instrument in
His hands] to win obedience from the
Gentiles, by word and deed.

ROMANS 15:18

The Father has sent to us a Counselor —
the Spirit of Truth — who teaches us all
things (see John 14:16,17,26). As we stay sensitive
to God's leading, He will direct us. If we pray before
speaking, the Lord will keep us from overcommit-
ting our time, and from misleading people.

Jesus took time to listen to the Father before
speaking. God will also give us "a word in due season" for somebody (see Proverbs 15:23), if we listen for His input before we give what we may think
is a right answer. God will give us the right words to
say if we expectantly listen for His direction before
we speak.

Aim Higher!

Therefore I do not run uncertainly (without
definite aim). I do not box like one beating the air
and striking without an adversary. But [like a boxer]
I buffet my body [handle it roughly, discipline it
by hardships] and subdue it, for fear that after pro-
claiming to others the Gospel and things pertaining
to it, I myself should become unfit [not stand the test,
be unapproved and rejected as a counterfeit].

I CORINTHIANS 9:26—27

Excessive sleep causes the downfall of many good plans. You can set the clock to get up early and pray, but your flesh is not going to help you get up in the morning. Your body will nearly always beg for more sleep.

Don't let your flesh rob you of time with God. Aim for the higher goal, and wake up with your alarm to enjoy the best minutes of your day.

Start Moving

Bless (affectionately, gratefully praise) the
Lord . . . who satisfies your mouth [your necessity
and desire at your personal age and situation]
with good so that your youth, renewed, is like the
eagle's [strong, overcoming, soaring]!

PSALM 103:1, 5

Proverbs 6:4 says, "Give not [unnecessary] sleep to your eyes, nor slumber to your eyelids." The Bible is saying, "Get the sleep you need, but then wake up!" Too much sleep brings poverty. It is like a robber who steals from you and makes you helpless (see Proverbs 6:11).

Too little sleep will ruin your day too. Being tired and cranky doesn't help you hear from God. Make rest a priority, but then get up. Start moving first thing in the morning, saying, "Thank You, Lord, that I am alive for another day with You. I believe I am anointed to do what You ask me to do today. My youth is renewed like the eagle's, just as You promised."

Love Not Sleep

My eyes anticipate the night watches and *I am*
awake before the cry of the watchman, that I may
meditate on Your word.

PSALM 119:148

It is interesting that our popular greeting
is "Good morning." Somewhere along
the way, someone realized that if we get started off
right in the morning, we will have a good day.

Proverbs 20:13 says, "Love not sleep, lest you
come to poverty; open your eyes and you will be satisfied with bread." And Psalm 57:8–9 encourages us
to wake up ready to sing praises: "Awake, my glory
(my inner self); awake, harp and lyre! I will awake
right early [I will awaken the dawn]! I will praise *and*
give thanks to You, O Lord, among the peoples; I
will sing praises to You among the nations."

Make It a Habit

*Besides this you know what [a critical] hour this
is, how it is high time now for you to wake up out
of your sleep (rouse to reality). For salvation
(final deliverance) is nearer to us now than when
we first believed (adhered to, trusted in, and
relied on Christ, the Messiah).*

ROMANS 13:11

The Word says that Jesus had a habit of
going up the mountain to spend time
with God. Luke 22:39 says, "And He came out and
went, as was His habit, to the Mount of Olives, and
the disciples also followed Him." Jesus formed a
habit of communicating with God every morning.

It has been said that if you do something consistently for thirty days, it will become a habit. You
can either make or break a habit by consistently doing the same thing. Follow Jesus, and form a habit of
starting your day with prayer.

Require God's Presence

*One thing have I asked of the Lord, that will I
seek, inquire for, and [insistently] require: that I may
dwell in the house of the Lord [in His presence] all
the days of my life, to behold and gaze upon the
beauty [the sweet attractiveness and the delightful
loveliness] of the Lord and to meditate, consider,
and inquire in His temple.*

PSALM 27:4

When I first became a Christian, I didn't
desire to pray as much as I do now.
Although I do spend time with God every morning,
I also spend time with Him all day. It seems that I
walk in prayer.

In her powerful book, *Experiencing God through
Prayer*, Madame Guyon says there is a difference between praying *to* God and experiencing Him. At
first you must discipline yourself to pray, but eventually you will give yourself to the ocean of God's
love, and experience His continual presence.

Pray Anywhere

*Blessed (happy, fortunate, to be envied) are those
who dwell in Your house and Your presence; they will
be singing Your praises all the day long. Selah
[pause, and calmly think of that]!*

PSALM 84:4

Once in the habit of spending time with God, you will miss these encounters if you start your day without talking and listening to Him. You can spend time with God anywhere, while doing anything — in the grocery store, or while cleaning house, for example. I have had great encounters with God while driving my car.

God is always listening for the sound of your voice calling out to Him. Develop a ready ear for His voice too. Whatever you have to do today, do it with the Lord. Acknowledge Him and talk to Him about everything. You will greatly enjoy His company.

Today May Be "One of Those Days"

Be alert and on your guard; stand firm in your faith (your conviction respecting man's relationship to God and divine things, keeping the trust and holy fervor born of faith and a part of it). Act like men and be courageous; grow in strength!

1 CORINTHIANS 16:13

Have you ever had "one of those days" where nothing went right, yet you were hesitant to pray because you didn't know where God might lead you? God won't always ask you to *do* something; sometimes He just wants to talk to you.

If He does ask you to do something, He will anoint you to do it. You will enjoy the presence of His power, and someone will be blessed by your obedience. Those are the best days of your life. Take time to pray this morning. Today may be "one of those days" that God has a special assignment for you.

Praise God

Enter into His gates with thanksgiving and *a thank offering and into His courts with praise! Be thankful* and *say so to Him, bless* and *affectionately praise His name!*

PSALM 100:4

There are many opportunities to praise God throughout the day. If thankfulness for your many blessings suddenly rises in your heart, stop right then and tell the Lord how grateful you are for all He has given you.

Say, "I worship You, Lord, for You are worthy to be praised. I need You, and I just want to tell You that I love You. Thank You, Father, for everything."

Then go on with what you are doing as if it is for Him. You will be amazed at how much fun everyday life becomes in the presence of the Lord.

Be Fully Satisfied

*Planted in the house of the Lord, they shall flour-
ish in the courts of our God. [Growing in grace] they
shall still bring forth fruit in old age; they shall be
full of sap [of spiritual vitality] and [rich in the]
verdure [of trust, love, and contentment].*

PSALM 92:13–14

Many people pursue possessions and
awards to satisfy their inner need for contentment. But we can be fully satisfied in lean times
and in times of abundance, whether we abase or
abound (see Philippians 4:12), when we learn to enjoy fellowship with the Lord as soon as we wake up.

Before you are fully awake, you can start talking
to God. Just thank Him for seeing you through yesterday, and for being with you today. Praise Him for
providing for you, and for working out all the situations in your life for your good.

Ask Him to make you aware of His presence all
day long. Peace fills your heart when your mind is on
the Lord. Nothing is more satisfying than walking
with God.

Have a Glad Heart

From the fruit of his words a man shall be
satisfied with good, and the work of a man's hands
shall come back to him [as a harvest].

PROVERBS 12:14

I used to live with an ongoing sense of dread until I asked God to show me what was wrong. He spoke the words "evil forebodings," and then showed me His Word concerning this subject: "All the days of the desponding *and* afflicted are made evil [by anxious thoughts and forebodings], but he who has a glad heart has a continual feast [regardless of circumstances]" (Proverbs 15:15).

Anxious thoughts make the day evil. If you expect to have a dismal day, you will be unpleasant yourself. Evil forebodings ruin the day, but faith makes the heart glad and brings miraculous results. If you want to have a good day, raise your expectations to be in line with God's Word.

Don't Dread It

The hand of the diligent will rule, but the
slothful will be put to forced labor.

PROVERBS 12:24

Don't spend your day looking for something easy to do instead of tackling the hard things that need to be done. Do the hard things first, the ones you dislike the most, and get them out of the way. For example, don't look at your distasteful jobs and think, *I will do those later.* The hard tasks will nag at you all day long and drain your energy for doing the things you want to do.

The spirit of passivity will rob you of productive energy, but you have the power of God in you to overcome procrastination. Pray and ask God to help you finish the tasks you have been dreading. Work on what is important first, and soon they will no longer be ruling or ruining your day.

Have Confidence in God

*No unbelief or distrust made him waver
(doubtingly question) concerning the promise of God,
but he grew strong and was empowered by faith as he
gave praise and glory to God, fully satisfied and
assured that God was able and mighty to keep His
word and to do what He had promised.*

ROMANS 4:20—21

No one believed David could defeat the giant, but David wasn't discouraged. David had sought the Lord early, which gave him confidence in God to do what he was supposed to do that day. When David killed Goliath, he ran quickly to the battlefield and proclaimed victory in the name of the living God (see 1 Samuel 17:20—54).

People who rise early and seek God go forth to do what they must do with courage. Ask God for confidence to slay any giants in your life that have set themselves against God's plan for you.

Be a Blessing

You will guard him and keep him in perfect and constant peace whose mind [both its inclination and its character] is stayed on You, because he commits himself to You, leans on You, and hopes confidently in You.

ISAIAH 26:3

Galatians 6:10 says, "Be mindful to be a blessing, especially to those of the household of faith." Second Corinthians 10:5 speaks of casting down imaginations and every high and lofty thing that exalts itself against the knowledge of God. In other words, keep (set) your mind on God's promises and on what is relevant to His plan for your life.

Don't let your mind be taken captive by the enemy. Instead, "lead every thought and purpose away captive into the obedience of Christ." Decide to be a blessing to everyone you meet today. Forgive anyone who has hurt you, and leave unresolved circumstances in God's hands. Don't use today to relive yesterday. Say, "I am moving forward today, in Jesus' name."

God Gives Us All We Need

*And they who know Your name [who have
experience and acquaintance with Your mercy]
will lean on and confidently put their trust in You,
for You, Lord, have not forsaken those who seek
(inquire of and for) You [on the authority of God's
Word and the right of their necessity].*

PSALM 9:10

In His Word God has given us the tools
we need to help us through each new day.
He has given us "the garment of praise for the spirit
of heaviness" (Isaiah 61:3 KJV). So, when you wake
up in the morning, decide that no matter what happens, you will not be depressed today.

Put on the garment of praise first thing in the
morning. Listen to worshipful music, read the Word,
and renew your thoughts to bring them into line with
what God says you are — righteous and blessed. You
can think right, talk right, and act right all day, if you
spend time with God before trials come your way.

Some Things Never Happen

*You will show me the path of life; in Your
presence is fullness of joy, at Your right hand
there are pleasures forevermore.*

PSALM 16:11

Many times we get upset about things
that never happen. Satan likes to get us
anxious about things that are not even real problems. Jesus said, "The thief comes only in order to
steal and kill and destroy. I came that they may have
and enjoy life, and have it in abundance (to the full,
till it overflows)" (John 10:10).

The Bible says that the kingdom of God is internal righteousness, peace, and joy in the Holy Ghost
(see Romans 14:17). When we make Jesus Lord of
our heart, we have joy in our lives. Satan has no right
to steal from you today, so enjoy the good life that
Jesus paid for you to have.

Love Yourself

Keep out of debt and *owe no man anything,
except to love one another; for he who loves his
neighbor [who practices loving others] has fulfilled
the Law [relating to one's fellowmen, meeting
all its requirements].*

ROMANS 13:8

Jesus said, "Love your neighbor *as your-self*" (see Matthew 22:39). So we need a healthy respect for ourself if we want to enjoy our relationships with other people. If we don't have a balanced love for ourselves, it is difficult to love others. Life is no fun if we can't enjoy other people, because they are everywhere we go!

Sometimes it is difficult to get along with people because they seem so different from us, but it is our differences that make us need one another. God designed us to need each other's friendships and talents. Do something nice for someone today. Let someone know that you appreciate him or her.

Get Along with Others

*But the meek [in the end] shall inherit the
earth and shall delight themselves in the
abundance of peace.*

PSALM 37:11

We can *learn* to get along with people.
It is especially important to learn to get
along with our immediate family members and co-
workers. There are many informative books about
personality differences to help us understand why
people feel and act the way they do. Understanding
helps to smooth over strained relationships.

People make decisions differently. Some give an
immediate answer, while others want time to think
about things first. Try to understand the people you
will see today. Ask God to show you ways to get
along with them. He will give you favor as you trust
in Him.

Positive Change

Bear (endure, carry) one another's burdens and
troublesome moral faults, and in this way fulfill and
observe perfectly the law of Christ (the Messiah)
and *complete what is lacking [in*
your obedience to it].

GALATIANS 6:2

Our happiness and joy are not dependent
on whether or not other people do what
we want them to do. We may never be able to influence anyone else to do what we think is right. But
with God's help, we can change ourselves to bring
about the results we want in life.

I have discovered that if I change in a positive
way, and if it is a permanent and stable change, it almost always provokes change in the people around
me. If you want your life to be different, ask God
to show you how *you* need to change. Accept others
for who they are, and see how God works in you to
complete your joy.

Live to Full Potential

*For you are becoming progressively acquainted
with and recognizing more strongly and clearly the
grace of our Lord Jesus Christ (His kindness, His
gracious generosity, His undeserved favor and
spiritual blessing), [in] that though He was [so very]
rich, yet for your sakes He became [so very] poor,
in order that by His poverty you might become
enriched (abundantly supplied).*

2 CORINTHIANS 8:9

I used to wake up feeling guilty and condemned. I was full of judgment and criticism for every little mistake I made. But that outlook
creates pressure inside of us that is apt to explode in
the face of the first person who comes around.

If you struggle this way, begin your day by reading the Word. Knowledge of God's mercy and forgiveness is vital in learning to love yourself so that
you can love others. Live today to its fullest potential.

A Useful Vessel

*So whoever cleanses himself [from what is ignoble
and unclean, who separates himself from contact with
contaminating and corrupting influences] will [then
himself] be a vessel set apart and useful for honorable
and noble purposes, consecrated and profitable to the
Master, fit and ready for any good work.*

2 TIMOTHY 2:21

The Bible refers to us as earthen vessels
(see 2 Corinthians 4:7); we are made of
clay (see Isaiah 64:8). God formed Adam out of
the dirt (see Genesis 2:7), and King David said,
"Remember Lord, that I am but dust" (see Psalm
103:14).

When we fill ourselves with God's Word, we become containers of His blessing, ready to be poured
out for His use. God can even use cracked pots! We
are all valuable to the Lord. We can offer His truth
to people everywhere we go.

Read God's Word before you go about your routine today, and see how many people you can bless
with the truth of His love.

Show Jesus

And become useful and helpful and kind to one
another, tenderhearted (compassionate, understand-
ing, loving-hearted), forgiving one another [readily
and freely], as God in Christ forgave you.

EPHESIANS 4:32

I hope to show to everyone I meet the character of Jesus through my words and actions. I pray that everyone who contacts our ministry team will say: "Those people are full of Jesus. They are patient, kind, and sweet."

We are containers capable of being filled to overflowing with the Spirit of Jesus, who dwells in our hearts. If we understand that everywhere we go we can demonstrate His character and virtue, we will be as the Word says — lights in a dark world (see Philippians 2:15).

Jesus called us the salt of the earth (see Matthew 5:13). Salt gives flavor to what is otherwise bland or tasteless. Be salt today — at home, at your job, wherever you go.

Stay Plugged In

*Let your light so shine before men that they may
see your moral excellence and your praiseworthy,
noble, and good deeds and recognize and honor and
praise and glorify your Father Who is in heaven.*

MATTHEW 5:16

Jesus is the Light of the world and He lights up those who come into relationship with Him. When Moses spent time in God's presence, his face became so bright that he wore a veil because people feared to come near him (see Exodus 34:29–30).

As a lamp must be plugged into the electrical outlet to illuminate the darkness around it, so we must stay plugged into God if we want our light to shine before others. The only way we can walk in love and behave the way we should is to pray, read the Word, and experience fellowship with God. Stay plugged in, and be a light wherever you go.

Don't Get Upset

May He grant you out of the rich treasury of His glory to be strengthened and reinforced with mighty power in the inner man by the [Holy] Spirit [Himself indwelling your innermost being and personality].

EPHESIANS 3:16

The devil sets us up to get upset so that we act ugly, throw fits, and ruin our witness of what God has done in our lives. Without God's love flowing through us, it is hard to be nice to nice people, let alone to treat difficult people nicely. We need God's help to live well.

The Holy Spirit will give you the power to walk in love everywhere you go. Don't leave home without inviting Him to fill you with the grace to demonstrate God's love and compassion toward everyone you meet.

Really Come to Know God

[I pray] that you may be filled [through all your being] unto all the fullness of God [may have the richest measure of the divine Presence, and become a body wholly filled and flooded with God Himself]!

EPHESIANS 3:19

Paul was praying for us (the church) when he said, "I pray that you might really come to know, practically and experientially for yourselves, the love of Christ, which far surpasses mere knowledge without experience" (see Ephesians 3:19). He knew that we needed to experience the love of God personally.

Our faith is not dependent on experiences, but our relationship with God *is* real, and we can expect visitations from God. We need times of God's outpouring in which we know, without a doubt, that He is moving in our lives.

Begin the journey of getting to know God better and better. Be aware of His love for you all day.

Desire More of God

*I pray You, if I have found favor in Your sight,
show me now Your way, that I may know You
[progressively become more deeply and intimately
acquainted with You, perceiving and recognizing and
understanding more strongly and clearly] and that
I may find favor in Your sight. And [Lord, do]
consider that this nation is Your people.*

EXODUS 33:13

As you get to know God better, you will undergo a transition from just praying during times of trouble to wanting to serve Him with everything you are, every breath you take, and every talent you possess. When you fall in love with Jesus, you will crave more and more time with Him.

Once you offer your time, your money, and your gifts to the Lord, you will want to spend every day getting to know Him more intimately. Ask God to fill your entire being with His fullness as you seek Him with all of your heart.

Be Filled with God

*My mouth shall be filled with Your praise
and with Your honor all the day.*

PSALM 71:8

Consider again the verse from Ephesians 3:19: "That you may be . . . a body wholly filled and flooded with God Himself!" Imagine what your day will be like if your body is *wholly filled* with God. You will be a container, carrying God everywhere you go. It will affect your thoughts, emotions, and actions. Being filled with the divine presence of God will change what you say, the entertainment you choose, and the people with whom you elect to spend time.

When we are born again, Jesus comes to live in us as a seed. Caring for that seed of new life by watering it with the Word, nurturing it through direction, and weeding out the sins in our lives makes the seed of His presence grow bigger and bigger until it fills our entire being.

Bearing Fruit

*You have not chosen Me, but I have chosen you
and I have appointed you [I have planted you], that
you might go and bear fruit and keep on bearing,
and that your fruit may be lasting [that it may
remain, abide], so that whatever you ask the Father
in My Name [as presenting all that I AM],
He may give it to you.*

JOHN 15:16

The Bible says that we are blessed if our confidence is in the Lord. We will be like trees planted by the waters that continue to bear fruit (see Jeremiah 17:7–8).

I admit that sometimes, at the end of a day, we may feel that all of our fruit has been picked! But God will replenish us if we abide in Him. If we put our trust in God, we will bear all kinds of fruit, and will have new fruit to share with others every morning.

Use the Keys

They who seek (inquire of and require) the Lord
[by right of their need and on the authority of His
Word], none of them shall lack any beneficial thing.

PSALM 34:10

Jesus said, "I will give you the keys of the kingdom of heaven; and whatever you bind (declare to be improper and unlawful) on earth must be what is already bound in heaven; and whatever you loose (declare lawful) on earth must be what is already loosed in heaven" (Matthew 16:19).

As a believer, you have authority to live a life of victory and to forbid the devil to torment you. It is not lawful for him to destroy you in heaven, so it is not lawful for him to destroy you during your days on earth. Use the keys of the kingdom of heaven that Jesus has passed to you. Loose God's blessings upon your efforts and bind the evil works that come against the fruit of your labors today.

Brokenness Is Good

Show Your marvelous loving-kindness, O You Who
save by Your right hand those who trust and take
refuge in You from those who rise up against them.
Keep and guard me as the pupil of Your eye;
hide me in the shadow of Your wings.

PSALM 17:7–8

David said, "Lord, I am like a broken vessel" (see Psalm 31:12). Brokenness seems
bad, but through brokenness we rid ourselves of the
outer shell, the fleshly parts of us, that need to be
thrown off in order to bring forth the good things
that are in us.

All of us need to be broken as David was; we
need to be totally dependent on God to deliver us
from evil. Pray today as David did: "But I trusted in,
relied on, *and* was confident in You, O Lord; I said,
You are my God" (Psalm 31:14).

Broken and Poured Out

For the Son of Man is going to come in the glory
(majesty, splendor) of His Father with His angels, and
then He will render account and reward every man
in accordance with what he has done.

MATTHEW 16:27

Be willing to give your best to the Lord, and He will use your gifts in ways beyond your imagination. The lady with the alabaster jar of perfume that was worth a year's wages wanted to do something for Jesus because she loved Him. So she poured out the expensive perfume on Him, not realizing at the time that she was anointing Him for His burial (see Mark 14:1—9).

God led her to give what she had, no matter how costly. As you pour out the gifts God has given you, He will use them to prepare the world for the second coming of His son. Your obedience today will reap rewards in heaven that you are not aware of now.

Bless People

For you, brethren, were [indeed] called to freedom;
only [do not let your] freedom be an incentive to your
flesh and an opportunity or excuse [for selfishness],
but through love you should serve one another.

GALATIANS 5:13

As a believer in Jesus Christ, you have wonderful, wonderful gifts on the inside of you. You have the ability to make others happy today. You can encourage. You can edify. You can exhort and uplift. You can believe. You can pray. You can lead somebody else to Christ.

People don't have to have desperate needs before we bless them. The Holy Spirit will lead us to be good to people every day, if we will be sensitive to His voice. Offer your gifts and talents to the Lord, and see what happens.

Do Good

This message is most trustworthy . . . so that those
who have believed in (trusted in, relied on) God may
be careful to apply themselves to honorable occupa-
tions and *to doing good, for such things are [not*
only] excellent and *right [in themselves], but [they*
are] good and *profitable for the people.*

TITUS 3:8

What an awesome thing it is to be good to
people. The Bible says that God anointed
Jesus with the Holy Spirit and with strength, ability,
and power; and that He went about doing good, for
God was with Him (see Acts 10:38). Jesus spent His
days being good to people — all people. He helped
and encouraged people everywhere He went.

We are anointed to bless people as Jesus did.
God has given us the strength, ability, and power to
do awesome works in His name. Do good all day —
today.

Humble Yourself

Let this same attitude and *purpose* and *[humble]*
mind be in you which was in Christ Jesus: [Let Him
be your example in humility].

PHILIPPIANS 2:5

Humility comes from brokenness; brokenness hurts so bad, but it "hurts good."
Brokenness comes when we learn that we are not
hotshots after all. Brokenness comes when we judge
others, and then realize that we do the same things
they do. Brokenness comes when we think *we are* going to step out and do something great, and then fall
flat on our face because we forgot to stay plugged in
to God.

Brokenness comes when we give our opinion,
knowing that we are absolutely right to the point of
arguing about it, and then find that we are wrong.
Brokenness is good for us. Brokenness leads to humility, and humility precedes honor (see Proverbs
15:33).

Let God Be Exalted

The proud looks of man shall be brought low, and
the haughtiness of men shall be humbled; and the
Lord alone shall be exalted in that day.

ISAIAH 2:11

None of us are where we need to be, but, thank God, we are not where we used to be. Don't look at what you are *going through* right now; look at the person you are *becoming*. We are always in the process of becoming like Christ (see 2 Corinthians 3:18).

Brokenness hurts, but the alternative is much worse. The Word says, "Haughtiness comes before disaster, but humility before honor" (Proverbs 18:12). Pray to be bendable, pliable, and moldable so that you will be more like Christ in all that you do today. Pray to be broken so that the Lord may be exalted in your life.

A Precious Treasure

All these [gifts, achievements, abilities] are
inspired and brought to pass by one and the same
[Holy] Spirit, Who apportions to each person
individually [exactly] as He chooses.

1 CORINTHIANS 12:11

In 2 Corinthians 4:7, Paul says, "We possess this precious treasure [the divine Light of the Gospel] in [frail, human] vessels of earth, that the grandeur *and* exceeding greatness of the power may be shown to be from God and not from ourselves." God uses frail people (cracked pots!) to proclaim the power of His gospel.

He could send angels to preach the gospel, but He uses plain, ordinary, everyday people to demonstrate His power. He fills us with divine gifts, inspired and brought to pass by the Holy Spirit, and distributes them throughout His body of believers. Let us network with God's people today for the greater good, as we work together to accomplish His purpose.

It Must Be God

For You cause my lamp to be lighted and *to shine;
the Lord my God illumines my darkness.*

PSALM 18:28

The Bible says that God works through our weakness so that the grandeur and exceeding greatness of the power in our lives may be shown to be from Him and not from ourselves (see 2 Corinthians 4:7). God uses ordinary people like us with flaws and cracks in our pots (our earthen vessels), so that people will know that it has to be God working in us if we are doing good works.

If people knew us before we trusted in Jesus, they especially notice the difference that a few years of walking with the Lord has made in our lives. We become totally different creatures when we allow His love to shine through our weaknesses. We may look the same, but we don't act the same. We just ooze with love when we are filled with God's exceeding greatness. Let His glorious light shine through you all day.

Light Shines Through Cracked Pots

Let not those who wait and hope and look for You,
O Lord of hosts, be put to shame through me; let not
those who seek and inquire for and require You
[as their vital necessity] be brought to confusion
and dishonor through me, O God of Israel.

PSALM 69:6

Everyone is like a pot that carries life. But not everyone carries a presence that blesses others. Religion tries to force people to follow laws to make them perfect, like pots without cracks. But if a light is put within a flawless pot and then covered, no one is able to see the light inside the pot. Perfect pots are not able to reveal internal light to illumine the way for others.

God chooses to shine through imperfect, cracked pots. People are blessed when our cracked pots let the light of Jesus shine through. Choose to be a glory-filled, cracked pot rather than an empty, pretty vessel.

Die to Sin

And Peter answered them, Repent (change your views and purpose to accept the will of God in your inner selves instead of rejecting it) and be baptized, every one of you, in the name of Jesus Christ for the forgiveness of and release from your sins; and you shall receive the gift of the Holy Spirit.

ACTS 2:38

Dying to sin requires a daily commitment. We all have weaknesses, but that is why we need Jesus. He would have died for us in vain if we didn't need Him. Each day we must ask Him to help us with our problems and our flaws.

He will save us from our sins, tempers, selfishness, jealousy, and greed. When we become Christians, our fleshly desire to sin doesn't die *in* us, but Jesus will save us *from* our sins if we ask Him for strength to die to selfish desires and follow Him.

Identify Who You Are

*Let him turn away from wickedness and shun it,
and let him do right. Let him search for peace
(harmony; undisturbedness from fears, agitating
passions, and moral conflicts) and seek it eagerly.
[Do not merely desire peaceful relations with God,
with your fellowmen, and with yourself, but
pursue, go after them!]*

1 PETER 3:11

Paul said, "I want to do what is right, but
I can't" (see Romans 7:15–25). He was a
new person on the inside because he was born
again, but he still had to resist the temptation to sin.

Paul explained that "the sin [principle]" (v. 20)
continues to dwell in us. We want to do right, but
we don't have the power to perform it, because evil
is ever present to tempt us to do wrong. Only God
can deliver us from this tendency to sin; that is why
we must ask Him to deliver us from evil each day.

Enlarge Your Circle of Love

Behold, how good and how pleasant it is
for brethren to dwell together in unity!

PSALM 133:1

We can dress up and look pretty on the outside, but God is more concerned about what is going on inside us. When we judge others by the way they look, we fall into the devil's trap of rejecting everyone who does not appear to be like us.

Purposely enlarge your circle of love today. Seek ways to include others you may have previously overlooked. Ask God to help you enlarge your circle of love by taking in people of all types, colors, and backgrounds. Pray for eyes to see into people's heart, and expect to enjoy a great day.

We Need Each Other

Again I tell you, if two of you on earth agree
(harmonize together, make a symphony together)
about whatever [anything and everything] they may
ask, it will come to pass and be done for them by
My Father in heaven.

MATTHEW 18:19

We need each other in the body of Christ. Men and women need each other — denominations need each other. I believe that when we get to heaven, we will learn the truth about our differences. We will learn that all of us were right about some things and wrong about others.

But even the things we were right about won't matter. God wants us to get along, to stop fighting with everyone over petty things we disagree about, and to begin to find the things we can agree about so that we may get along with one another. Practice looking for ways to agree with other believers, and then watch what God does through the unity of faith.

Christ Is the Power

*And God also selected (deliberately chose) what in
the world is lowborn and insignificant and branded
and treated with contempt, . . . so that no mortal
man should [have pretense for glorying and]
boast in the presence of God.*

1 CORINTHIANS 1:28—29

"But to those who are called, . . . Christ
[is] the Power of God and the Wisdom of
God" (1 Corinthians 1:24). When God calls us to do
something, He enables us to do it. Remember, God
uses inadequate people to do important things because that way He gets the glory.

So if God calls you to do something today that
seems too big for you to handle, Christ will give
you the power and the wisdom that you need to
do it. God has said to each of us, "*My* strength *and*
power are made perfect (fulfilled and completed)
and show themselves most effective in [your] weakness"
(2 Corinthians 12:9).

God Uses What Others Throw Away

And the Lord said to him, Who has made man's mouth? Or who makes the dumb, or the deaf, or the seeing, or the blind? Is it not I, the Lord? Now therefore go, and I will be with your mouth and will teach you what you shall say.

EXODUS 4:11—12

God purposely calls people to serve Him who don't know how to do what He tells them to do. His tool chest is full of weak individuals who can't seem to do things right, "cracked pots" whom the world treats with contempt (1 Corinthians 1:28).

But God knows that these individuals will depend on Him and will pray, "Lord, help me," "so that no mortal man should [have pretense for glorying and] boast in the presence of God" (1 Corinthians 1:29).

Qualify yourself for God's tool chest today by telling someone what you have seen God do in your life.

God Enables Us

It is through Him that we have received grace
(God's unmerited favor) and [our] apostleship to
promote obedience to the faith and make disciples for
His name's sake among all the nations, and this
includes you, called of Jesus Christ and invited
[as you are] to belong to Him.

ROMANS 1:5—6

God gives us beauty for ashes, the oil of joy for mourning, and the garment of praise for the spirit of heaviness (see Isaiah 61:3). God gives us whatever we need to be victorious. Because He enables us, we credit Him for all the good things in our lives.

Get up today and do the best you can, and then let God do the rest. Don't try to make mistakes, don't try to fail; but when you do, repent and get things straight with God. If you need to apologize to somebody, go and apologize. Receive your forgiveness, and go on.

Grow Continually

For this reason, since the day we heard about you,
we have not stopped praying for you and asking God
to fill you with the knowledge of his will through all
spiritual wisdom and understanding. And we pray
this in order that you may live a life worthy of the
Lord and may please him in every way: bearing fruit
in every good work, growing in the knowledge of God.

COLOSSIANS 1:9–10 NIV

God's Word encourages us to strive for perfection by growing into complete maturity of godliness in mind and character, having integrity, as our heavenly Father is perfect (see Matthew 5:48).

Paul said that even though he had not attained the ideal of perfection, he pressed on to grasp and make his own that for which Christ had laid hold of him (see Philippians 3:12). We, too, should press toward maturity and integrity today.

Repent, and Move On

If we [freely] admit that we have sinned and
confess our sins, He is faithful and just (true to His
own nature and promises) and will forgive our sins
[dismiss our lawlessness] and [continuously] cleanse
us from all unrighteousness [everything not in con-
formity to His will in purpose, thought, and action].

1 JOHN 1:9

It is important to be sincerely sorry if we do something wrong, but it doesn't help anybody for us to openly mourn over everything that is wrong with us. We will never mature in our faith if we stay angry at ourselves.

We are to repent of our sin, receive forgiveness of it, and then forget it. We must not drag memories of our old behavior around with us all the time. Sooner or later we have to let go and say, "Well, I made a mistake because I am just an old cracked pot." Then we must let God's light shine through the holes in our surface.

God Wants Your Heart

*But the Lord said to Samuel, Look not on his
appearance or at the height of his stature, for I have
rejected him. For the Lord sees not as man sees;
for man looks on the outward appearance,
but the Lord looks on the heart.*

1 SAMUEL 16:7

Religious teaching turns our attention to our outward appearance, but it doesn't empower us to clean up our inside thoughts and intentions. Jesus called the religious Pharisees "white-washed tombs full of dead man's bones" (see Matthew 23:27), because they boasted of their perfect obedience to the Hebrew laws.

But God didn't see them as perfect, because their hearts were not merciful as is His. God would rather have someone with a sweet, wonderful heart toward Him, who makes mistakes, than somebody with a slick performance, who is rotten inside.

When God looks at your heart today, let Him find it wholly seeking Him.

God Likes the Way
He Made You

*My frame was not hidden from You when I was
being formed in secret [and] intricately and curiously
wrought [as if embroidered with various colors]
in the depths of the earth [a region of
darkness and mystery].*

PSALM 139:15

Have you ever asked God, "Why did You
make me this way?" Sometimes the things
that we think are our worst faults, God will use to
His greatest glory: "But who are you, a mere man,
to criticize *and* contradict *and* answer back to God?
Will what is formed say to him that formed it, Why
have you made me thus?" (Romans 9:20).

Jesus died so that we might enjoy our life in
abundance and to the fullest until it overflows. You
are not going to enjoy your life if you don't enjoy
yourself. Be satisfied with yourself, and celebrate
the unique way God made you.

Live to Serve God

*For even the Son of Man came not to have
service rendered to Him, but to serve, and to give
His life as a ransom for (instead of) many.*

MARK 10:45

As the potter forms clay into vessels, some for honorable use and some for menial use, so God forms us to serve His purpose. Regardless of how our position in life may look to others, we are all formed to serve the Lord in some way.

If God made you to be a helper, then help with all your heart. If you enjoy cleaning houses for people, then do so as if you are cleaning the Lord's house. If you want to stay home with your children instead of earning extra income, don't worry that God has called others to paying positions outside the home. Do whatever the Lord puts in your heart to do — and enjoy fulfilling your God-given purpose.

Only God Can Change You

The Lord will sustain, refresh, and *strengthen him*
on his bed of languishing; all his bed You [O Lord]
will turn, change, and *transform in his illness. I said,*
Lord, be merciful and *gracious to me; heal my inner*
self, for I have sinned against You.

PSALM 41:3–4

Don't obsess over your faults, or you will
never enjoy the life that Jesus died to give
you. Only God can change you, so talk to Him about
your desires. The Word says that those who wait on
the Lord will *change* (see Isaiah 40:31).

Meanwhile, quit taking your flaws so seriously.
Don't let discouragement or depression rob you of
your energy and make you angry. If you do, you may
take that anger out on other people and miss the
blessings God has in store for you today. Enjoy yourself, and lighten up! Take the right steps today
toward the change you want to make by asking God
to help you all day long.

We Are Carriers

*The Lord make His face to shine upon and
enlighten you and be gracious (kind, merciful, and
giving favor) to you; the Lord lift up His [approving]
countenance upon you and give you peace
(tranquility of heart and life continually).*

NUMBERS 6:25–26

Looking at seemingly successful people
and thinking, *Oh, I wish I was like them,*
wastes much time. We don't know their problems
or their flaws. Everyone has trials, and we should
thank God for our own, because if we didn't have
problems, we wouldn't need Jesus anymore.

Reveal to others the glory of God's presence
in your life by being grateful for what He is doing
for you. Understand that God puts His treasures in
earthen vessels, like us, so that those who don't know
Him will see His grandeur and glory in us (see 2
Corinthians 4:7). Let the light of God shine through
your life today.

In Our Weakness
He Is Strong

Yes, You are my Rock and my Fortress; therefore
for Your name's sake lead me and guide me.

PSALM 31:3

Each of us has our own unique flaws, like cracked pots. But if we will allow it, Jesus will use our flaws to grace His Father's table. In God's great economy, nothing goes to waste.

So as we seek ways to minister together and as God calls you to the tasks He has appointed for you, don't be afraid of your flaws. Acknowledge them and allow Him to take advantage of them so that you too can be a thing of beauty in His pathway.

Go out boldly, knowing that in our weaknesses we will always find His strength. In Christ the answer to every one of His promises is "Yes," and for this reason we say, "Amen, so be it!" (see 2 Corinthians 1:20).

His Strength Is Perfect

*And [God] Who provides seed for the sower and
bread for eating will also provide and multiply your
[resources for] sowing and increase the fruits of
your righteousness [which manifests itself in active
goodness, kindness, and charity].*

2 CORINTHIANS 9:10

There are people who have a lot, but who do nothing for others with what they have. And there are people who have little, but who are able to do much with what they have. Use what you have today, and don't worry about what you don't have. God will make up the difference of what you lack, if you will just give Him what you can.

God's strength is always made perfect in your weaknesses. Don't apologize for your shortcomings; instead, watch for God's presence to fill your void. Be the best that you can possibly be, and enjoy the glory God receives through your testimony every single day.

Decide to Be Positive

For the rest, brethren, whatever is true, whatever is worthy of reverence and is honorable and seemly, whatever is just, whatever is pure, whatever is lovely and lovable, whatever is kind and winsome and gracious, if there is any virtue and excellence, if there is anything worthy of praise, think on and weigh and take account of these things [fix your minds on them].

PHILIPPIANS 4:8

Negative people don't enjoy life. Viewing each day with positive expectations is one of the key principles to godly happiness.

We act on what we believe, so positive thoughts cause positive actions. If you want a positive life, begin thinking positive thoughts. It is easy to do so if you read the Word and meditate on all that God wants to do for you and through you. Get alone today, and think about all the good, positive things God has done for you in the past, and all He has planned for you in the future.

Bless Someone Today

*In everything I have pointed out to you [by
example] that, by working diligently in this manner,
we ought to assist the weak, being mindful of the
words of the Lord Jesus, how He Himself said, It is
more blessed (makes one happier and more to be
envied) to give than to receive.*

ACTS 20:35

To have a healthy love walk today, spend time this morning thinking about what you can do for somebody else. Don't wait for God to *ask* you to do something; take the initiative and say, "Okay God, what can *I* do to be a blessing on Your behalf today?"

The best days you live are the ones you spend loving other people. Choose a particular person, and think about ways to bless him or her. If you don't know what to do, just listen to what he or she says, and before long you will hear of that individual's needs.

God Knows and Sees

The secret [of the sweet, satisfying companionship]
of the Lord have they who fear (revere and worship)
Him, and He will show them His covenant and
reveal to them its [deep, inner] meaning.

PSALM 25:14

Nobody else may see the things you do, but God sees them all. Every time you pray, God sees it. Every time you do an act of kindness secretly, God sees it and plans a reward to give you openly (see Matthew 6:1–6).

Serve the Lord in all that you do today. The Word says, "In the morning sow your seed, and in the evening withhold not your hands, for you know not which shall prosper, whether this or that, or whether both alike will be good" (Ecclesiastes 11:6). God will prosper what you do for Him.

You Can Change

We were buried therefore with Him by the baptism into death, so that just as Christ was raised from the dead by the glorious [power] of the Father, so we too might [habitually] live and behave in newness of life.

ROMANS 6:4

You will never reach your destiny by thinking negative thoughts. When you first wake up in the morning, start saying, "I love my life. It is wonderful. I thank God for everything He has given me."

You will do yourself a favor if you start thinking right thoughts so that you will also choose right actions. Sowing the right actions into your day will form new habits. As you begin to operate in those new habits, you will change in your character. And as your character changes, you will move into the destiny that God has for you. By God's power you can live in newness of life.

Enjoy Challenges

But it is good for me to draw near to God; I have put my trust in the Lord God and made Him my refuge, that I may tell of all Your works.

PSALM 73:28

Another key to starting your day right is not to dread things. Don't lie in bed dreading the whole day before you even get up. Dread is a close relative of the spirit of fear. When dread enters, joy leaves. Dread sets you up for misery, because by choosing to dread you decide that you cannot enjoy what you must do today.

Be excited when you face new tests. Close the door to the mindset of dread. Decide early to enjoy every challenge that faces you today, knowing that God will be with you to make your path straight and to prosper in everything you set out to do.

Have a New Mindset

Create in me a clean heart, O God, and renew a
right, persevering, and steadfast spirit within me.

PSALM 51:10

We set ourselves up either for misery or for joy by the mindset that we have toward the things in our life. Mindsets are the patterns in which our mind normally operates toward a certain determination. For example, when we look at our schedule today, it may seem that there is far too much to do. But if we choose the mindset that God will help us through it, we will enjoy watching how everything falls into place.

Refuse to dread what must be done. Greet the day with a right attitude and a thankful heart that you have a Savior who is ready to rescue you from more than you can handle. Enjoy yourself and say, "I refuse to live in dread; I am going to enjoy my life today."

Perfect Love Casts Out Fear

I have strength for all things in Christ Who
empowers me [I am ready for anything and equal to
anything through Him Who infuses inner strength
into me; I am self-sufficient in Christ's sufficiency].

PHILIPPIANS 4:13

Dread is a relative of fear. The devil tempts us with dread to get us to confess fear instead of faith. But 1 John 4:18 says, "There is no fear in love [dread does not exist], but full-grown (complete, perfect) love turns fear out of doors *and* expels every trace of terror! For fear brings with it the thought of punishment, and [so] he who is afraid has not reached the full maturity of love [is not yet grown into love's complete perfection]."

Enjoy your day, knowing that God loves you perfectly. Don't dread the hard things that you must do today, because God is on your side and is ready to help you.

God Is on Your Side

For the Lord takes pleasure in His people; He will
beautify the humble with salvation and
adorn the wretched with victory.

PSALM 149:4

If you never face trials, you will never have to exercise your faith. But even when facing hard times, you shouldn't dread life. Isaiah 8:13 says, "The Lord of hosts — regard Him as holy *and* honor His holy name [by regarding Him as your only hope of safety], and let Him be your fear and let Him be your dread [lest you offend Him by your fear of man and distrust of Him]."

If you dread life and fear people, you are not trusting the Lord to save you. Keep your reverential fear and awe of God; dread displeasing Him, but don't fear anything else. If God is for you, who can be against you? "No, in all these things we are more than conquerors through him who loved us" (Romans 8:37 NIV).

Be Ready

*Forsake not [Wisdom], and she will keep, defend,
and protect you; love her, and she will guard you.*

PROVERBS 4:6

Philippians 4:13 promises that Christ will empower you for anything you must face. This means that He will make you ready for anything and equal to all challenges by infusing you with inner strength.

God will never put you in a position to do something without giving you the strength and the ability to do it. You can relax and enjoy your life, for God will "strengthen (complete, perfect) *and* make you what you ought to be *and* equip you with everything good that you may carry out His will; [while He Himself] works in you *and* accomplishes that which is pleasing in His sight, through Jesus Christ" (Hebrews 13:21).

Renew Your Joy

Honor and majesty are [found] in His presence;
strength and joy are [found] in His sanctuary.

1 CHRONICLES 16:27

Emotional trauma drains people of their energy. But the Word says, "Be not grieved *and* depressed, for the joy of the Lord is your strength *and* stronghold" (Nehemiah 8:10). The devil wants to steal your joy because he knows that joy is your strength. He wants you to be weak so that you won't resist the turmoil he sets against you. That is why sometimes we need each other.

Some days God will send messengers to build you up in faith and renew your joy. Some days He will send you to someone else who is in a weakened condition because Satan has been pounding on them. Be someone's friend today. They may need a friend to stand beside them and encourage them and to lift them up and pray for them.

Think Ahead

But rather what we are setting forth is a wisdom
of God once hidden [from the human understanding]
and now revealed to us by God — [that wisdom]
which God devised and decreed before the ages
for our glorification [to lift us into the
glory of His presence].

1 CORINTHIANS 2:7

Look ahead to the reward God has for you in heaven. God has already written the end of the Book which says that good news is in store for those who put their faith in Jesus.

Even if you live to be a hundred years old, and have trials every day of your life, Paul said that our momentary troubles are achieving for us an eternal glory that far outweighs all the trials we face now (see 2 Corinthians 4:17–18 NIV). Keep your eyes on the finish line and not on the turmoil around you.

Be Satisfied

The poor and *afflicted shall eat and be satisfied;*
they shall praise the Lord — they who [diligently]
seek for, inquire of and *for Him,* and *require Him*
[as their greatest need]. May your hearts be
quickened now and *forever!*

PSALM 22:26

Many people constantly seek the thrill of a new experience, but every new thing eventually becomes an old thing. Sooner or later, people have to be happy with old things too, or they will never reach God's higher goal of contentment (see 1 Timothy 6:6).

In Philippians 4:11–12, Paul said that he had learned how to be content and satisfied to the point where he wasn't disturbed or disquieted, no matter what state he was in. He could live in humble circumstances or enjoy plenty. He had learned that the secret of facing every situation, whether well-fed or hungry, was to be content. Seek contentment in God today, and you will be satisfied.

Enjoy Your Life

*Whatever may be your task, work at it heartily
(from the soul), as [something done] for the Lord and
not for men, knowing [with all certainty] that it is
from the Lord [and not from men] that you will
receive the inheritance which is your [real] reward.*

COLOSSIANS 3:23—24

Jesus died so that you can enjoy abundant life, not just the days you are off work or on vacation or when you get to go shopping or golfing — but every day of your life.

He wants you to enjoy going to the grocery store. He wants you to enjoy driving the kids to school. He wants you to enjoy paying the bills. He wants you to enjoy cleaning the house or mowing the yard.

You can enjoy life if you determine to do so. Say, "I am going to enjoy every aspect of my life, because Jesus died so that I could have joy unspeakable and full of glory."

Follow God's Spirit

And He Who searches the hearts of men knows
what is in the mind of the [Holy] Spirit [what His
intent is], because the Spirit intercedes and pleads
[before God] in behalf of the saints according to
and in harmony with God's will.

ROMANS 8:27

Many people follow their own desires or other people's advice instead of following the Spirit of God. The Holy Spirit is given to each one of us to lead us into the fullness of our destiny, and into the fullness of what Jesus died to give us.

Your faith in Jesus gives you the promise of heaven, but God wants to work all things together for your good in this life too (see Romans 8:28). Don't be satisfied with receiving half of what Jesus died to give you. Follow the Spirit's leading so that you will get all that God has for you. Seek God for clear guidance to remain right in the center of His perfect will for every single day.

Go Where God Sends You

Let us all come forward and *draw near with true
(honest and sincere) hearts in unqualified assurance*
and *absolute conviction engendered by faith (by
that leaning of the entire human personality on God
in absolute trust and confidence in His power,
wisdom, and goodness).*

HEBREWS 10:22

One of the main reasons people don't enjoy their lives is that they don't follow the
leading of the Holy Spirit. Because Jesus fulfilled the
law, we have full freedom to enter into the Holy of
Holies and fellowship with the Father. Hebrews calls
this "a fresh (new) and living way" to enjoy our relationship with God (see Hebrews 10:20).

Spend time with God today, and go wherever
the Spirit of God leads you. He will always give you
the grace to do what He calls you to do.

A New Desire

For I endorse and *delight in the Law of God
in my inmost self [with my new nature].*
ROMANS 7:22

When we are born again, we get a new
"want to." The law says we "have to,
should, and ought to," but we want to do the right
thing because God has put a new heart in us to replace the hard stony one that used to be indifferent
to Him and His will (see Ezekiel 36:26).

Learn to recognize the difference between the
desires of your flesh and the desires placed in you
by the Holy Spirit. Psalm 1:1–2 says, "BLESSED
(HAPPY, fortunate, prosperous, and enviable) is the
man who walks *and* lives not in the counsel of the
ungodly . . . But his delight *and* desire are in the law
of the Lord, and on His law (the precepts, the instructions, the teachings of God) he habitually meditates (ponders and studies) by day and by night."

Everyone Is Different

*Having gifts (faculties, talents, qualities) that
differ according to the grace given us, let us use them.*

ROMANS 12:6

Don't feel bad about yourself if you are
not able to do what someone else is
anointed to do. God anoints each of us to contribute
to the body of Christ in some unique way. What
God enables you to do is no more or less important
than what He has called someone else to do.

God made you different from everyone else to
fulfill the desire of His heart, and He promises to fulfill the desires of your heart too (see Psalm 37:4).
He will anoint whatever He's given you, so place
your gifts in His power today, and enjoy yourself.

Change "Must" to "Want"

Therefore, [there is] now no condemnation (no adjudging guilty of wrong) for those who are in Christ Jesus, who live [and] walk not after the dictates of the flesh, but after the dictates of the Spirit.

ROMANS 8:1

Many of us compare ourselves and our achievements to others and what they accomplish for the Lord, thinking we *have to* do certain things to please God. But God didn't send Jesus into the world to condemn us (see John 3:17). What pleases God most is our deep craving to know Him better, which is achieved by spending time with Him through study and prayer.

We are called to enjoy fellowship with God. Don't let condemnation rob you of your joy today. Pray: *Lord, I want to follow the law of my new being. By Your grace, help me follow Jesus, because He has done what the law could not do and has saved me from my sins.*

Follow Peace

*Now the mind of the flesh [which is sense and
reason without the Holy Spirit] is death [death that
comprises all the miseries arising from sin, both here
and hereafter]. But the mind of the [Holy] Spirit is
life and [soul] peace [both now and forever].*

ROMANS 8:6

People hesitate to follow their desires,
because they don't know how to divide
their soul from their spirit. If they can't discern the
difference between the desires of their flesh and
Spirit-led desires, then they don't know when God
is truly leading them to do something.

But you can learn to know if God is leading you
or not. When God gives you a desire for something,
He will give you peace along with it. You may not be
excited, but you will have peace, if the thing you desire is from God. Wait for peace today.

166 ~ Joyce Meyer

Recognize Your Calling

That is why I would remind you to stir up
(rekindle the embers of, fan the flame of, and keep
burning) the [gracious] gift of God, [the
inner fire] that is in you.

2 TIMOTHY 1:6

Before I knew I was called to preach, I would privately repreach entire sermons I had just heard, thinking, *I would have said this, and, I would have done that.* Then, I would think, *Women don't preach!* But my spirit was stirred by the preacher's anointing because I had the same anointing.

If you are called to do something, you will get stirred up in the presence of someone operating in that same anointing. For example, if you have an anointing to lead worship, or to do special music, you will probably get more excited about the music than the sermon being preached. When in doubt, ask God to make clear your calling.

Iron Sharpens Iron

Iron sharpens iron; so a man sharpens the counte-nance of his friend [to show rage or worthy purpose].

PROVERBS 27:17

If you want to do something for God, then don't associate with people who do nothing. You may have to drastically change your life if you want to move on with what God has called you to do. Spend time with people who know how to use their days well.

Just as iron sharpens iron, positive people will inspire you to be positive. Godly people will inspire you to use your faith to do for the Lord what is in your heart to do. Spend time with people who are doing something for the Lord. Elisha got a double portion of Elijah's anointing, but he had to associate with Elijah for a long time to get it (see 2 Kings 2:1–14).

Follow Your Heart's Desires

*Who is the man who reverently fears and worships
the Lord? Him shall He teach in the way that
he should choose. He himself shall dwell at ease,
and his offspring shall inherit the land.*

PSALM 25:12—13

To enjoy your life, start following the God-given desires of your heart instead of the desires of your flesh. You may need to mature in faith before you can tell the difference between your flesh and Spirit-led desires.

One way to tell if you are following a desire of your flesh is that when you step out to do it, you will lose your peace and face a struggle. If it is not of God, you will feel like you are pushing a dead horse uphill. If it is a God-given desire of the Spirit, it will work like a well-oiled machine. It will flow, with what I call a "Holy ease." Start your day right, and follow your heart.

Get Peace from God

If any of you is deficient in wisdom, let him ask of
the giving God [Who gives] to everyone liberally and
ungrudgingly, without reproaching or faultfinding,
and it will be given him.

JAMES 1:5

Be careful when somebody makes a suggestion that sounds good; not every good
idea is a God-idea. Don't rush into making a decision or accepting a new responsibility without praying about it first.

Slow down long enough to ask God for wisdom,
and listen for His guidance. Take a little bit of time
to see if you have peace about the idea. If you don't
have peace, you don't even have to understand *why*
you don't have peace. Just don't do it!

Quality Is Better than Quantity

I call to remembrance my song in the night; with
my heart I meditate and my spirit searches diligently.

PSALM 77:6

God cares more about the quality of what you learn than the quantity of teaching to which you are exposed. He would rather you read one scripture verse and get revelation out of it than to read two whole books in the Bible and not have a clue about what you read.

Listen for key messages that the Lord is specifically speaking to you when you hear good teaching through television, radio, sermon tapes, a church service, or weekly Bible study. Ask God to show you how to apply what you hear to your own life. Meditate on His Word each day and look for ways to use what you have learned. Then you will know that you are engaging in and enjoying true quality time with Him.

Study Daily

Practice and *cultivate* and *meditate upon these duties; throw yourself wholly into them [as your ministry], so that your progress may be evident to everybody.*

I TIMOTHY 4:15

Second Timothy 2:15 says, "Study *and* be eager *and* do your utmost to present yourself to God approved (tested by trial), a workman who has no cause to be ashamed, correctly analyzing *and* accurately dividing [rightly handling and skillfully teaching] the Word of Truth."

It is difficult to grow if you don't like to read the Word. If Satan has created obstacles to keep you from reading the Word, take authority over him. Declare your love for the Word, and then read it — even if only a couple of pages a day. Your desire for more will quickly increase. If you truly don't like to read, then pray that God will give you a brand new desire to do so right now.

Choose How to Live

*For it is by free grace (God's unmerited favor) that
you are saved (delivered from judgment and made
partakers of Christ's salvation) through [your] faith.
And this [salvation] is not of yourselves [of your
own doing, it came not through your own striving],
but it is the gift of God.*

EPHESIANS 2:8

You can live under the law of sin and death, with its rules and regulations; or you can live under the law of the Spirit of life in Christ Jesus, which by grace sets you free from the law of sin and death (see Romans 8:2).

Galatians 5:4–5 explains that the law brings us to nothing and separates us from Christ. But the Holy Spirit will help us conform to God's will in purpose, thought, and action. Choose the law of life and say, "Today I will enjoy a grace-filled day."

Let God Lead Others

Yes, let none who trust and wait hopefully and look for You be put to shame or be disappointed; let them be ashamed who forsake the right or deal treacherously without cause.

PSALM 25:3

Our day might seem better if everyone would just do what we tell them to do. But God doesn't override people's will, and we are not to do so either. Instead of trying to control people, pray that they will "hear" God leading them.

If someone persists in doing something his or her own way today, show your confidence in God by stepping aside. You may learn that you were wrong, or they may learn that you were right. God is big enough to get both you and them out of any mess they may make. Either way, He will get the glory, if you put your trust in Him.

Don't Be Afraid to Stop

The thoughts and *purposes of the [consistently]*
righteous are honest and *reliable, but the counsels*
and *designs of the wicked are treacherous.*

PROVERBS 12:5

Don't be ashamed to back off if you get out in the middle of something and find that God is not in it. Just be secure enough to simply say, "I thought this was God, but it's not, so I am not going to do it anymore."

You can apologize to others if you caused them any trouble or confusion. But there is no shame in quickly admitting that you were wrong. It is more important not to perpetuate a mistake than it is to keep people from thinking you were wrong. Don't be afraid to say, "I didn't hear from God." Honesty will keep your day going right, all day long.

Wait for Peace

*A man's mind plans his way, but the Lord
directs his steps and makes them sure.*

PROVERBS 16:9

You may have to step out to find out the right thing to do. If you don't hear clearly from God, just step in the direction you think you should go, and then wait for peace. If you lose your peace, back out of wherever you were headed.

Dave and I almost bought two different buildings to house our ministry. We were in negotiations until, one morning after praying, Dave said, "Joyce, I don't have peace about buying that building. I feel like God is saying, 'If you buy that building, you are going to be sorry later.'" So we waited for peace, and now we have a building that is completely paid for with room to grow. Pray until you find peace.

Follow God's Leading

*Roll your works upon the Lord [commit and trust
them wholly to Him; He will cause your thoughts to
become agreeable to His will, and] so shall your
plans be established and succeed.*

PROVERBS 16:3

Trying to figure everything out before
you obey God will steal your joy. God
doesn't have to answer you when you ask, "Why
God, why?" Trust means that you won't always have
answers when you want them. Sometimes you just
have to get to the other side of a situation to see the
whole picture of what God is doing in your life.

God may be trying to separate you from some
influence in your life that is keeping you from receiving the better plan He has for you. He may be
"pruning" you to encourage new, healthier growth
(see John 15:1–8). Use uncertain times to demonstrate your faith by trusting Him.

Let Disappointments Go

But he who keeps (treasures) His Word [who bears
in mind His precepts, who observes His message in its
entirety], truly in him has the love of and for God
been perfected (completed, reached maturity).

I JOHN 2:5

It can be disappointing when people who are close to us don't do what we would like for them to do. But if we really love them, we should encourage them to follow the Holy Spirit rather than try to keep us happy all the time.

Help others grow spiritually by encouraging them to listen for God's voice. Remind them that God will help them through mistakes and lead them to a good life. Soon they will be making Spirit-led, rather than people-led, decisions. It is tremendously gratifying to see loved ones mature spiritually in Christ.

The Law of the Spirit

Behold, God, my salvation! I will trust and not be
afraid, for the Lord God is my strength and song;
yes, He has become my salvation.

ISAIAH 12:2

Life is not just one long party; there will always be hard things and easy things mixed together in the events of your life. Regardless of what today brings, you can still have joy in the Lord, and that joy will give you strength to handle whatever comes your way on any given day.

When you follow Jesus, the law of the Spirit of life keeps you free to enjoy yourself because you can cast any burdens on the Lord (see Romans 8:2). God will lead you to know what to do, and He will energize you to do what needs to be done. You won't feel drained by life, but will grow through both the trials and the triumphs as you walk with God today.

Do Whatever God Says

*So that the righteous and just requirement of the
Law might be fully met in us who live and move not
in the ways of the flesh but in the ways of the
Spirit [our lives governed not by the standards
and according to the dictates of the flesh,
but controlled by the Holy Spirit].*

ROMANS 8:4

"In Him we live and move and have our being" (Acts 17:28). God is everything. Talk to Him all day long, every time you need to make a decision or overcome anything negative. Whatever He says to do, do it. If He says don't do it, don't do it. You don't belong to yourself; you belong to God.

Religious teaching tries to predetermine what God wants from you. But He will write on your heart what is good and what is bad for you to do. He will speak to your inner conscience and keep you safe, as long as you pay attention to His voice and do what He tells you. Throughout the day today, occasionally stop what you are doing and ask Him if there is anything He wants to say to you.

Love Is the Higher Law

Love does no wrong to one's neighbor [it never hurts anybody]. Therefore love meets all the requirements and is the fulfilling of the Law.

ROMANS 13:10

There are things that we shouldn't do, simply because we love God, and because we don't want to hurt somebody else's conscience. We may have the freedom to do these things, but our freedom could offend others, or cause them to do something against their conscience, and thus sin against God.

If you walk in love today, there may be things that you have the right to do, but the Holy Spirit will prompt you not to exercise your right out of love for someone who is watching you. Love never demands its own way (see 1 Corinthians 13:5). Love is always the higher law.

Wear the Right Armor

And all this assembly shall know that the Lord
saves not with sword and spear; for the
battle is the Lord's.

I SAMUEL 17:47

When David went out to face Goliath, everyone around him said, "David, you can't do this!" But God put a sense of "knowing" within David that he would succeed in the name of the Lord. When King Saul decided to let David fight, he gave David his armor, but David said, "I cannot, because I am not used to this" (see 1 Samuel 17:31–39). David *knew* he was to go in the name of the Lord with only his slingshot (see vv. 40–50).

If you have battles to face in life, don't let others tell you how to fight. God will personally direct you in the way you should go. His Word is your weapon; that is why it is a vital necessity to arm yourself with knowledge and to spend time in God's presence before you have to face any giants.

God's Plan Is Greater

For the law of the Spirit of life [which is]
in Christ Jesus [the law of our new being] has
freed me from the law of sin and of death.

ROMANS 8:2

The law of the Spirit of life in Christ Jesus sets us free from the law of sin and death. We are free from the law of sin and death only to the degree that we follow the law of the Spirit. If we know what is right but insist on doing wrong, our actions may still lead us to miss out on the abundant life God has for us on earth.

Follow the law of the Spirit, and you will remain completely free from the law of sin and death. The Holy Spirit will lead you into holiness, into righteousness, and into the complete destiny that God has for your life. God's will for you is greater than anything you can imagine for yourself. Be willing to obey God even when you don't understand what He is doing with you.

Follow God's Priorities

*The sheep that are My own hear and are listening
to My voice; and I know them, and they follow Me.*

JOHN 10:27

Many people try to feel spiritual by obeying religious laws. But they never get
around to feeling good, because there is always one
more law to follow. That is why God does not define
our righteousness by our works, but by our faith in
Jesus. We feel inner peace when we obey the voice
of the Holy Spirit.

God may tell you that it is more important to
give away your favorite personal possession, than to
try to please Him by reading the Bible through in a
year. He may say that it is more important to just remain silent, if He tells you to, than to volunteer for
every activity at church. His ways are not our ways
(see Isaiah 55:8–9), so learn to listen for His direction each day.

Have Fun

*For the kingdom of God is not a matter of eating
and drinking, but of righteousness, peace and joy in
the Holy Spirit, because anyone who serves Christ in
this way is pleasing to God and approved by men. Let
us therefore make every effort to do what leads to
peace and to mutual edification.*

ROMANS 14:17—19 NIV

Everything in your life doesn't have to be serious in order to be spiritual. If you are filled with God's Spirit, whatever you do has a spiritual connotation to it. You can live a holy life, and still enjoy your day.

God measures holiness by how quick we are to obey His voice. He promises that goodness and mercy will follow us if we seek His presence (see Psalm 23:6). He may even encourage you just to have fun today.

Pamper Yourself

Why are you cast down, O my inner self? And why should you moan over me and be disquieted within me? Hope in God and wait expectantly for Him, for I shall yet praise Him, my Help and my God.

PSALM 42:5

God gave you your emotions, so it doesn't work to ignore them completely. You make a big mistake if you refuse to meet any of your emotional needs. If you are tired, you need rest. If you are stressed, you need some fun.

If you need encouragement, spend time with someone who knows how to build you up. Don't ignore your emotional needs in the name of Christianity. You are a whole person — body, soul, and spirit (see 1 Thessalonians 5:23). God will show you how to be strong in all areas of your life.

Set Priorities

*Your eyes saw my unformed substance, and in Your
book all the days [of my life] were written before ever
they took shape, when as yet there was none of them.*

PSALM 139:16

Be *determined* to enjoy the abundant life
that Jesus Christ desires for you to have.
The devil will always try to set you up to get upset.
The busy activities of today's society can make life
seem like a blur. Most people have a lot of stress,
continuous pressure, and really too much to do.

Set priorities. Start your day with God. Be determined to follow His lead all day, and you will enjoy every day of your life — not just on weekends,
vacations, or sunny days when the weather's perfect.
Walking with God will give you pleasure and relax-
ation even when things aren't going your way.

Clean Up

Let us throw off everything that hinders and the sin that so easily entangles, and let us run with perseverance the race marked out for us. Let us fix our eyes on Jesus, the author and perfecter of our faith.

HEBREWS 12:1−2 NIV

Have you ever gone on a cleaning rampage to straighten up your home or office? Did you enjoy pitching junk, straightening objects, and organizing materials so that you could find them when you need them?

You may need to get on a Holy Ghost rampage and do the same thing with your life. Say, "I've had enough bondage. I've had enough negative thoughts. I've had enough of the lies of the devil. I am not going to have any more bad days. I am not going to be discouraged, depressed, or despondent. I am going to enjoy my life!"

Jesus is ready to help you live life to the fullest!

Joy Unspeakable

Now to Him Who is able to keep you without
stumbling or slipping or falling, and to present
[you] unblemished (blameless and faultless) before
the presence of His glory in triumphant joy and
exultation [with unspeakable, ecstatic delight].

JUDE 1:24

I used to be so miserable when I went to bed that I wished it was time to get up. And when I got up, I was still so miserable I wanted to go back to bed. I was under the curse of not obeying the voice of the Lord or serving Him with joyfulness (see Deuteronomy 28:15–48).

Obedience to God fills our lives with so much joy that we don't even know how to talk about it. The Bible calls it "joy unspeakable and full of glory" (1 Peter 1:8 KJV). Experience the joy of being in God's awesome presence. Start your day by praising God for your blessings, and worshiping Him with a heart ready to serve Him.

The Key to Joy

And may the God of peace Himself sanctify you through and through [separate you from profane things, make you pure and wholly consecrated to God]; and may your spirit and soul and body be preserved sound and *complete [and found] blameless at the coming of our Lord Jesus Christ (the Messiah).*

I THESSALONIANS 5:23

Righteousness is a key to enjoying every single day of your life. Being in right relationship with God is available to us simply through our faith in Jesus Christ. That security gives us peace through every situation, and having peace brings joy.

The Word says to listen with expectancy to what God the Lord will say to you, for He will speak peace to His saints (those who are in right standing with Him), and those who don't turn again to self-confident folly (see Psalm 85:8). Before making plans today, listen for God's voice to make sure you follow His peace for your day.

The Key to Loving Others

Now may the Lord of peace Himself grant you
His peace (the peace of His kingdom) at all times
and in all ways [under all circumstances and
conditions, whatever comes].

2 THESSALONIANS 3:16

The Bible says to love your neighbor as yourself (Luke 10:27); the key is to love yourself. You won't enjoy your day until you learn to accept and enjoy yourself, because you have to eat with yourself, sleep with yourself, and be with yourself all day. Until you are happy with who you are and where you are in life, you will never learn to love others or get to where you want to be.

Don't get down on yourself about everything you didn't do right yesterday. Today is a new day. Learn to love your life, right now, right where you are now. Say, "I am grateful to be a child of God, redeemed and made righteous in His eyes. I am going to enjoy myself all day long."

No Matter What

For you shall go out [from the spiritual exile
caused by sin and evil into the homeland] with joy
and be led forth [by your Leader, the Lord Himself,
and His word] with peace; the mountains and the
hills shall break forth before you into singing, and all
the trees of the field shall clap their hands.

ISAIAH 55:12

Peace is not dependent on circumstances.
Our peace and joy are found in *the Holy
Ghost*. Jesus said:

He who believes in Me [who cleaves to *and*
trusts in *and* relies on Me] as the Scripture has
said, From his innermost being shall flow [con-
tinuously] springs *and* rivers of living water. But
He was speaking here of the Spirit, Whom those
who believed (trusted, had faith) in Him were
afterward to receive (John 7:38–39).

No matter what is going on today, you can drink
from your own well of joy through the indwelling
presence of God's Spirit.

Enjoy Whatever
You Are Doing

*And there you shall eat before the Lord your God,
and you shall rejoice in all to which you put your
hand, you and your households, in which the
Lord your God has blessed you.*

DEUTERONOMY 12:7

I used to hate waiting in the airport, but Dave always wanted to arrive early. I finally changed my mind. It is amazing what happens when you decide to enjoy God every day. It is easy to get so caught up in all your responsibilities that you forget to enjoy what you are doing.

You can get so busy raising your children that you forget to enjoy them. You can get so caught up in cleaning your house, trying to pay for it, and remodeling it, that you forget to enjoy it. But you can learn to enjoy God so much that no matter what you do today, you can truly say, "I enjoyed it."

Don't Worry

For You make him to be blessed and *a blessing forever; You make him exceedingly glad with the joy of Your presence.*

PSALM 21:6

It is a learning process to keep the devil from stealing your joy, because he constantly tempts you in new ways to lose your peace. If Satan gets your peace, then he will get your joy. Be strong and resist his temptation to make you worry.

The Word says that God gives riches and possessions, and the power to enjoy them. To accept our appointed lot and to rejoice in our work is the gift of God. We won't remember seriously the days of our life, because the tranquility of God is mirrored in us (see Ecclesiastes 5:19–20). Determine that from this day forward you will do everything you can to keep your peace and enjoy your life.

Triumph Over Troubles

Moreover [let us also be full of joy now!] let us exult and triumph in our troubles and rejoice in our sufferings, knowing that pressure and affliction and hardship produce patient and unswerving endurance.

ROMANS 5:3

Some days it seems that everything goes wrong, one thing after another, after another. Don't just talk to yourself, saying, "I just can't take anymore of this." Don't talk to your friends, saying, "I just can't put up with anymore of this."

Don't struggle with the same tests day after day; instead, talk back to the devil as Jesus did (see Luke 4:1–13). If you feel your peace and joy slipping away, talk out loud to Satan. If he is trying to steal from you, say, "Forget it, devil; you are not getting me upset today!"

Joy Makes You Strong

*As for God, His way is perfect; the word of the
Lord is tried. He is a Shield to all those who trust
and take refuge in Him.*

2 SAMUEL 22:31

Nehemiah 8:10 says, "Be not grieved *and*
depressed, for the joy of the Lord is your
strength *and* stronghold." Being happy and joyful
makes you strong, and being mad or sad makes you
weak. But the Lord is a Shield, and the Lifter of your
head (see Psalm 3:3).

Satan isn't after your joy; he is after your strength.
The devil wants you too weak to pray. He wants you
worn out and burned out. But the Lord will lift your
head and shield you from the devil's plot against
you, if you put your trust in Him.

One Day at a Time

My God, my Rock, in Him will I take refuge;
my Shield and the Horn of my salvation; my
Stronghold and my Refuge, my Savior —
You save me from violence.

2 SAMUEL 22:3

Trials can come like a freight train — one car after another, after another — but eventually the last car passes. When problems seem unceasing, remind yourself, "This too shall pass." Deal with one trial at a time in the power of the Holy Ghost until each series of events is over. God will give you fresh anointing daily to handle everything that comes into your life.

Each time you endure a tough day, you can sleep it off and start again the next day. So you may as well enjoy the tough days too, because God's favor is for a lifetime; weeping may endure for a night, but joy comes in the morning (see Psalm 30:5).

Experience *His* Joy

Yet I will rejoice in the LORD, *I will joy in*
the God of my salvation.

HABAKKUK 3:18 KJV

God created us with the ability to laugh, so we must *need* to laugh. The Word says, "A happy heart is good medicine *and* a cheerful mind works healing" (Proverbs 17:22). Jesus said that His joy would be *in* us so that we may experience His delight; He wants to fill our hearts with His gladness (see John 17:13). Jesus wants us to *experience* His joy, not just preach about it, or read books about it. He wants us to *experience* His joy.

Joy greatly depends on how you view life, so if you need help getting your sense of humor back, ask God to show you the lighter side of life today. Don't hesitate to laugh when you suddenly feel joyful; you will quickly find that joy is very contagious.

Go with the Flow

*Brethren, for this reason, in [spite of all] our stress
and crushing difficulties we have been filled with
comfort and cheer about you [because of] your faith
(the leaning of your whole personality on God in
complete trust and confidence).*

1 THESSALONIANS 3:7

Go with the flow, and stop being anxious about things that may never happen. If you really trust God, you don't need a backup plan. Faith means that you have peace even when you don't have all the answers.

Life will always be stressful if you constantly try to rearrange it. For example, getting upset in a traffic jam doesn't get you out of it any sooner. But planning for obstacles will inspire you to leave a little earlier for your appointments and keep you from hurrying. Grow in wisdom, and place high priority on keeping your peace in spite of any jams you get into today.

Enjoy Ordinary Days

*They who sow in tears shall reap
in joy* and *singing.*

PSALM 126:5

Our days in the kingdom of God are like seeds scattered upon the ground. We must continue to sleep and rise, night and day, while the seeds that we sow through our words and deeds sprout and grow and increase (see Mark 4:26–28).

Most days are not full of excitement, and some days are more difficult to endure than others. But we can learn to enjoy the ordinary and the challenging days of our lives. As the earth produces first the blade, then the ear, and finally the full grain in the ear, so will our lives produce a great harvest from our faithfulness in sowing righteousness.

Continue to do what you know is right to do, and enjoy this ordinary day. You are one day closer to a joyful harvest.

Stay Stable

*The [uncompromisingly] righteous shall flourish
like the palm tree [be long-lived, stately, upright,
useful, and fruitful]; they shall grow like a
cedar in Lebanon [majestic, stable,
durable, and incorruptible].*

PSALM 92:12

James 1:12 says, "Blessed (happy, to be
envied) is the man who is patient under
trial *and* stands up under temptation, for when he
has stood the test *and* been approved, he will receive
[the victor's] crown of life which God has promised
to those who love Him."

Don't get upset if somebody gives you a hard
time today. Don't get upset if you don't get your way,
or if somebody says or does something you don't like.
If you are set up for an upset, stay stable — it is only
a test.

Do Your Best

*But if anyone should sin, we have an Advocate
(One Who will intercede for us) with the Father —
[it is] Jesus Christ . . . And He [that same Jesus
Himself] is the propitiation (the atoning sacrifice)
for our sins, and not for ours alone but also for
[the sins of] the whole world.*

I JOHN 2:1—2

You are responsible *to* people, but God
has not made you responsible *for* their
joy. You may have children, or siblings, or a spouse
God has given you to love and nurture who seem
uninterested in your testimony. Some people just
refuse to be happy, so don't let them steal your joy.

You cannot *fix* anyone, and you shouldn't take the
blame for everything that goes wrong in someone
else's life. Obviously, you cannot make everybody
you know believe in Jesus. But you can get up every
day and do your best, and then trust God for the rest.

God Is Always Working

Furthermore, brethren, we beg and admonish
you in [virtue of our union with] the Lord Jesus, that
[you follow the instructions which] you learned from
us about how you ought to walk so as to please and
gratify God, as indeed you are doing, [and] that you
do so even more and more abundantly [attaining yet
greater perfection in living this life].

1 THESSALONIANS 4:1

In 1 Thessalonians 2:13, Paul wrote, "When you received the message of God [which you heard] from us, you welcomed it not as the word of [mere] men, but as it truly is, the Word of God, *which is effectually at work in you who believe* [exercising its superhuman power *in those who adhere to and trust in and rely on it*]" (emphasis mine).

The Bible says that God's Word works in those who believe it. So no matter what you see today, believe that God is working on your breakthrough.

Look to What Is Unseen

*Clothe yourselves therefore, as God's own chosen
ones (His own picked representatives), [who are]
purified and holy and well-beloved [by God Himself,
by putting on behavior marked by] tenderhearted pity
and mercy, kind feeling, a lowly opinion of yourselves, gentle ways, [and] patience [which is tireless
and long-suffering, and has the power to endure
whatever comes, with good temper].*

COLOSSIANS 3:12

When you pray for other people, it may
seem that they get worse before they get
better. The devil wants to discourage you from believing that God is answering your prayers. The
apostle Paul said that he learned not to be discouraged even when going through terrible trials. He
said to look to the things that are unseen, not to the
things that are seen (see 2 Corinthians 4:18).

Keep believing, and the power of the Holy Spirit
will fill you with joy and peace until you are overflowing with hope (see Romans 15:13). Always trust
God to answer your prayers.

Ignore Distractions

And when they raised their eyes,
they saw no one but Jesus only.
MATTHEW 17:8

Our own flaws can distract us from keeping our eyes on Jesus. If we think too much about what is wrong with us, we will forget what God can do through us. If we look too much at what we lack, we will forget to be thankful for what we have.

The Bible says to look away from all that will distract us from focusing on Jesus (see Hebrews 12:2). If your faith begins to waver, quickly get your eyes on Jesus, who is the Source of your faith and the Incentive for your belief. Remember how He endured the cross, despising and ignoring the shame of it, for the joy of winning you to Himself. He promises to bring your faith to maturity and perfection.

Be Thankful

Be happy [in your faith] and rejoice and be glad-
hearted continually (always); be unceasing in prayer
[praying perseveringly]; thank [God] in everything
[no matter what the circumstances may be, be
thankful and give thanks], for this is the will of
God for you [who are] in Christ Jesus [the Revealer
and Mediator of that will]. Do not quench
(suppress or subdue) the [Holy] Spirit.

I THESSALONIANS 5:16–19

Be thankful for everything, and be careful not to quench the Holy Spirit by complaining, or you will lose your joy. You can be glad-hearted no matter what your circumstances are.

Renew your mind to God's ideals and attitude (see Romans 12:2). If you spend time in God's presence, you will think differently about yourself, and about the people around you. You will have the mind of Christ, and be full of His love.

Discipline Brings Success

But if from there you will seek (inquire for and
require as necessity) the Lord your God, you will find
Him if you [truly] seek Him with all your heart
[and mind] and soul and life.

DEUTERONOMY 4:29

Proverbs 5:23 says that a person "will die
for lack of discipline *and* instruction, and
in the greatness of his folly he will go astray *and* be
lost." That doesn't necessarily mean that a person
will die immediately, but a lack of discipline leads
toward deathly situations.

In his book *A Pursuit of God*, A. W. Tozier said
(paraphrased) that God puts a desire in us to seek
Him. But we have to discipline ourselves to seek
Him. We can become too passive waiting for God to
initiate a relationship with us. If you want to have a
successful life, discipline yourself to seek God every
day.

Balance Life

Blessed (happy, fortunate, to be envied) is the man
whom You discipline and instruct, O Lord, and teach
out of Your law, that You may give him power to
keep himself calm in the days of adversity.

PSALM 94:12—13

A person who is lazy and passive is not happy. A passive person is someone who *wants* something good to happen, but who just sits still and waits to see if it does. Successful people live disciplined lives.

First Peter 5:8 says, "Be well balanced (temperate, sober of mind), be vigilant *and* cautious at all times." The devil would like you to go overboard in some area, but stay steady and God "will Himself complete *and* make you what you ought to be, establish *and* ground you securely, and strengthen, and settle you" (v. 10).

God Works While You Rest

Now to Him Who, by (in consequence of) the
[action of His] power that is at work within us, is
able to [carry out His purpose and] do super-
abundantly, far over and above all that we [dare]
ask or think [infinitely beyond our highest prayers,
desires, thoughts, hopes, or dreams].

EPHESIANS 3:20

Being well-balanced means that you don't do too much of one thing and not enough of another. If you go overboard to be disciplined, you can become legalistic, rigid, and boring! Learn to have fun too.

Don't spend the whole day working, but don't be lazy either. Ask God to help you balance hard work and rest. Stop working long enough to be thankful for all God gives you to celebrate through-out the day. As you rest in God, He will continue working in you to help you become all He plans for you to be.

Make Time with God a Priority

Then Jesus, knowing that they meant to come and seize Him that they might make Him king, withdrew again to the hillside by Himself alone.

JOHN 6:15

If the devil can't convince you to be idle and passive, he will drive you to do too much. As soon as you are out of balance, he can devour you (see 1 Peter 5:8). The word *disciple* comes from the word *discipline.* To be a disciple of Jesus, you must discipline yourself to follow His ways.

Jesus spent a great deal of time going about doing good for people, but He balanced His time by getting alone to pray and commune with the Father. Time with God renews your strength to do good things that you want to do for others. Live a balanced life by spending time with Him.

Walk in Love

*And walk in love, [esteeming and delighting in
one another] as Christ loved us and gave Himself up
for us, a slain offering and sacrifice to God [for you,
so that it became] a sweet fragrance.*

EPHESIANS 5:2

Jesus said, "If anyone intends to come after Me, let him *deny himself [forget, ignore,
disown, and lose sight of himself and his own interests]*
and take up his cross, and [joining Me as a disciple
and siding with My party] follow with Me [continu-
ally, cleaving steadfastly to Me] (Mark 8:34, emphasis mine).

Living a disciplined life means laying aside personal feelings, deciphering which choice is most important in God's eyes, and then allowing that choice
to take preeminence over the others. As Jesus laid
down His life for you, He is asking you to lay down
your interests for His greater cause.

Crucify Selfish Attitudes

All of you must keep awake (give strict attention, be cautious and active) and watch and pray, that you may not come into temptation. The spirit indeed is willing, but the flesh is weak.

MATTHEW 26:41

To live in victory, we can't make decisions according to the way we feel, or by what we think we want. The Word teaches that we are born with appetites sensitive to our human nature. Our natural flesh is carnal and unspiritual. It will keep us slaves to sin, unless we crucify it and follow what the Spirit of God leads us to do.

Studying God's Word will build your faith and keep you on the right path: "The wise also will hear and increase in learning, and the person of understanding will acquire skill *and* attain to sound counsel [so that he may be able to steer his course rightly]" (Proverbs 1:5).

Choose the Narrow Path

Enter through the narrow gate; for wide is the gate and spacious and *broad is the way that leads away to destruction, and many are those who are entering through it. But the gate is narrow (contracted by pressure) and the way is straitened* and *compressed that leads away to life, and few are those who find it.*

MATTHEW 7:13−14

Even when we know the right thing to do, it can be difficult to do if we don't *feel* like it. We may feel like lying in bed much longer than we should, even when we aren't sleepy anymore. Sometimes we know we ought to keep our mouth shut, but we don't *feel* like it.

The way to victory is a narrow path that requires discipline regardless of our feelings. Sometimes it may look too narrow to even squeeze through. But victory comes by obeying God's Word to us, in spite of our feelings. Follow faith, not feelings, today.

Don't Avoid Hard Work

*For the time being no discipline brings joy, but
seems grievous and painful; but afterwards it yields a
peaceable fruit of righteousness to those who have
been trained by it [a harvest of fruit which consists in
righteousness — in conformity to God's will in
purpose, thought, and action, resulting in right
living and right standing with God].*

HEBREWS 12:11

An undisciplined person looks for ways
to avoid hard work. Passivity prevails in
our culture; everything is geared toward making life
easier: ride the escalator, take the elevator, get fast-
food carryout. But the easy way is not always the
best way.

Just as we need to exercise our bodies, so we
also need to exercise our faith by facing difficult
challenges. Use faith to forgive those who offend
you and to trust God when you can't see how problems will be solved. Soon you will enjoy a harvest of
righteousness from the discipline you endure today.

Make the Most of Time

Where is the wise man (the philosopher)? Where is the scribe (the scholar)? Where is the investigator (the logician, the debater) of this present time and age? Has not God shown up the nonsense and the folly of this world's wisdom?

1 CORINTHIANS 1:20

In Ephesians 5:15–17 God's Word says that we are to live purposefully, using wisdom as sensible, intelligent people. This means to make the most of the time we are given. Equal time is given to us all, but we don't always use wisdom to keep from wasting it.

We are to buy up every opportunity we can to fulfill our purpose on earth, which is to love God and others. Verse 17 says, "Therefore do not be vague *and* thoughtless *and* foolish, but understanding *and* firmly grasping what the will of the Lord is." Get alone with God to make sure you know how to use your time today.

Words Are Power

Exercise foresight and *be on the watch to look
[after one another], to see that no one falls back from
and fails to secure God's grace (His unmerited favor
and spiritual blessing), in order that no root of resentment (rancor, bitterness, or hatred) shoots forth
and causes trouble* and *bitter torment, and the many
become contaminated* and *defiled by it.*

HEBREWS 12:15

Jesus said, "If you have faith (a firm relying trust) and do not doubt . . . even if
you *say* to this mountain, Be taken up and cast into
the sea, it will be done. And *whatever you ask* for in
prayer, having faith *and* [really] believing, you will
receive" (Matthew 21:21–22, emphasis mine).

Don't misuse the power of words by *talking too
much* without faith or *talking too little* about your
faith. Choose kind and gentle words that lift people
and quiet gossip and strife. Believe that God's grace
will prevail through what you say.

Balance Discipline

And I will walk at liberty and *at ease, for I have
sought and inquired for [and desperately
required] Your precepts.*

PSALM 119:45

It takes discipline to balance your life.
You should be disciplined to pray, disciplined to read and study the Word, and disciplined
to spend quality time in fellowship with the Lord.
But you must also be disciplined to spend quality
time with your family, and to take care of your
health. You should even discipline yourself to rest
and have fun.

Examine your life today, and do what is needed
to bring balance to the way you use your time. God
wants your life to be full of joy. Psalm 23:2–3
teaches that He will lead you beside still and restful
waters. He will refresh and restore your life. And
He will lead you in the paths of righteousness for
His name's sake.

Write the Vision

Where there is no vision [no redemptive revelation
of God], the people perish; but he who keeps the law
[of God, which includes that of man] — blessed
(happy, fortunate, and enviable) is he.

PROVERBS 29:18

The Lord told Habakkuk to write the vision that God had given him, and to en-
grave it so plainly on tablets that everyone who
passed could read it easily. God promised that His
vision would be fulfilled on its appointed day (see
Habakkuk 2:2–3).

If you have been asking God to lead you in the
way you should go, you will have a sense of purpose
building in you. You can ask Him to help you plan
your day, your week, and your life. I encourage you
to write down the things that God imprints on your
heart to do. Writing the vision, and placing it where
you can routinely see it, will help settle the plan
God puts inside of you.

Live with Purpose

Therefore, my beloved brethren, be firm (steadfast),
immovable, always abounding in the work of the Lord
[always being superior, excelling, doing more than
enough in the service of the Lord], knowing and being
continually aware that your labor in the Lord is not
futile [it is never wasted or to no purpose].

1 CORINTHIANS 15:58

Life without purpose is vanity. Webster's definition of *purpose* is "something set up as an object or end to be attained." Christians ought to be people with purpose. We are all purposed to seek the kingdom of God, which is His righteousness, peace, and joy in the Holy Spirit (see Romans 14:17).

Today is an opportunity to willfully and deliberately seek God with the intent to know Him better than we knew Him yesterday. Today we can deliberately move forward with the intent to accomplish good things for the kingdom.

Stay on Course

Let your eyes look right on [with fixed purpose],
and let your gaze be straight before you. Consider well
the path of your feet, and let all your ways be estab-
lished and *ordered aright. Turn not aside to the right*
hand or to the left; remove your foot from evil.

PROVERBS 4:25–27

Jesus knew what His purpose was. He disciplined Himself to stay on course, living His life to fulfill that purpose for which He came. As Christians, we need to follow in His steps and focus on our purpose. We were bought with a price to live our lives in such a way that we become the salt of the earth, the light of the world (see Matthew 5).

We are to lay down our selfish, self-centered life-styles, and gear our lives toward doing something for the betterment of someone else. Then we will experience that "joy unspeakable, and full of glory" (1 Peter 1:8).

Keep Alert

Blessed (happy, fortunate, and to be envied) are
those servants whom the master finds awake and alert
and watching when he comes. Truly I say to you, he
will gird himself and have them recline at table and
will come and serve them!

LUKE 12:37

In Ephesians 6:10 God's word teaches, "Be strong in the Lord [be empowered through your union with Him]; draw your strength from Him [that strength which His boundless might provides]." We are to put on God's armor so we won't be deceived by the devil. Verse 16 says, "Lift up over all the [covering] shield of saving faith, upon which you can quench all the flaming missiles of the wicked [one]."

In verse 18 we are also told to "pray at all times (on every occasion, in every season) in the Spirit, with all [manner of] prayer and entreaty. *To that end keep alert and watch with strong purpose and perseverance*, interceding in behalf of all the saints (God's consecrated people)" (emphasis mine).

Act Now

*The Spirit of the Lord [is] upon Me, because He
has anointed Me [the Anointed One, the Messiah] to
preach the good news (the Gospel) to the poor;
He has sent Me to announce release to the captives
and recovery of sight to the blind, to send forth as
delivered those who are oppressed [who are downtrod-
den, bruised, crushed, and broken down by calamity].*

LUKE 4:18

Good intentions are not acts of obedience, and procrastination devours opportunities to live a purposeful life. Whatever God
has inspired you to do — do it today.

Just do what needs to be done, even if the first
thing you tackle is the dishes in the kitchen sink or a
garage that needs cleaning. If God has specifically
told you to bless someone, and you have intended to
do it, remember that *now* is the acceptable time, *now*
is the day of salvation (see 2 Corinthians 6:2).

Win the Race

*But [like a boxer] I buffet my body [handle
it roughly, discipline it by hardships] and subdue
it, for fear that after proclaiming to others the
Gospel and things pertaining to it, I myself
should become unfit [not stand the test, be unapproved and rejected as a counterfeit].*

1 CORINTHIANS 9:27

It is easy to leave unpleasant tasks for
later. But God wants His people to finish
the race that He sets before them to run (see 2 Timothy 4:7). Don't be afraid to do what seems to be
hard. God will anoint you to do whatever He tells
you to do.

Paul spoke of this race for the sake of the gospel
in 1 Corinthians 9:23–26: "So run [your race] that
you may lay hold [of the prize] *and* make it yours."
He said to run with definite aim, and to discipline
yourself to finish the race. Grace will make winning
easier than you imagined.

Brace Your Mind

I am able to do nothing from Myself [indepen-
dently, of My own accord — but only as I am taught
by God and as I get His orders].

JOHN 5:30

One of the reasons people don't get things done is that they mentally see their unfinished assignments as monstrous undertakings. If they would just take care of those projects, they would find they aren't that big of a deal.

First Peter 1:13 says, "Brace up your minds; be sober (circumspect, morally alert); set your hope wholly *and* unchangeably on the grace (divine favor) that is coming to you when Jesus Christ (the Messiah) is revealed." Don't let your mind rule you. When thoughts of inadequacy fill your head, stop and remember that God's grace is sufficient to meet all your needs. Just do things one at a time, and keep your mind on God's ability, not your own.

Keep a Positive Attitude

*Keep your foot [give your mind to what
you are doing] when you go [as Jacob to sacred
Bethel] to the house of God. For to draw near to
hear and obey is better than to give the sacrifice of
fools [carelessly, irreverently] too ignorant to
know that they are doing evil.*

ECCLESIASTES 5:1

People who take a positive attitude and say, "I can do it. I am going to do it right now. It is no problem. Everything will work out fine," are wonderful to be around and work with because they tackle things and get them done.

If you put off something you should have done already, it will start to threaten you with fear. Don't allow an assignment to get out of proportion in your mind. Keep your mind on what you set out to do today. If you get interrupted, make yourself come back to that task and finish it up. Nothing is so hard that you can't handle it, if you will keep a positive attitude and do it God's way.

Have a Plan

Make me go in the path of Your commandments,
for in them do I delight.

PSALM 119:35

Go to sleep at night with a plan in mind for the next day. Don't be vague about what you hope to accomplish. One morning I was lying in bed when the Spirit of the Lord said to me, "Stop being ambiguous." The dictionary defines *ambiguous* as "doubtful or uncertain," and "capable of being understood in two or more possible senses or ways."

Don't be double-minded. Don't just wait to see what happens. Wake up with a plan that puts God first in all you do. God's Word is a lamp to your feet, and a light to your path (see Psalm 119:105). Talk to Him before you even get out of bed; ask Him to make clear what you need to achieve today.

Develop Self-control

He who has no rule over his own spirit is like a
city that is broken down and without walls.

PROVERBS 25:28

Self-control is a fruit of the Spirit (see Galatians 5:22–23). It develops as we spend time fellowshipping with God and practicing obedience to Him. Sometimes we would rather that God control us and make us do the right thing. But He wants us to rule over our spirit.

Proverbs 16:32 says, "He who is slow to anger is better than the mighty, he who rules his [own] spirit than he who takes a city." It takes self-control not to get offended, not to become angry every time somebody doesn't do something the way we want it done. Self-control is needed over our thoughts, our words, and our appetites. But once we master our own spirit, we are considered to be powerful in the eyes of God — stronger than one who takes a city.

Don't Be Lazy

Do you see a man diligent and skillful in his business? He will stand before kings; he will not stand before obscure men.

PROVERBS 22:29

Proverbs 24:30–34 gives a clear warning about being lazy. Laziness allows everything in our lives to get overgrown or broken down. We are to observe the fate of a lazy man and receive this instruction: "Yet a little sleep, a little slumber, a little folding of the hands to sleep — so shall your poverty come as a robber."

God will help you with anything in your life that has become overgrown or broken down. If you put your trust in Him, He can turn your mess into your message. Set your way to follow God from this day forth. Guard against the spirit of laziness. Get rid of procrastination, and do whatever God has been telling you to do.

Appreciate Correction

*Happy (blessed, fortunate, enviable) is the man
who finds skillful and godly Wisdom, and the man
who gets understanding [drawing it forth from God's
Word and life's experiences], for the gaining of it
is better than the gaining of silver, and the
profit of it better than fine gold.*

PROVERBS 3:13–14

Ask God to reveal areas in which you need to apply self-control. You can even enjoy the journey to becoming all that He has in mind for you to be, if you learn to appreciate godly correction from others. Remember, God loves you just the way you are, but He corrects those He loves (see Proverbs 3:12).

Only mature Christians enjoy the meat of God's Word, and He has much to share with His grown-up sons and daughters. There will always be more to learn, so don't make excuses for your weak points. Accepting the truth will set you free (see John 8:32), and God will give you strength to overcome in those areas in which you are weak.

Fruit of the Spirit

If we live by the [Holy] Spirit, let us also walk
by the Spirit. [If by the Holy Spirit we have our
life in God, let us go forward walking in line,
our conduct controlled by the Spirit.]

GALATIANS 5:25

People crave love, happiness, and peace. They try to buy these things and pay therapists to help them find them. All these qualities are available by trusting as their Savior, Jesus, who sends the Holy Spirit to help them walk in obedience to God. Living the Spirit-filled life will eventually produce those things that people want most in their lives.

Galatians 5:22–23 says, "But the fruit of the [Holy] Spirit [the work which His presence within accomplishes] is love, joy (gladness), peace, patience (an even temper, forbearance), kindness, goodness (benevolence), faithfulness, gentleness (meekness, humility), self-control (self-restraint, continence). Against such things there is no law [that can bring a charge]." Let the work of God's presence within you shine through you to others today.

Be Diligent

*But we do [strongly and earnestly] desire for
each of you to show the same diligence and sincerity
[all the way through] in realizing and enjoying
the full assurance and development of [your]
hope until the end.*

HEBREWS 6:11

Proverbs 22:29 says, "Do you see a man
diligent *and* skillful in his business? He
will stand before kings; he will not stand before obscure men." A diligent man lives by the principle of
"just do it!" He is the one who does it, does it, does
it, and then does it some more, until whatever he set
out to do is finished.

Never give up on anything God has told you to
believe for; never quit doing anything He has clearly
shown you to do. Your diligence will pay off with a
blessing from God.

Complete Your Work

Jesus said to them, My food (nourishment) is to do the will (pleasure) of Him Who sent Me and to accomplish and completely finish His work.

JOHN 4:34

I believe the Lord wants us to finish whatever He calls us to do, even when it requires patience, perseverance, and hard work. God wants us to grow roots and learn to endure until the fruit of His promise is manifested.

Be willing to endure patiently to see God's plan take place in your life. If God has given you a vision of something He wants you to accomplish, keep doing whatever He has given you to do, even when the excitement for the work is over, and all the goose bumps are gone. If you don't have a vision, ask God to show you something that you need to do, and then commit your work to the Lord until it is completed.

Rid Yourself of Clutter

"You will keep him *in perfect peace,* whose *mind*
is *stayed* on You, *because he trusts in You."*

ISAIAH 26:3 NKJ

Sometimes we complicate our life by taking on things that God has not told us to do. We add stress, confusion, and clutter with the unnecessary things we take on and hold on to. We need to use our faith to let go of whatever clutters our mind and keeps us from peace.

Ask God to show you ways to simplify your life. Take an inventory today, and start throwing out whatever is filling your life with unproductive distractions. God wants you to enjoy your day, so get rid of whatever He shows you to give up.

Love Your Critics

He who heeds instruction and *correction is
[not only himself] in the way of life [but also]
is a way of life for others.*

PROVERBS 10:17

Love your critics. Appreciate people's
correction. Appreciate God's correction
also. Proverbs 3:12 says, "For whom the Lord loves
He corrects."

Self-discipline is the mark of maturity. If you
don't have control of yourself in a certain area, you
are undisciplined. In that area you are not mature. If
you want to be a mature Christian, then you must be
disciplined.

If you want to be free to truly enjoy your life,
you must face the truth. You cannot be free if you
make excuses for any area of weakness that God has
pointed out to you. Everyone has weaknesses: give
thanks to God if you discover one of yours today,
and trust Him to be strong in that area in your behalf.

Get Rid of Hindrances

Purge (clean out) the old leaven that you may
be fresh (new) dough, still uncontaminated
[as you are], for Christ.

1 CORINTHIANS 5:7

If you are serious about growing in the Lord and reaching a maturity of faith, you will embrace Matthew 5:29–30. It is a powerful Scripture which basically says: "If your eye offends you, pluck it out; if your hand offends you, cut it off."

In 1 Corinthians 9:24–27, Paul said, "I am running a race, and *I am running it to win*. Therefore, I buffet my body, I subdue it, and I handle it roughly" (paraphrased).

If you have habits or hindrances in your life that are fouling you up, get rid of them. Do it *now!* Don't waste today with regret. Ask God to show you any area in your life that needs discipline, and then draw from His vast supply of grace to make the changes you need to make.

Control Your Moods

Receive instruction in wise dealing and the
discipline of wise thoughtfulness, righteousness,
justice, and integrity.

PROVERBS 1:3

Moods can bring strange impulses that we dare not heed. When we get moody, we want to do weird things, or neglect our responsibilities.

"I don't feel like doing anything today. I am in a bad mood. Just leave me alone."

Disciplined people submit their emotions to wisdom. They say, "These are my feelings, but I don't live by my feelings. I may have moods, but they don't dictate my actions. I am going to do exactly what I would do if I felt better." You will enjoy your day more when you discipline yourself to do what you believe, instead of what you feel.

Control Your Speech

A gentle tongue [with its healing
power] is a tree of life.

PROVERBS 15:4

The Bible says that if a person can control his speech, he can curb his entire nature: "For we all often stumble *and* fall *and* offend in many things. And if anyone does not offend in speech [never says the wrong things], he is a fully developed character *and* a perfect man, able to control his whole body *and* to curb his entire nature"(James 3:2).

No one is completely mature in the Lord, so there is always room for improvement. If your mouth is out of control, other areas of your life will also be out of control. Give your speech to God today. Ask Him to direct the words you speak, and allow Him to fill your mouth with words of life that lift up everyone around you.

Choose Excellence

I am Your servant; give me understanding
(discernment and comprehension), that I may know
(discern and be familiar with the character of)
Your testimonies.

PSALM 119:125

The Word says, "Learn to sense what is vital, *and* approve *and* prize what is excellent *and* of real value [recognizing the highest and the best, and distinguishing the moral differences], and . . . be untainted *and* pure and unerring *and* blameless [so that with hearts sincere and certain and unsullied, you may approach] the day of Christ [not stumbling *nor* causing others to stumble]" (Philippians 1:10).

People make choices and selections all day long. A truly disciplined person has the ability to subordinate the lesser choice to the greater, more excellent choice. Think about that as you choose the way you will go today. Select the greater cause, and subordinate the lesser options to it.

You Are Secure

Lean on, trust in, and *be confident in the Lord*
with all your heart and *mind and do not rely on your*
own insight or *understanding. In all your ways know,*
recognize, and *acknowledge Him, and He will direct*
and *make straight* and *plain your paths.*

PROVERBS 3:5—6

Following God is not a part-time lifestyle. The Bible clearly teaches that we
are to be cautious *at all times* because the devil looks
for opportunities to devour us (see 1 Peter 5:8).

But God gives us grace to withstand the devil
and to be firm in faith against his onset. You can be
rooted, established strong, immovable, and determined, knowing that whatever you face today is
identical to what Christians throughout the world
are facing. And God Himself will complete you and
make you what you ought to be. He will establish
you and ground you securely, strengthen and settle
you today (see vv. 9—10).

Use Self-Control

*For this very reason, make every effort to add
to your faith goodness; and to goodness, knowledge;
and to knowledge, self-control; and to self-control,
perseverance; and to perseverance, godliness; and
to godliness, brotherly kindness; and to brotherly
kindness, love. For if you possess these qualities in
increasing measure, they will keep you from being
ineffective and unproductive in your knowledge
of our Lord Jesus Christ.*

2 PETER 1:5–8 NIV

The Word says that a person will die for lack of discipline and instruction, and in his folly he will go astray and be lost (see Proverbs 5:23). You can't buy discipline, but you have an inner ability to develop self-control.

By spending time with God, you can be filled with His Spirit and controlled by His power to live a calm life with a well-balanced mind of discipline and self-control (see 2 Timothy 1:7). Consciously add self-control to your behavior today.

Give God Control

*And endurance (fortitude) develops maturity of
character (approved faith and tried integrity). And
character [of this sort] produces [the habit of]
joyful and confident hope of eternal salvation.*

ROMANS 5:4

You will not enjoy your day if anything is out of control. You can keep your temper, moods, emotions, appetite, mouth, and thoughts in line with God's Word if you give Him control over the areas you want to subdue with faith. God created us with a free will, and we can choose the thing that is best for us.

Be free from old destructive habits by simply forming new ones. Don't let your emotions get out of control today. If, for instance, you feel your temper begin to rise, pray quickly for God to fill you with the fruit of the Spirit. Use the self-control that He freely makes available to you.

Desire God's Heart

*Arm yourselves with the same thought and pur-
pose [patiently to suffer rather than fail to please
God]. For whoever has suffered in the flesh [having
the mind of Christ] is done with [intentional] sin
[has stopped pleasing himself and the world, and
pleases God], so that he can no longer spend the rest
of his natural life living by [his] human appetites
and desires, but [he lives] for what God wills.*

I PETER 4:1—2

You have desires of the flesh, but you also
have desires inspired by the Holy Spirit.
You have a mind of flesh, but you also "have the mind
of Christ" and "hold the thoughts (feelings and purposes) of His heart" (1 Corinthians 2:16).

Learn to determine where your desires are coming from. Desires from your flesh don't bring peace,
but desires from God's Spirit bring joyful rewards.
Exercise self-control, and choose those desires that
are planted in you by the Holy Spirit.

Don't Waste Time

Look carefully then how you walk! Live pur-
posefully and worthily and accurately, not as the
unwise and witless, but as wise (sensible, intelligent
people), making the very most of the time
[buying up each opportunity].

EPHESIANS 5:15–16

We need to be so self-controlled that we don't waste time. That doesn't mean that we can never do anything fun. It doesn't mean we can't do things that we enjoy.

We don't need to be rigid, stiff, or boring. But we do need to use our time wisely, choosing to give the best part of our day to spend time with God.

The Word encourages us to be prepared, saying, "Hear counsel, receive instruction, *and* accept correction, that you may be wise in the time to come" (Proverbs 19:20). Starting your day with God's instruction will keep you walking in wisdom, making the most of your time.

Initiate Solutions

I have set before you life and death, the blessings
and the curses; therefore choose life.

DEUTERONOMY 30:19

Sometimes we complain about things that we could change if we would stop feeling sorry for ourselves long enough to do something about them. For example, if we are lonely, we can make the effort to be a friend to someone else. We can choose to be free or remain in bondage to self-pity. We can choose to be pitiful or powerful.

Psalm 25:12–14 says, "Who is the man who reverently fears *and* worships the Lord? Him shall He teach in the way that he should choose. He himself shall dwell at ease, and his offspring shall inherit the land. The secret [of the sweet, satisfying companionship] of the Lord have they who fear (revere and worship) Him, and He will show them His covenant *and* reveal to them its [deep, inner] meaning."

Admirable Virtues

But I say, walk and live [habitually] in the
[Holy] Spirit [responsive to and controlled and
guided by the Spirit]; then you will certainly not
gratify the cravings and desires of the flesh
(of human nature without God).

GALATIANS 5:16

"The fruit of the [Holy] Spirit, [the work which His presence within accomplishes] is love, joy (gladness), peace, patience (an even temper, forbearance), kindness, goodness (benevolence), faithfulness, gentleness (meekness, humility), self-control (self-restraint, continence)" (Galatians 5:22–23).

People throughout the world try to acquire these virtues through counseling or self-help books. Yet the Bible says that if we walk with God, the Spirit-filled life will produce all these things within us. Give your life to God each day, and He will create a right heart in you, one that will want to do the things He would have you do.

Sowing and Reaping

So then, as occasion and *opportunity open up to
us, let us do good [morally] to all people [not only
being useful or profitable to them, but also doing
what is for their spiritual good and advantage].
Be mindful to be a blessing, especially to those of the
household of faith [those who belong to God's
family with you, the believers].*

GALATIANS 6:10

"For he who sows to his own flesh (lower nature, sensuality) will from the flesh reap decay *and* ruin *and* destruction, but he who sows to the Spirit will from the Spirit reap eternal life" (Galatians 6:8).

We can enjoy our life (and avoid trouble) if we follow the Holy Spirit's leading. The Word tells us not to grow weary from doing what is right, because God promises that whatever we sow today we will also reap sometime in the future (see v. 9). Be courageous, act nobly, and continue doing what you know is right.

A New Direction

O Lord, You have heard the desire and *the longing of the humble* and *oppressed; You will prepare*
and *strengthen* and *direct their hearts.*

PSALM 10:17

Sometimes we come to an unhappy place
in our lives. If we examine ourselves on
those days, we will most likely discover that the
things that make us most unhappy are the fruit of the
choices that we made earlier.

Today can be a new start. I think God gave us
twenty-four-hour days because He knew that was all
we could handle. His mercies are new every morning (see Lamentations 3:22–23). You can start over
this morning and live today for the Lord. Determine
to follow wherever God leads you, and do whatever
He tells you to do. You can expect better tomorrows
when you live right today.

Walk in Integrity

The Lord rewarded me according to my righteousness (my conscious integrity and sincerity with Him); according to the cleanness of my hands has He recompensed me.

PSALM 18:20

Talking about the Word isn't enough; we need to do what we say we believe. God will bless us if we are people of integrity. As believers, we need to keep our promises and do what we say we will do.

Look for ways to demonstrate integrity today. If you can't follow through with something you said you would do for someone, at least call or write a letter, saying, "Please forgive me; I was not being led by God, and I just cannot do what I said." This way you will honor God and keep your steps going in the right direction.

Stay Out of Strife

He who is of a greedy spirit stirs up strife,
but he who puts his trust in the Lord
shall be enriched and blessed.

PROVERBS 28:25

Probably 80 percent of the places we visit in our ministry have church members who are riddled with strife. Strife is the devil's tool against us. It takes personal self-control to stay out of strife.

If you want to keep peace, you can't always say everything you want to say. Sometimes you have to control yourself and apologize even when there is nothing in you that wants to do so. But if you sow the godly principle of harmony and unity today, a time will come when you will reap the blessings of all it can bring to you.

Keep Your Promises

He who honors those who fear the Lord (who revere
and worship Him); who swears to his own hurt and
does not change; [he who] does not put out his
money for interest [to one of his own people] and
who will not take a bribe against the innocent. He
who does these things shall never be moved.

PSALM 15:4—5

There are times when I make a commitment to do something that later I regret.
Then I try to figure out some way to get out of doing what I said I would do. I argue, "God, surely You
don't want me to do this thing and miss this other
great opportunity."

The only thing the Lord ever says to me is, "You
gave your word, Joyce. Be a woman of integrity, and
I will bless you." If we are people of integrity, God
will bring other good opportunities around another
time with even more blessings.

Ask for Help

Confess to one another therefore your faults
(your slips, your false steps, your offenses, your sins)
and pray [also] for one another, that you may be
healed and restored [to a spiritual tone of mind and
heart]. The earnest (heartfelt, continued) prayer of a
righteous man makes tremendous power available
[dynamic in its working].

JAMES 5:16

Addictions, habits, or negative attitudes can wear you out. If you need deliverance from some wrong behavior, the Bible teaches that the Holy Spirit is your Helper (see John 14:16). Confess your need to God, and ask Him to deliver you.

He may lead you to confess your faults to other believers whom you can trust to pray for you. The Word says that we are to confess our faults to one another *so that we may be healed and restored.* If you are out of control in some area, be honest about it. Today can be your day of deliverance.

Eliminate Excuses

For the Lord your God walks in the midst of
your camp to deliver you and to give up your enemies
before you. Therefore shall your camp be holy,
that He may see nothing indecent among
you and turn away from you.

DEUTERONOMY 23:14

If a habit is controlling you, you will not enjoy the best that God offers you. Don't make excuses for bondages that seem to have a hold on you. Denial and excuses will keep you from enjoying your life.

Whether it is an eating disorder or a bad temper, you cannot blame it on your genes or your family. God makes a way of escape for us and promises a good life for those who are born again. Claim your rights as a child of God. Say, "I am a new person in Christ; I can do all things through Christ who strengthens me" (see Philippians 4:13).

God Will Change You

*Many plans are in a man's mind, but it is the
Lord's purpose for him that will stand.*

PROVERBS 19:21

Even though you may still be operating in old habits, you still have hope of change, but you can't change yourself. God will change you, if you seek Him with your whole heart.

Don't be in a hurry for God to finish working in your life. We want everything to be done instantly, but God is not interested in our schedule. The enemy may thwart *your* plans, but *God's* plans don't get thwarted, and He has a unique plan for you.

Seek God's plan for your life. Stay on fire, red hot, zealous. Pursue His purpose for you with every ounce of energy you have. There is nothing in this world that is worth seeking more.

Seek God Wholeheartedly

Seek, inquire of and *for the Lord,* and *crave Him*
and His strength (His might and inflexibility
to temptation); seek and *require His face* and *His*
presence [continually] evermore.

PSALM 105:4

If you have a need today, seek God with your whole heart. The Bible says to "aim at *and* seek the [rich, eternal treasures] that are above" (Colossians 3:1). If you seek the fruit of the Spirit wholeheartedly, God will do a work in your life so that you will enjoy the abundant life Jesus died to give you.

God promises, "And the Lord shall make you the head, and not the tail; and you shall be above only, and you shall not be beneath, if you heed the commandments of the Lord your God which I command you this day and are watchful to do them" (Deuteronomy 28:13).

Be Positive

*I thank my God at all times for you because of
the grace (the favor and spiritual blessing) of God
which was bestowed on you in Christ Jesus, [so] that
in Him in every respect you were enriched, in full
power* and *readiness of speech [to speak of your
faith] and complete knowledge* and *illumination
[to give you full insight into its meaning].*

I CORINTHIANS 1:4–5

The Word of God says, "Depart from evil
and do good; seek, inquire for, *and* crave
peace and pursue (go after) it!" (Psalm 34:14). "Do
all things without grumbling *and* faultfinding *and*
complaining [against God] and questioning *and*
doubting [among yourselves]" (Philippians 2:14).

Be positive. Get rid of gossiping and complaining. Start your day by reading the Bible so that you
will know how to speak from the authority of God's
Word. Spend time listening to God, and then tell
others what you hear Him say. Bring life to whatever
situations you face.

Control Your Temper

He who is slow to anger has great understanding.

PROVERBS 14:29

It is uncomfortable for others to be around us if we are easily angered. We need to learn how to *respond* to life instead of *react* to it, so that we can enjoy God's power in our lives. God says that a person who can control his or her anger is better and mightier than an individual who can take a whole city (see Proverbs 16:32).

God's Word says, "Understand [this], my beloved brethren. Let every man be quick to hear [a ready listener], slow to speak, slow to take offense *and* to get angry. For man's anger does not promote the righteousness God [wishes and requires]" (James 1:19–20). Be a ready listener, and enjoy the freedom from anger that God offers you.

Be Slow to Speak

For let him who wants to enjoy life and see
good days [good — whether apparent or not] keep
his tongue free from evil and his lips from guile
(treachery, deceit).

I PETER 3:10

Have you ever regretted something you said as soon as the words were out of your mouth? You can't take back the words you speak to others — and words can damage relationships. The Bible says that if you can control your mouth, you can control your whole body (see James 3:2).

Before you respond to people too quickly, stop and listen to what the Holy Spirit has to say about your situation. James taught, "Let every man be quick to hear [a ready listener], slow to speak, slow to take offense *and* to get angry" (James 1:19). Commit your mouth to God's service today, and use words that speak healing to others.

Love Isn't Touchy

Love (God's love in us) does not insist on its own rights or its own way, for it is not self-seeking; it is not touchy or fretful or resentful; it takes no account of the evil done to it [it pays no attention to a suffered wrong].

1 CORINTHIANS 13:5

The Bible says that God's love in us is not touchy. If we wear our emotions on our sleeve all the time, we may need to spend more time in His presence before we face the day. Our tears can provoke sympathy, but it is better to be a giver instead of a taker all the time.

Starting your day with God will keep you "sweetened up" and full of confidence. As you enjoy His gentleness and kindness, you will be built up in your spirit and better able to overlook the offenses of others. Ask God to give you a strong heart, one ready to love people today as He does.

Get in Balance

Love bears up under anything and everything that comes, is ever ready to believe the best of every person, its hopes are fadeless under all circumstances, and it endures everything [without weakening].

1 CORINTHIANS 13:7

We all get emotional occasionally or lose our temper once in a while. But if you are out of balance in either one of these areas, it is very important to get back in balance if you want your day to go right.

If your feelings get hurt because someone looks at you crossways or because friends or family forget your birthday, you need to spend more time with God. He will fill you with so much love and such a sense of self-worth that you won't feel ill-tempered or touchy toward anyone. Seek God with your whole heart today. Talk to Him about your problems, and then enjoy yourself, knowing that He cares for you.

Don't Procrastinate

*But the fruit of the [Holy] Spirit [the work
which His presence within accomplishes] is love, joy
(gladness), peace, patience (an even temper, forbearance), kindness, goodness (benevolence), faithfulness,
gentleness (meekness, humility), self-control
(self-restraint, continence). Against such things
there is no law [that can bring a charge].*

GALATIANS 5:22–23

The Bible says that we are to "be doers of
the Word [obey the message], and not
merely listeners to it" (James 1:22). In other words,
we are to apply its teaching to our everyday lives.

Procrastination is one of the greatest barriers to
putting God's word into action in our lives. It takes
self-control to *do* something, and it also takes self-
control *not* to do something. Self-control is a fruit of
the Spirit that comes into our lives by spending time
with God. Ask God to fill you with the power of
self-control in order to overcome procrastination
and be a doer of the Word.

Break Strongholds

For the weapons of our warfare are not physical
[weapons of flesh and blood], but they are mighty
before God for the overthrow and destruction of
strongholds, . . . and we lead every thought and
purpose away captive into the obedience of Christ
(the Messiah, the Anointed One).

2 CORINTHIANS 10:4–5

The Bible teaches that Satan tries to build strongholds in our lives. One way to identify the strongholds in your life is to watch for repetitive situations that pull you down in spirit.

We all know inside when something is not right in our life or is getting out of control. If that happens to you, seek God early to find out what is going on. If a negative behavior becomes repetitive, that is a signal that Satan is building himself a stronghold in your life. God will destroy the devil's strongholds within you, if you draw near to Him.

Find Truth

And you will know the Truth, and
the Truth will set you free.

JOHN 8:32

If you lose your temper easily, you will never enjoy your day as God meant for it to be. Seek God with your whole heart and find out what is wrong. The way to get free from things that upset you is to find truth — the truth will always set you free.

We don't always want to face truth because sometimes it is painful. Sometimes it shows us that we need to change. If we are behaving badly, we make excuses for our wrong behavior. But excuses will never make us free. Let God get involved with your day; when you feel your temper flare, ask Him to reveal the truth of that situation. The truth will always set you free to enjoy the rest of your day.

Get Free

Out of my distress I called upon the Lord;
the Lord answered me and set me free.

PSALM 118:5

If you find yourself running late everywhere you go (even 50 percent of the
time), that is evidence of a stronghold that Satan has
built in your life. Get free from it, or the devil will
use it to keep you under pressure. You may have an
excuse for every time you are behind schedule, but
something is wrong if that behavior pattern is repetitive.

Ask God to show you how to get free from the
pressure of always hurrying and being late. Starting
your day with God will help you set priorities for
your day. Get to the root of the problem, and enjoy
the fruit of God's indwelling presence to get you
where you need to be — on time and without hurrying.

Run the Race

I press on toward the goal to win the
[supreme and heavenly] prize to which God in
Christ Jesus is calling us upward.

PHILIPPIANS 3:14

We live in a society that is used to doing whatever feels good *right now*. But instant gratification never brings lasting satisfaction.

If you operate in self-control through the power of the Holy Spirit living in you, you will choose to do things that contribute to the goal that you have in mind. You must discipline yourself now so you will reap the reward of reaching your goal later.

Paul taught, "Do you not know that in a race all the runners compete, but [only] one receives the prize? So run [your race] that you may lay hold [of the prize] *and* make it yours" (1 Corinthians 9:24). Stay focused on the goal. God will give you the grace to continue moving toward it.

Get Fit

*For God did not give us a spirit of timidity
(of cowardice, of craven and cringing and fawning
fear), but [He has given us a spirit] of power and
of love and of calm and well-balanced mind
and discipline and self-control.*

2 TIMOTHY 1:7

"Every athlete who goes into training conducts himself temperately *and* restricts himself in *all* things" (1 Corinthians 9:25, emphasis mine). That word *all* is a difficult concept for us to grasp.

We need to live a disciplined life, physically, spiritually, and emotionally, if we want to enjoy God's plan for us. The fruit of the Spirit is self-control, and the fruit of the flesh is no control.

Paul said, "I buffet my body [handle it roughly, discipline it by hardships] and subdue it, for fear that after proclaiming to others the Gospel *and* things pertaining to it, I myself should become unfit [not stand the test, be unapproved and rejected as a counterfeit]" (1 Corinthians 9:27).

Be a Doer of the Word

My life makes its boast in the Lord.

PSALM 34:2

I have found three principles to be life-changing when followed faithfully every day:

1. Eliminate excuses and avoid procrastination. Being a doer of the Word is putting your faith into action. Faith without action is dead faith (see James 2:20 KJV).

2. Face the truth no matter how painful it is. Truth is the only thing that will set you free (see John 8:32). God's Word is full of truth. Start your day in the Word of God.

3. Stop feeling sorry for yourself. Understand who you are in Jesus Christ. You are more than capable in Him (see Philippians 4:13).

Enjoy the Power to Love Others

So speak and so act as [people should] who are to be judged under the law of liberty [the moral instruction given by Christ, especially about love].

JAMES 2:12

It can be difficult to grasp the idea of the "law of liberty," because law and liberty seem to be worlds apart: A law says one thing, while liberty says another. I believe the law of liberty spoken of in James 1:25 refers to the freedom of self-control, because God puts a new heart in us that *wants* to obey His law of love.

With this new heart that Jesus gave you, you have the ability to be led of the Spirit, who gives you the power and freedom to love others. Enjoy your day by allowing the Lord to love others through you.

Be Responsible

But you are not living the life of the flesh, you are
living the life of the Spirit, if the [Holy] Spirit of
God [really] dwells within you [directs and controls
you]. But if anyone does not possess the [Holy] Spirit
of Christ, he is none of His [he does not belong to
Christ, is not truly a child of God].

ROMANS 8:9

Romans 8:8 declares: "Those who are living the life of the flesh [catering to the appetites and impulses of their carnal nature] cannot please *or* satisfy God, *or* be acceptable to Him."

God wants us to enjoy the good life. Here He is saying to us, "If you walk in the Spirit, you will reap blessings from the Spirit-controlled life both now and hereafter."

Be responsible for your choices today. You cannot choose to live in the flesh and still expect everything to work out well. Choose to be obedient to the leading of the Holy Spirit.

Sow What You Want to Reap

*Sow for yourselves according to righteousness
(uprightness and right standing with God); reap
according to mercy and loving-kindness. Break up
your uncultivated ground, for it is time to seek the
Lord, to inquire for and of Him, and to require His
favor, till He comes and teaches you righteousness
and rains His righteous gift of salvation upon you.*

HOSEA 10:12

There is never a harvest without a time
of sowing (see Ecclesiastes 3:1–2). God
can do anything He wants to, but He has established
a life principle that works for everyone: "First you
sow, and then you reap." It always happens in that
order.

Those who sow trouble and mischief reap the
same. Those who sow righteousness reap mercy. If
God tells you to do something, and you sow obedience, and once you have passed the test, you will
reap a good harvest. Remember the sequence: What
you sow *today,* you will reap *tomorrow.*

Sow Generously

*[Remember] this: he who sows sparingly and
grudgingly will also reap sparingly and grudgingly,
and he who sows generously [that blessings may
come to someone] will also reap generously
and with blessings.*

2 CORINTHIANS 9:6

We don't sow now and reap a harvest five minutes later. We need to endure patiently in order to reap the blessing of righteousness. Ten to fifteen years may pass before a harvest comes, but God's Word is still true.

Be willing to go through the test of time in order to enjoy the harvest God promises. His Word says, "In the morning sow your seed, and in the evening withhold not your hands, for you know not which shall prosper, whether this or that, or whether both alike will be good" (Ecclesiastes 11:6). Sow good seeds generously today.

Reap the Good Life

I have told you these things, so that in Me you may have [perfect] peace and confidence. In the world you have tribulation and trials and distress and frustration; but be of good cheer [take courage; be confident, certain, undaunted]! For I have over-come the world. [I have deprived it of power to harm you and have conquered it for you.]

JOHN 16:33

God showed me that my life was in a mess because of the decisions I had made. He said, "Joyce, you have to change; start sowing good seeds, and down the road somewhere, you will reap."

If trials come against you, don't try to figure out whether you sowed some bad seeds that produced them. Trials will come, but if you will obey the Word of God long enough (not just five minutes of trial and error), sooner or later, you will come into the good life that God has prearranged for you to live.

Plant Purposefully

Do not be deceived and *deluded* and *misled;*
God will not allow Himself to be sneered at (scorned,
disdained, or mocked by mere pretensions or pro-
fessions, or by His precepts being set aside). [He
inevitably deludes himself who attempts to delude
God.] For whatever a man sows, that and *that*
only is what he will reap.

GALATIANS 6:7

Choose carefully what you sow through your words and actions, and plant only what you want to reap: "For he who sows to his own flesh (lower nature, sensuality) will from the flesh reap decay *and* ruin *and* destruction, but he who sows to the Spirit will from the Spirit reap eternal life" (Galatians 6:8).

Everything you do, all day long, is an opportunity to sow good seeds, or bad ones, that can drastically change things in your life. Get an early start in sowing only what you want to come back to you.

Depend on God

*And I am convinced and sure of this very thing,
that He Who began a good work in you will continue
until the day of Jesus Christ [right up to the time of
His return], developing [that good work] and perfecting and bringing it to full completion in you.*

PHILIPPIANS 1:6

Whatever you may be struggling with today, the Holy Spirit will help you live a
self-controlled life, because the Bible says that self-
control is a fruit of the indwelling presence of the
Holy Spirit (see Galatians 5:22–23).

Allow the Holy Spirit to help you admit when
you have a problem that you need His help to overcome; then ask God for help from the Holy Spirit.

Jesus said, "Behold! I have given you authority
and power . . . and [physical and mental strength and
ability] over all the power that the enemy [possesses]"
(Luke 10:19).

God's Way Works

*Blessed (happy, fortunate, to be envied) is
everyone who fears, reveres, and worships the Lord,
who walks in His ways and lives according to
His commandments.*

PSALM 128:1

The Bible says, "Do not be deceived *and*
deluded *and* misled; God will not allow
Himself to be sneered at (scorned, disdained, or
mocked . . . For whatever a man sows, that *and* that
only is what he will reap" (Galatians 6:7). God's
Word is true; He will not be mocked.

If it seems that the enemy has erected walls to
keep you from your purpose, just keep doing what
is right anyway. Speaking of the Lord, the psalmist
says, "You have broken down all his hedges *and* his
walls; You have brought his strongholds to ruin"
(Psalm 89:40). God is in control; if you do right today, you will be blessed.

Keep on Keeping On

*To those who by patient persistence in well-doing
[springing from piety] seek [unseen but sure]
glory and honor and [the eternal blessedness of]
immortality, He will give eternal life.*

ROMANS 2:7

In Proverbs, Wisdom says: "Blessed (happy, fortunate, to be envied) is the man who listens to me, watching *daily* at my gates, waiting at the posts of my doors" (8:34). Many people seem to jump from one thing to another, when what they need is wisdom and consistency.

It is important to keep on keeping on — doing what you know is right, even if you are the only one doing it. God is on your side (see Romans 8:31), and He has already written the end of the Book. Those who obey Him will win!

Obedience Brings Success

Every Scripture is God-breathed (given by His inspiration) and profitable for instruction, for reproof and conviction of sin, for correction of error and discipline in obedience, [and] for training in righteousness (in holy living, in conformity to God's will in thought, purpose, and action).

2 TIMOTHY 3:16

The Bible says that we will reap what we sow. The dividing line between success and failure is doing what God tells us to do. We pray for fruit in our lives, but we don't always want to pray for roots.

If we want our days to go right, we need to do whatever God tells us to do. If we don't walk in obedience, then we can't complain if we wind up in a mess. If we are lonely and God tells us to invite somebody over, but we decide it is too much trouble, then we will stay lonely.

Obedience brings the fruit of the Spirit in your life. Dig deep into God's Word before you walk away from blessings today.

Jesus Is Our Standard

*His intention was . . . that [we might arrive]
at really mature manhood (the completeness of
personality which is nothing less than the standard
height of Christ's own perfection), the measure of
the stature of the fullness of the Christ and the
completeness found in Him.*

EPHESIANS 4:12—13

One time I was comparing myself to the
way I used to be, and I thought, *I am not
doing too badly.*

Then God said to me, "But Who is your standard? How are you doing compared to Me?"

I said, "Lord, I have a long way to go!"

Refuse to live beneath the standard that Jesus
has set for you. Keep your eyes on Him and tell
Him, "Many . . . are the wonderful works which
You have done . . . no one can compare with You"
(Psalm 40:5).

Receive His Grace

*For we are God's [own] handiwork (His work-
manship), recreated in Christ Jesus, [born anew] that
we may do those good works which God predestined
(planned beforehand) for us [taking paths which He
prepared ahead of time], that we should walk in them
[living the good life which He prearranged and
made ready for us to live].*

EPHESIANS 2:10

The Bible doesn't say that you have to
have self-control in order to go to heaven.
You are free to be out of control if you want to; it is
entirely up to you. The Word does say that you have
to believe that Jesus Christ is your Lord and Savior
(see Romans 10:9–10).

But if you want to live the good life that God has
prearranged and laid out for you before the foundation of the world, you will need to discipline
yourself to do whatever His Word says to do or
whatever the Holy Spirit speaks to your heart to do.
God offers you the grace to live a holy life that will
reap many blessings in the days to come.

Enjoy the Good Life

You have put more joy and rejoicing in my heart
than [they know] when their wheat and new wine
have yielded abundantly. In peace I will both lie
down and sleep, for You, Lord, alone make me
dwell in safety and confident trust.

PSALM 4:7–8

God has prearranged and made ready a good life for you, but that good life is a choice. You have to decide to follow God's leading in order to walk in it.

The Bible contains guidelines for that good life. It is not a book of laws; it is about the liberty and freedom to live the life that reaps good things. It is a book of wisdom that will lead you to peace and joy. If you do what the Word says to do, blessings will chase you and find you wherever you are (see Deuteronomy 28:1–2).

The Grace of God

*I have raised you up for this very purpose of dis-
playing My power in [dealing with] you, so that My
name may be proclaimed the whole world over.*

ROMANS 9:17

If you want victory over something, prepare yourself to work at it. But it is not a
matter of depending on yourself or winning at life
through your own determination. God gives us grace
to do good works. But grace doesn't mean that our
human flesh gets a free ride while we just lie down
and go to sleep.

You are made for good works, to be a servant of
righteousness. You are built to take responsibility,
and God will help you accomplish all He gives you
to do. He set you free from the bondage of sin so
that you can conform to His divine will in thought,
purpose, and action (see Romans 6:18). Victory is
achieved through God's grace, but you have to
choose to trust Him every step of the way.

Choose Liberty

You were washed clean (purified by a complete atonement for sin and made free from the guilt of sin), and you were consecrated (set apart, hallowed), and you were justified [pronounced righteous, by trusting] in the name of the Lord Jesus Christ and in the [Holy] Spirit of our God.

1 CORINTHIANS 6:11

As a believer, you are free to do anything you please: "All things are legitimate [permissible — and we are free to do anything we please], but not all things are helpful (expedient, profitable, and wholesome)" (1 Corinthians 10:23).

God trusts you with liberty because He has also given you a new heart full of desire to please Him. You don't have to struggle against immorality and sin when you allow Him to fill you with His Spirit each day. As a born-again, Spirit-filled believer, you have been given the liberty to lead a good life. Choose today what is wholesome, edifying, and constructive.

Accept God's Invitation

I [the Lord] will instruct you and teach you in the
way you should go; I will counsel you
with My eye upon you.

PSALM 32:8

The devil wants to keep us believers subject to legalism. If he can't condemn us for what we *do*, he will try to torment us for what we *don't do*. He wants us to feel guilty when we don't read the Word and pray, suggesting that God isn't pleased with us, or that He is even mad at us for what we *haven't done*.

God never condemns us for not being disciplined, but He lovingly invites us to spend time with Him. Heaven is available to us through simple trust in Jesus, but the good life is enjoyed when we act the way Jesus acts. We should *want to* read the Word because it holds the keys to knowing God intimately and enjoying Him fully.

Bless Yourself

*I love those who love me, and those who seek me
early and diligently shall find me.*

Our motives are misplaced if we think we read the Bible and pray to please God or to keep from making Him mad at us. God once told me, "You think, when you read the Bible, that you are making Me happy. I am going to be happy whether you read it or not. No, Joyce, if you read the Bible, *you're* happy. If you pray, *you're* happy. If you *give*, you *receive*."

Every single thing that God tells us to do, He tells us to do so to bless ourselves. He doesn't ask us to devote ourselves to study and prayer for Him; it is for us. The good life is our choice.

It's a Promise

Let Your mercy and *loving-kindness come*
also to me, O Lord, even Your salvation
according to Your promise.

PSALM 119:41

Some Christians want to make a law out of studying the Bible or spending a certain amount of time with God. But we should be motivated to read God's Word and spend time with Him because of our love relationship with Him, not because of a commandment to do so.

Jesus said, "If you [really] love Me, you will keep (obey) My commands" (John 14:15). What He really meant was, "If you love Me and walk in fellowship with Me, you *will* keep My commandments." If you concentrate on loving God, then keeping His commandments will become a natural part of what you do. It is a promise He makes to you.

God Does the Work

Work out . . . your own salvation . . . [not in your own strength] for it is God Who is all the while effectually at work in you [energizing and creating in you the power and desire], both to will and to work for His good pleasure and satisfaction and delight.

PHILIPPIANS 2:12—13

The Word of God brings liberty, not legalism; promises, not laws; and guidelines to a good life, not condemnation. Many work at following a Christian lifestyle, but they are not happy because they are focused on rules instead of on their relationship with God.

If you are trudging along, believing you *have to* give, *have to* read the Bible, *have to* pray, *have to* walk in the fruit of the Spirit, I encourage you to stop thinking you *have* to *do* anything. You will discover that God will give you the grace to *want* to do the things that lead to a victorious life in Him.

Balance Is Safety

So everyone who hears these words of Mine and acts upon them [obeying them] will be like a sensible (prudent, practical, wise) man who built his house upon the rock.

MATTHEW 7:24

Being out of balance opens the door for the devil to rob people of the good life. The devil tempts them to live in excess and extremes. He pushes some to be workaholics and others to be lazy, whichever works to keep them unproductive. He drives some to seek wealth above God, and convinces others that poverty is godliness.

I believe that the only safe life is a balanced life. And a balanced life is obtained by keeping its priorities in line with God's truth. Build your life on solid, safe ground by praying to God and listening to His plan for you.

Live Victoriously through Moderation

Let your moderation be known unto all men.

PHILIPPIANS 4:5 KJV

God demonstrates our need for balance through the great varieties of foods He made available to us. We need some of all of it, but not all of any of it. If we overdo anything, it is just as bad as underdoing it.

Some people think, *If it is a good thing, then more of a good thing ought to be better.* But that is not necessarily true. Too much or too little can both be big problems. Balance is the key to powerful, victorious living. Ask God to show you how to stay in balance today.

Learn to Pray

Establish my steps and direct them by [means of] Your word; let not any iniquity have dominion over me. Deliver me from the oppression of man; so will I keep Your precepts [hearing, receiving, loving, and obeying them].

PSALM 119:133–134

You may pray fifteen minutes every morning, and know you are touching heaven because things happen as a result of your prayers. But if you have a friend who prays for four hours every day, you may feel that you should pray more too.

Trust God to lead you individually in how long to pray and what to pray about. Spending an extra three hours and forty-five minutes can become a work of the flesh, if you do it just to be like your friend. You can wind up miserable and unproductive if you follow what someone else is doing, instead of simply saying, "Lord, teach *me* to pray."

Show the Blessings

And the grace (unmerited favor and blessing) of
our Lord [actually] flowed out superabundantly and
beyond measure for me, accompanied by faith and
love that are [to be realized] in Christ Jesus.

1 TIMOTHY 1:14

God wants to bless you today. You may feel that you shouldn't have nice things, but let God balance your thinking when it comes to His blessings. He will help you understand what you should have and what you shouldn't have. God blesses you so that you will be a blessing to others.

When God provides for you, it offers hope to unbelievers that He is faithful to provide for those who serve Him. You are an ambassador for Christ (see 2 Corinthians 5:20); expect His provision today, and don't hide His blessings when they come.

Communicate Love

If you then, evil as you are, know how to give
good gifts [gifts that are to their advantage] to
your children, how much more will your heavenly
Father give the Holy Spirit to those who
ask and continue to ask Him!

LUKE 11:13

One day, my son sent me a text message on my phone while he was away on a ministry trip. It read: "Mom, I love you." That blessed me so much. Of course, the next time I went shopping, I wanted to find something for him to bless him and let him know how proud I am of him.

Send God a message today, and tell Him how much you love Him. Just like a loving parent, God enjoys meeting your needs, filling your desires, and blessing you for the love you demonstrate to Him through your obedience. He can't wait to give you what you need.

Know God's Character

*And my God will liberally supply (fill to the
full) your every need according to His
riches in glory in Christ Jesus.*

PHILIPPIANS 4:19

I believe Jesus tries to get us to sow a good seed by making a statement that He is first in our lives. I believe if we do that, we will receive more than we give up. I am tested in this way all the time.

There have been many times when God has asked me to give my last, my only, and my all. But every time I have done so, I have ended up better off than I was before.

Offer up your best to God today, and you will see His character, that He is *El-Shaddai* — the God of more than enough (see Exodus 6:3).

Imitate God's Goodness

For You make him to be blessed
and a blessing forever.

PSALM 21:6

God made a covenant with Abraham, that He would bless him, and cause him to be a blessing to others (see Genesis 12:2). You too are an heir to the true riches of God (see James 1:9). As you mature spiritually and are able to handle your inheritance, God wants you to have an abundance to bless others in His name.

Before you get involved with your daily routine today, seek God and feed your soul with His truth for your life. Experiencing God will cause you to imitate His goodness, and prosper in His abundance.

Don't Let Feelings Rule

This is my comfort and *consolation in my afflic-*
tion: that Your word has revived me and *given me life.*

PSALM 119:50

God showed me that we are always going to have feelings, and that denying the existence of them is not godly. We do have to learn how to manage them, so they don't manage us.

If we live by our feelings, we will be destroyed, because our feelings aren't always in line with God's truth. We are to walk by faith in His promises, and not by sight or how things appear or the way we feel (see 2 Corinthians 5:7). Ask God to keep your feelings balanced with the truth of His Word today.

Temptation Isn't Sin

In the day when I called, You answered me; and
You strengthened me with strength (might and inflex-
ibility to temptation) in my inner self.

PSALM 138:3

Temptation to do wrong can make you feel horrible. You may think, *I shouldn't be going through this; I shouldn't be having a problem with this.* But God taught me that temptation isn't sin; we sin when we give in to temptation.

The Bible says temptation will come. It doesn't say, "Woe unto him to whom it comes," it says, "Woe unto him by whose hand it comes" (see Matthew 17:7). Jesus told us to pray that we would not give in to the temptation when we are tempted (see Luke 22:40).

Psalm 105:4 is a great way to start your day right. It says, "Seek, inquire of *and* for the Lord, *and* crave Him and His strength (His might and inflexibility to temptation); seek *and* require His face *and* His presence [continually] evermore."

Forgiveness Wins

For if you forgive people their trespasses [their reckless and willful sins, leaving them, letting them go, and giving up resentment], your heavenly Father will also forgive you.

MATTHEW 6:14

Unforgiveness will ruin your day. If someone hurts you, pray quickly, "God, I forgive them in Jesus' name." If your emotions feel strained when you see that person, stand firm in your decision to forgive them.

Pray for them, asking God to show you how to bless them. Do whatever God leads you to do for them, and let God's love work through you to heal the rift between you. If you do your part, God will bring your feelings in line with your decision, and you will enjoy your day and your life.

Be Truthful

Do not say, I will repay evil; wait [expectantly]
for the Lord, and He will rescue you.

PROVERBS 20:22

God doesn't mind if you tell Him how you honestly feel. Actually, telling God how you feel will give you relief. If you repress your feelings and pretend you aren't angry or hurting, and try to be superspiritual, you will miss the healing that God can give to you.

Be truthful with God. Don't carry a grudge all day. Get in touch with what is going on inside of you and talk to God about it. Truth is the only thing that will set you free to enjoy the rest of your day (see John 8:32).

Get Over It

Open rebuke is better than love that is hidden.

PROVERBS 27:5

Hiding your true feelings, like resentment or unforgiveness, keeps you in bondage to them. It is impossible to get your day started right if you keep waking up with pain from yesterday's wounds. If you carry around this kind of "emotional baggage," it will poison your day.

Sometimes you have to confront things to make them better. But use wisdom. While it is good to talk about things, don't dump all your thoughts and emotions on every person who comes along today.

Talk to God about your situation before you meet anyone. He may lead you to speak with someone you trust. But if He doesn't, learn to trust it completely to Him, and let it go.

Minister to Your Emotions

Keep and *protect me, O God, for in You
I have found refuge,* and *in You do I put
my trust* and *hide myself.*

PSALM 16:1

God gave us feelings, and it is all right to minister to your emotions or to the emotions of other people. Do something kind for yourself to keep your emotions healthy; just don't be ruled by them.

Treat yourself to a hot bath or a walk in the fresh air. Do what you need to do to get emotional release. If yesterday wore you out, get refreshed spiritually and emotionally before starting a new day. Find some time alone with God, listen to teaching or music tapes, and refill your heart with an awareness of God's presence.

Find Balance

*Since all this is true, we ought to pay much
closer attention than ever to the truths
that we have heard, lest in any way we drift past
[them] and slip away.*

HEBREWS 2:1

When Satan finds people out of balance, he has an inroad to destroy their lives. There are people who get out of balance in everything: from not sleeping, to sleeping too much; from not cleaning their house, to trying to keep it so clean that nobody can move in it.

Find balance; balance keeps your day going right. Satan doesn't much care if you don't do enough of something, or if you do too much of it, as long as you don't stay balanced. Take time to examine yourself prayerfully, and ask God to show you how to remain balanced.

Appreciate Your Calling

So we, numerous as we are, are one body in Christ
(the Messiah) and individually we are parts one of
another [mutually dependent on one another].

ROMANS 12:5

Learn to appreciate the call of God on your life. He has a different call for everybody. None of us are called to do *all* the work that needs to be done, but we can each enjoy the assignments we are given. We can also enjoy the work God does through others.

Today holds an opportunity to mature in the knowledge of God and to enjoy whatever God has called you to do. Your part is needed. Ask God early in the day to show you where to use your gifts to help others.

Speak Positively

Behold, You desire truth in the inner being; make
me therefore to know wisdom in my inmost heart.

PSALM 51:6

 Focus on speaking words in faith today; keep your confession truthful but positive. Don't deny the existence of your circumstances, but confess what God's Word has to say about your situation.

For example, if you are sneezing, coughing, and finding it difficult to breathe, it isn't truthful to say you aren't sick. But you can learn to present a negative situation in a positive way. You can say, "I believe God's healing power is working in me, and that I am getting better all the time."

Avoid Extremes

Apply your mind to instruction and *correction and your ears to words of knowledge.*

PROVERBS 23:12

When I first became a Christian, I heard a message about keeping my mouth shut, so I made a decision that the next day I wouldn't open my mouth to say anything. I was determined not to get myself in any trouble with my words.

The next morning I did not say a word for several hours. Then somebody asked me, "What is your problem?" That made me mad all over again. Eventually I learned that extremes never make our days go right. Reading God's Word helps us find balance to face everything that comes our way. The Word says we are to be *well-balanced* because the devil seeks someone to devour (see 1 Peter 5:8).

Unseen Promises Exist

And whatever you ask for in prayer, having faith
and [really] believing, you will receive.

MATTHEW 21:22

Before the fulfillment of God's promise to multiply Abram, He changed his name from Abram ("high exalted father") to Abraham, ("father of a multitude") (see Genesis 17:1–6). God spoke the promise long before it was visible to anyone.

Anything that is in the Word of God is a promise that can be rightfully and legally spoken forth even before it visibly exists. Reach into the spiritual realm, that you cannot see, and pull the promises of God out of there, with the words of your mouth, and prophesy them into existence. Read God's Word and speak as the Holy Spirit leads you to do so today.

God's Word Changes Things

Yet we have the same spirit of faith as he had who wrote, I have believed, and therefore have I spoken. We too believe, and therefore we speak.

2 CORINTHIANS 4:13

God created with words everything that we see. God *said,* "Let there be light," and there was light. Hebrews 11:3 says that everything that is visible was made from the invisible. God has blessings stored up for you in the spiritual realm that you may not be experiencing, but they do exist.

Speak positive words today, and call those things that are not (that are invisible) into your life (see Romans 4:17). If you face a problem today, say, "My problem is temporary. God's Word says that I am an overcomer because of Christ's love for me. Even though I don't see the answers now, God will provide for all of my needs."

Esteem Others

*Let each one of us make it a practice to please
(make happy) his neighbor for his good and for his
true welfare, to edify him [to strengthen him and
build him up spiritually].*

ROMANS 15:2

There are people who make "ministries"
out of criticizing everybody else. But
most people who judge others who are actually doing something are the ones who are doing nothing
themselves. They put down other people to try to lift
up themselves.

The Word of God calls us to build up others, es-
teeming them more highly than ourselves (see
Philippians 2:3). Avoid people who constantly criticize others so their negative comments will not rob
you of godly enthusiasm. God can use you today to
help strengthen someone's faith. Ask Him to make
you aware of these opportunities today.

Love Truth

*Instead, speaking the truth in love, we will in
all things grow up into him who is
the Head, that is, Christ.*

EPHESIANS 4:15 NIV

If you want to become fully mature in the Lord, you must learn to love truth. Otherwise, you will always leave open a door of deception for the enemy to take what is meant to be yours.

Some people have a difficult time facing truth and reality. They prefer to live in a make-believe world, pretending that certain things aren't happening. But we cannot deny the existence of problems or act as if they are not real.

The devil is real, life is real, people are real, pain is real, and poverty is real. The good news is that no matter how real our pain may be, or how big our problems may seem, we can overcome all of them with the Word of God.

Enjoy Your Whole Day

I will praise You, O Lord, with my whole heart;
I will show forth (recount and tell aloud) all Your
marvelous works and wonderful deeds!

PSALM 9:1

Some Christians feel guilty when they are doing something that isn't "spiritual." Somehow or another, they feel the need to hurry through the grocery store, dash through the house cleaning, and rush through all the daily aspects of life that seem irrelevant to their faith. They want to get back to doing something "spiritual" so God will be pleased with them again.

God did not intend for you to *hate* the secular side of life. You can enjoy *holiness* and time with God even when you are doing daily chores, running errands, or taking the children somewhere they need to go. Don't begrudge the routine things of life; see every activity as an opportunity to serve God with your whole heart.

Encourage, Don't Criticize

*Therefore encourage (admonish, exhort) one an-
other and edify (strengthen and build up) one another.*

We can improve our relationships with others by leaps and bounds if we become encouragers instead of critics. It is the greater person who does the right thing; Christ's righteousness dwells in you to help you do what is right. You are great in God's eyes when you choose to do right and bless others.

No matter how rough your day is today, speak words that uplift and encourage those around you. Encourage others if you notice them doing a good job — not just those who work with you, but people wherever you go, such as store clerks, auto mechanics, and waiters. Say something like, "I ap-preciate the extra effort you are making to do your job well." You can change your life and someone else's by choosing to speak positive words.

Keep Balanced

For we who have believed (adhered to and trusted
in and relied on God) do enter that rest.

HEBREWS 4:3

It is easy to get overcommitted, burned out, bummed out, worn out, and stressed out if you are trying to keep up with too many commitments. It is out of balance to try to do everything. If you are happy doing what you do, keep doing it. But if it wears you out and robs you of peace, don't do it. What sense does it make to commit to something, and then murmur and complain about it while you are doing it?

Being overcommitted will frustrate you. Anxiety is usually a sign that God never told you to do what you are doing in the first place. To avoid frustration in your life, keep in balance.

Talk to God Anywhere

Do you not know that your body is the temple (the very sanctuary) of the Holy Spirit Who lives within you, Whom you have received [as a Gift] from God?

1 CORINTHIANS 6:19

The angel of the Lord said to Moses, "Take the shoes off your feet, for the ground on which you stand is holy ground" (see Exodus 3:5). The ground was holy because the Holy One was there. Now through faith in Jesus, you are the temple of the Holy Ghost. Everywhere you go becomes a holy place because the Holy One dwells in you.

God is not in a building, where you can only visit Him on Sunday morning. He is with you everywhere you go. You can talk to Him while you vacuum, or while you change the oil in your car. When you let God become involved in every aspect of your life, every day becomes exciting.

Pray All Day

Let my prayer be set forth as incense before You,
the lifting up of my hands as the evening sacrifice.

PSALM 141:2

God wants to be the center of your life: the center of your conversation, the center of your entertainment, and the center of your relationships. Prayer keeps Him in the center of all you do.

Years ago I could have told you that I prayed an hour every day. But now, I couldn't even determine how long I pray, because I just pray every time I see or feel a need. I pray while driving. I pray while working, and while relaxing. Sometimes I just stop what I am doing and praise God, and that is prayer too. I cast my cares on Him and say, "Lord, I am not going to worry about anything today; I am giving it to You."

Prayer should be like breathing, natural to do anywhere you are.

Loving Actions Speak Clearly

*[Living as becomes you] with complete lowliness
of mind (humility) and meekness (unselfishness,
gentleness, mildness), with patience, bearing with
one another* and *making allowances because
you love one another*

EPHESIANS 4:2

It is good for the unsaved members of your family to see you studying the Bible, going to church, and bearing the fruit of the Spirit. But your family may be more receptive to the gospel if you minister to their needs. Ministering to them may require giving up a prayer meeting to do things with them, such as going fishing or shopping with your spouse, helping your son work on his car, or taking your daughter out for lunch.

The Bible says that the natural man does not understand the spiritual man (see 1 Corinthians 2:14). So spiritual talk doesn't always make sense to unsaved people, but loving actions speak clearly to them. Walk in love's anointing today: be kind, joyful, peaceful, and stable. Let God love others through you.

Be Wise to the Enemy

Be well balanced . . . for that enemy of yours, the
devil, roams around like a lion roaring . . . seeking
someone to seize upon and devour.

1 PETER 5:8

Satan cannot devour just anybody he pleases. He has to find someone who gives him an opening to do so. One of the ways we give him an opening to destroy us is through imbalance in our lives. A good example would be, if we eat improperly and in an unbalanced manner over a long period of time, we may open the door for the enemy to bring sickness or disease into our life.

Many times when people are recovering from illness, they follow a strict diet that brings balance back into their eating habits. Find balance in all you do, and keep the enemy away from your door.

Internal Blessings
Show Externally

*Therefore if any person is [ingrafted] in Christ
(the Messiah) he is a new creation (a new creature
altogether); the old [previous moral and spiritual
condition] has passed away. Behold, the
fresh and new has come!*

2 CORINTHIANS 5:17

When God baptized me in the Holy Ghost, I felt like He had filled me with liquid love. He did something on the inside of me, and it showed on the outside of me. Internal changes last, and keep showing up in everything we do.

That is why you can't really be a closet Christian. If you are saved, it will show to others. If you say you are saved, but nothing has changed in your life, something is wrong. When Jesus comes to live in you, He will get involved with how you live and how you look at life to make you more like Him. Welcome any changes He needs to make in you today.

Talk about God — Not the Devil

Leave no [such] room or foothold for the devil [give no opportunity to him].

EPHESIANS 4:27

God once said to me, "Quit talking so much about the devil, what he is saying and what he is doing. *I am* saying something! Talk about what I am saying. *I am* doing something! Talk about what *I am* doing."

Then one day God spoke a *life-changing* word to me, saying, "Why don't you study the Word, and see how Jesus waged spiritual warfare?"

I found that Jesus didn't talk or preach much about the devil and what he was saying or doing. He simply dealt with the devil by casting him out of people's lives. He told him to shut up. He quoted the Word to him (see Luke 4:1–13). Resist the devil today and tell someone about the good things God is doing for you.

Hold on to Your Peace

*In His [Christ's] days shall the [uncompromis-
ingly] righteous flourish and peace abound till
there is a moon no longer.*

PSALM 72:7

In the Bible, people are told to hold their peace, because peace is a place of power. God tells us not to be moved when our opponents and adversaries come against us. We are to remain constant, fearless, and at peace. His Word says, "The Lord will fight for you, and you shall hold your peace *and* remain at rest" (Exodus 14:14).

No matter what is happening, remain consistent; continue treating people well, continue walking in the fruit of the Spirit. You don't know what kind of fruit you have until somebody comes along and squeezes it. You don't know how much fruit you have until somebody is picking it all day.

Do What Is Right

Trust (lean on, rely on, and be confident) in the
Lord and do good; so shall you dwell in the land
and feed surely on His faithfulness, and
truly you shall be fed.

PSALM 37:3

Powerful results happen when you do what is right. Doing what is right is high-tech spiritual warfare! It puts you in a position where the devil can't affect you, because you have decided to stand and not be moved.

Remain in faith and trust God. The Bible says in Psalm 37:1 that evildoers, "those who work unrighteousness (that which is not upright or in right standing with God)," will be cut down like the grass. When problems arise against you, when your enemies attack you, or when evil makes an all-out assault upon you, trust in the Lord, and do good.

Don't Lose Focus

*For the weapons of our warfare are not physical
[weapons of flesh and blood], but they are mighty
before God for the overthrow and
destruction of strongholds.*

2 CORINTHIANS 10:4

Sometimes we lose our focus. We can be walking in love all day, going along fine, until someone comes along and offends us. As soon as we forget our focus of love, we stop making progress and come to a standstill — aggravated, upset, and offended.

Understand that the mind is a battlefield. If you don't stop Satan when he gets into your thoughts, you are not going to stop him from getting into your life. Stay focused. Ask God to help you remain full of love, no matter what comes your way today.

Build on Solid Foundations

For no other foundation can anyone lay than that
which is [already] laid, which is Jesus Christ (the
Messiah, the Anointed One).

I CORINTHIANS 3:11

We can know a lot of spiritual methods (or formulas) for getting things, but many such methods simply have no power flowing through them. Powerless methods are like empty containers — useless.

I had learned many spiritual methods, and I was busy trying them, until I realized that methods don't work. It was like building on a cracked foundation; nothing stood the test of time. If our foundations leak, we get into trouble every time it storms.

Build your life on who you are in Christ. Take time to meditate on the foundational things about being a Christian. Build your life on the solid foundation that you are an heir of God's grace and His unmerited favor.

Be Confident in God

For the Lord shall be your confidence, firm and strong, and shall keep your foot from being caught [in a trap or some hidden danger].

PROVERBS 3:26

Jesus knew where He came from, He knew what He was sent to do, and He knew where He was going. When you get that confidence of knowing God and His purpose for your life, you will not be affected by the judgments or criticisms of other people.

You know you belong to God. You know His hand is on you. You know His anointing is on you. You know what you are called to do. You know that with every breath you take, you are trying to follow Him, and you know where you are going when you are all finished. Say, "Nothing that happens today can separate me from God's love and His purpose for my life."

God's Promises
Will Be Fulfilled

*Little children, you are of God [you belong
to Him] and have [already] defeated and overcome
them [the agents of the antichrist], because He Who
lives in you is greater (mightier) than he
who is in the world.*

1 JOHN 4:4

Know who you are in Christ and understand that through salvation, you are seen
in the spiritual world as wearing a garment of salvation and covered with a robe of righteousness (see
Isaiah 61:10). God is on your side, and He is under
you, over you, around you, with you, for you, and
in you.

The devil *knows* you belong to Christ because
God "[has also appropriated and acknowledged us as
His by] putting His seal upon us and giving us His
[Holy] Spirit in our hearts as the security deposit
and guarantee [of the fulfillment of His promise]"
(2 Corinthians 1:22).

Powerful Christianity

*But you will receive power when the Holy Spirit
comes on you; and you will be my witnesses in
Jerusalem, and in all Judea and Samaria, and
to the ends of the earth.*

ACTS 1:8 NIV

Being *Spirit-filled* is not limited to one particular brand of Christianity. Spirit-filled people are found in every church and denomination. They are people who understand the need for the power of the Holy Ghost within them so they won't live a weak, defeated life.

The Word says to "ever be filled *and* stimulated with the [Holy] Spirit" (Ephesians 5:18), indicating that being Spirit-filled is something to which we submit ourselves. Ask God to fill you to overflowing with His Spirit so that everything you do today will be done through His power.

Stay in God's Presence

And now shall my head be lifted up above my enemies round about me; in His tent I will offer sacrifices and shouting of joy; I will sing, yes, I will sing praises to the Lord.

PSALM 27:6

The psalmist David said that the thing he wanted most was to be with God and to dwell in His presence all the days of his life (see Psalm 27:4). David loved God for who He is, not just for what He did for him.

The Word says that if we abide in the presence of God, He will defeat our enemies, and hide us in the day of trouble (see v. 5). God's attention is on us, but we must keep our attention on Him to enjoy the fullness of His presence in our lives. We must invite God to be involved in everything we do, and then remember to praise Him for His goodness.

Seek God First

> *[After all] the kingdom of God is not a matter of [getting the] food and drink [one likes], but instead it is righteousness (that state which makes a person acceptable to God) and [heart] peace and joy in the Holy Spirit. He who serves Christ in this way is acceptable and pleasing to God and is approved by men.*
>
> ROMANS 14:17–18

Forget all the *things* you think you need, and just admit to God that you need *Him.* Seek first the kingdom of God and His righteousness, and all that you need will be added to your life (see Matthew 6:33).

God knows your needs even before you ask. Don't become a seeker of promotion or position. Don't spend your life seeking prosperity. Seek the One who prospers. Seek the One who heals. Seek the One who is the giver of every good and perfect gift.

Remain Steadfast

And he [Abram] believed in (trusted in, relied on, remained steadfast to) the Lord, and He counted it to him as righteousness (right standing with God).

GENESIS 15:6

Spending time with God keeps you stable, steadfast, and calm. God says He "will strengthen and harden you to difficulties" (Isaiah 41:10). When your faith is fed daily by God's presence, the devil can't control you, because you don't get easily upset.

Being filled with God's truth makes it easier to live the life God has for you. Let God be your anchor in the midst of the raging waves of circumstances. Remain steadfast in God.

Don't Be Entangled

Put on God's whole armor [the armor of a heavy-armed soldier which God supplies], that you may be able successfully to stand up against [all] the strategies and *the deceits of the devil.*

EPHESIANS 6:11

We are called to be soldiers in the army of God. Paul told Timothy that no soldier gets entangled with civilian affairs, but "his aim is to satisfy *and* please the one who enlisted him" (2 Timothy 2:4). Likewise, as we serve the Lord, we should focus on His work, not our own concerns.

If we want to be a witness of God's power, we must first do what He says to do, and show others the fruit that comes from serving Him (see vv. 6–7). We do this by keeping our minds constantly on Jesus Christ. We must still handle the business of everyday life, but we are not to let the affairs of the world pull us down.

It's the Lord's Battle

*The Angel of the Lord encamps around those
who fear Him [who revere and worship Him
with awe] and each of them He delivers.*

PSALM 34:7

In the Old Testament, people carried banners when they went to war, sending the singers and praisers into the battle first. When the tribe of Judah sang, "Oh, give thanks to the Lord, for He is good, for His mercy endures forever" (see 2 Chronicles 20:21), the enemy was so confused they were self-slaughtered and self-defeated (see v. 22).

When King Jehoshaphat prepared for battle, he took the position of getting on his face to worship God (see v. 18). If you have battles to face, get in the position of warfare, and just worship the Lord. God's response to our worship is, "Be not afraid or dismayed at this great multitude; for the battle is not yours, but God's" (v. 15).

Spiritual Warfare

And let the peace (soul harmony which comes)
from Christ rule (act as umpire continually) in your
hearts [deciding and settling with finality all ques-
tions that arise in your minds, in that peaceful
state] . . . And be thankful (appreciative),
[giving praise to God always].

COLOSSIANS 3:15

You are waging spiritual warfare when you give radical praise to God in the midst of your need and lack. When you are thankful to God for all He has done and is doing, you are defeating the enemy. When you hold your peace in the midst of the storm, you are warring with spiritual weapons (see 2 Corinthians 10:4–5).

Jesus said, "Peace I leave with you; My [own] peace I now give *and* bequeath to you . . . [Stop allowing yourselves to be agitated and disturbed; and do not permit yourselves to be fearful and intimidated and cowardly and unsettled]" (John 14:27). Jesus has given you peace! Put it on, and wear it everywhere you go.

Stand!

[Earnestly] remember the former things, [which I did] of old; for I am God, and there is no one else; I am God, and there is none like Me, declaring the end and the result from the beginning, and from ancient times the things that are not yet done, saying, My counsel shall stand, and I will do all My pleasure and purpose.

ISAIAH 46:9–10

There may be times when it seems that you cannot go forward, but at least you do not have to go backward. You may not know how to forge ahead, but you can stand firmly on what you know of God.

Instead of passively yielding to the enemy, you can say, "This is the ground I have gained, and I am not giving it up, devil. You are not driving me back into the hole that God pulled me out of. I am going to stand strong in the power of God until He delivers me."

Submit Yourself to God

My soul, wait only upon God and *silently submit to Him; for my hope* and *expectation are from Him.*

PSALM 62:5

James 4:7–8 gives the best advice on how to wage spiritual warfare: "Be subject to God. Resist the devil [stand firm against him], and he will flee from you. Come close to God and He will come close to you."

When you humble yourself in the presence of the Lord, He will exalt you and lift you and make your life significant (see vv. 9–10). God will show you how to resist the devil. Spend time in God's presence, and do whatever He tells you to do!

Don't Stay Angry

Cease from anger and forsake wrath; fret not
yourself — it tends only to evildoing.

PSALM 37:8

The Word tells us another way to resist temptation: "When angry, do not sin; do not ever let your wrath (your exasperation, your fury or indignation) last until the sun goes down. Leave no [such] room or foothold for the devil [give no opportunity to him]" (Ephesians 4:26–27).

Paul said that we should forgive people to keep Satan from gaining an advantage over us (see 2 Corinthians 2:10–11). If someone offends you, get over it quickly so you won't leave open a door for the devil. It is a sin to hold anger and bitterness, so never go to sleep mad. If you forgive everyone before you fall asleep, freedom from wrong attitudes in your heart will help you start your day right the next morning.

Go on Through

Yes, though I walk through the [deep, sunless] valley of the shadow of death, I will fear or dread no evil, for You are with me; Your rod [to protect] and Your staff [to guide], they comfort me.

PSALM 23:4

Knowing God personally requires trusting Him through the hard times in life and not running away from trials. It requires being faithful to do whatever He says to do, being steadfast while waiting for Him to work out your problems.

You understand how faithful and how good God is when you see His deliverance in your life. You can't get that certainty by reading a book about Him. Your faith increases by *going through* tough times and seeing His presence make a difference in your life. Don't run away from God during tests and trials; draw near to Him, and listen for His voice of assurance.

Be Determined

*Even when we were dead (slain) by [our own]
shortcomings and trespasses, He made us alive
together in fellowship and in union with Christ;
[He gave us the very life of Christ Himself, the same
new life with which He quickened Him, for] it is
by grace (His favor and mercy which you did not
deserve) that you are saved (delivered from judgment
and made partakers of Christ's salvation).*

EPHESIANS 2:5

Paul said, "My determined purpose is,
that I may know Christ, and the power of
His resurrection, the power that lifts me out from
among the dead, even while I am in the body" (see
Philippians 3:10–11).

You can use every day to get to know God in a
deeper way. Read the Bible for understanding of what
He wants to reveal to you, and receive His grace to
be lifted out of every past fault. Let His power lift
you into life His way.

Don't Get Rattled

*Just think of Him Who endured from sinners such
grievous opposition* and *bitter hostility against
Himself [reckon up and consider it all in comparison
with your trials], so that you may not grow weary
or exhausted, losing heart* and *relaxing* and
fainting in your minds.

HEBREWS 12:3

We have authority over the devil, but that doesn't mean he will never come against us. Resisting the devil doesn't rid us of the problem. But standing in the faith of God's promises while we are waiting for God to do something keeps us from *acting like* the devil ourselves.

Don't get rattled about the devil. If he causes problems for you today, just say, "Forget it, devil! I am not staying hurt, bitter, wounded, or angry. My trust is in God. I am a Christian — watch me be happy."

Let Christ Live Through You

The life I now live in the body I live by faith
in (by adherence to and reliance on and complete
trust in) the Son of God, Who loved me and gave
Himself up for me.

GALATIANS 2:20

Some people need to unlearn some things before they can start learning what God wants for them. For example, some people try to manipulate others with their self-pity or anger. They believe these emotional tools will get what they want from others. Some people who have been hurt or abused feel that they have to take care of themselves because nobody else will.

Both attitudes display the common fear, "What about me? What about me?" But Paul offers us a life-changing principle to follow: "I have been crucified with Christ and I no longer live, but Christ lives in me" (Galatians 2:20 NIV). When Christ lives through you, you will enjoy every day of your life.

Trust God

But let all those who take refuge and *put their trust in You rejoice; let them ever sing* and *shout for joy, because You make a covering over them* and *defend them; let those also who love Your name be joyful in You* and *be in high spirits.*

PSALM 5:11

Many wounded people don't know how to get what they really need, so they wallow in self-pity. God once told me, "Joyce, you can be pitiful or powerful, but you can't be both."

Taking our eyes off of ourselves enables us to look to God. This positions us to trust Him to meet every need in our lives. God knows exactly what we need, and He promises to provide it through His abundant grace and mercy.

Ask Him to fill you with His power today, and trust Him as *Jehovah-Jireh,* the Lord our Provider (see Genesis 22:14 KJV).

Wait for God's Justice

Knowing [with all certainty] that it is from the Lord [and not from men] that you will receive the inheritance which is your [real] reward. [The One Whom] you are actually serving [is] the Lord Christ (the Messiah).

COLOSSIANS 3:24

God has brought a great reward in my life in recompense for the abuse that I suffered in my earlier days. Now I have a wonderful life. God blesses me. He does things for me. He opens doors of opportunity for me. He makes me happy. He gives me joy.

When you really trust God, He will bring justice into your life. In Isaiah 61:7 the Lord says, "For your former shame I will give you a double reward" (paraphrased). If someone has mistreated you, rejected you, abused you, or abandoned you, hold on to that promise. You have many blessings ahead of you. Trust God with your future, and enjoy your day as you wait for God's justice.

Choose to Be Changed

But we have the mind of Christ (the Messiah) and
do hold the thoughts (feelings and
purposes) of His heart.

1 CORINTHIANS 2:16

Do you get mad every time somebody tries to correct you, or tell you what to do, because you always have to be right? If you answered yes, I am sure that you are not a happy person. You cannot change others, but you can allow God to change you so that things don't bother you anymore.

With Jesus Christ as your Savior, you can learn how to live a different way. You can have peace. You can sleep well at night. You can like yourself. You can restore relationships that have been ruined. Your mind can be renewed to be like Jesus', if you read His Word and ask Him to help you live the abundant life He came to give you (see John 10:10).

Use Your Authority Well

Whoever wishes to be great among you must be
your servant, and whoever desires to be first among
you must be your slave — just as the Son of Man
came not to be waited on but to serve, and to
give His life as a ransom for many [the
price paid to set them free].

MATTHEW 20:26—28

God desires to restore us to our rightful position of authority in Christ. But first, we must learn to respect authority before we are fit to be in authority.

We all have authorities to whom God expects us to submit. Our government, our law officers, and even our merchants have the right to set rules for us to follow. If we are not submitting to God's appointed authority, it will soon be revealed.

Keep a submissive attitude in your heart, and enjoy the authority you have been given to spend time in God's presence today.

Change Things with Knowledge

*Commit your way to the Lord [roll and repose
each care of your load on Him]; trust (lean on,
rely on, and be confident) also in Him and He
will bring it to pass.*

PSALM 37:5

We are all eager for our situations and relationships to change, but nothing will change in our lives without knowledge of God's Word. In Hosea 4:6 God says, "My people are destroyed for lack of knowledge."

Change comes through prayer, and then through waiting patiently on God. While we are waiting for God to solve our problems, we are not to complain to everybody else about our situation.

God tells us to trust Him. He is not asking us to trust the people involved in our problems; He is asking us to trust Him. There is a difference. He is faithful to rescue us from all our troubles.

Lend a Helping Hand

He who is greatest among you
shall be your servant.

MATTHEW 23:11

If we help someone become what God wants them to be, God will send someone along to help us be everything God wants us to be.

One day I asked one of our musicians if he would like to do something that needed to be done. He said, "I will do whatever you tell me to do; I am here to serve you."

I said, "But do you *want* to do this? You don't have to do it; we can find someone else."

He said, "It doesn't matter if I want to or not. Tell me what you want me to do, and I will do it." He was anointed to help others and enjoyed doing whatever needed to be done.

To enjoy your day, be ready to help people with whatever God has called them to do.

Opportunity Brings Opposition

But he who looks carefully into the faultless law, the [law] of liberty, and is faithful to it and perseveres in looking into it, being not a heedless listener who forgets but an active doer [who obeys], he shall be blessed in his doing (his life of obedience).

JAMES 1:25

Many people agree with a sermon or a Scripture, but they don't apply it in their everyday life, so nothing changes. They think that just because they agree with the Word, it should bring change into their life.

But change doesn't happen automatically; a person has to be a *doer* of the Word, not a hearer only. Jesus said, "Keep awake (give strict attention, be cautious and active) *and* watch and pray, that you may not come into temptation. The spirit indeed is willing, but the flesh is weak" (Matthew 26:41).

Every time you have an opportunity to believe God for something, you will have a temptation to give up on it. Pray that you will overcome temptation when it comes.

Enjoy Liberty

Blessed (happy, to be envied) is the man who is patient under trial and stands up under temptation, for when he has stood the test and been approved, he will receive [the victor's] crown of life which God has promised to those who love Him.

JAMES 1:12

Life is miserable when we won't listen to anybody else, or when we get mad every time somebody doesn't agree with us. To be so emotionally ruled and controlled that we are stressed every time something doesn't go our way is bondage. When Jesus sets us free, it means that we are free *not* to get upset just because we don't get everything we want.

It is wonderful to be free. We can give thanks for the liberty to receive God's help and walk in patience despite our circumstances. Our lives can be happy, blessed, and peaceful. We can experience joy no matter what the situation may be.

Enjoy a New Beginning

But there is forgiveness with You
[just what man needs], that You may be
reverently feared and *worshiped.*

PSALM 130:4

People sometimes tell me, "I did something wrong, and I just don't know if
God can ever forgive me of it." Even when we have
made serious mistakes, there is always a place of forgiveness and a new beginning in Christ. When we
have a new beginning with Christ, we don't have to
mourn over the past. We just have to repent and go
on. We don't need to repent again and again.

If you know the character of God, you know He
will forgive any sin, no matter how terrible, because
to Him sin is sin. Remember, God can make miracles out of mistakes. If you need forgiveness today,
simply confess to the Lord what you have done, and
enjoy your new beginning (see 1 John 1:9). It begins
at the moment of forgiveness.

Accept Responsibility

Finally, brethren, farewell (rejoice)! Be
strengthened (perfected, completed, made what
you ought to be); be encouraged and *consoled*
and *comforted; be of the same [agreeable] mind one*
with another; live in peace, and [then] the God of
love [Who is the Source of affection, goodwill, love,
and benevolence toward men] and the Author and
Promoter of peace will be with you.
2 CORINTHIANS 13:11

Each one of us needs to accept our responsibility to do what is right in God's
eyes, whether others do the right thing or not. Otherwise we will have a standoff:

"Well, if you won't say you're sorry, then I won't
say I'm sorry."

"You're not nice, so I'm not going to be nice."

"You haven't given me a compliment in a year, so
I'm not giving you one either."

That attitude gets relationships in trouble. God
wants us to live above the pettiness of selfish argu-
ments by loving one another.

Start Something

*[Let your] love be sincere (a real thing); hate
what is evil [loathe all ungodliness, turn in horror
from wickedness], but hold fast to that which is
good. Love one another with brotherly affection
[as members of one family], giving precedence and
showing honor to one another. Never lag in zeal
and in earnest endeavor; be aglow and burning
with the Spirit, serving the Lord.*

ROMANS 12:9—11

If all of us started having a godly attitude,
it would catch hold and spread like a virus. Wouldn't it be great if we could spread a good
virus?

Imagine the whispers: "Have you heard? There's
something wonderful going around. Have you caught
it? It is running rampant all over the place. Everywhere you look, people have a *new attitude!*"

Let's start something today! Let's decide to think
like Christ. Let's decide to love everyone we meet
today, and pass the word so that everybody catches
on to it.

Start Something Good

For there shall the seed produce peace and *prosperity; the vine shall yield her fruit and the ground shall give its increase and the heavens shall give their dew; and I will cause the remnant of this people to inherit* and *possess all these things.*

ZECHARIAH 8:12

Start something good in someone's life today. Sow faith for a healing. Sow hope for a restoration. A sincere compliment can sow confidence in someone who is starving for encouragement. Your forgiveness of an ongoing offense can sow a seed for a miracle breakthrough in that situation.

Pray for someone else's need, or make a special offering to start something positive in the name of the Lord. Remember, God won't ask you to sow anything that He doesn't give you the grace to give. Enjoy the abundant harvest that is returned to your own life when you sow into someone else's life.

Be Christ's Bond Servant

Now the Lord is the Spirit, and where the Spirit of the Lord is, there is liberty (emancipation from bondage, freedom).

2 CORINTHIANS 3:17

Paul said that he would not become the slave of anything or anyone but Jesus Christ: "Everything is lawful for me, but I will not become the slave of anything *or* be brought under its power" (1 Corinthians 6:12)." He also said, "If I had been trying to be popular with people, I would not now be a bond servant of the Lord Jesus Christ" (see Galatians 1:10).

If you let other people control you, you will not fulfill the call of God on your life. If you let their rejection frighten you and change your focus, you won't do what God wants you to do. Be a slave only to God, and a servant to people on His behalf.

Follow Jesus

*All who keep His commandments [who obey His
orders and follow His plan, live and continue to live,
to stay and] abide in Him, and He in them. [They
let Christ be a home to them and they are
the home of Christ.]*

1 JOHN 3:24

Some people wanted to follow Jesus, but
they were afraid they would be put out of
the synagogue (see John 12:42). Some people are
still afraid to follow the Lord because they might be
put out of their family, their group, or even their
church.

Eventually, there will only be one Person to
face — God. You won't want Him to say, "I had so
much for you, but you didn't receive it because you
were too concerned about what people thought; you
were a people-pleaser." Jesus wasn't swayed by men's
opinions, threats, judgments, or criticisms. Follow
Jesus, and enjoy life.

Listen to God

Hear counsel, receive instruction, and *accept correction, that you may be wise in the time to come.*

PROVERBS 19:20

You may wonder, "How do I know when to confront someone about an issue, and when to let it go?" If you are too eager to set someone straight, it may not be God motivating you. Correction must be done in love to build up the person and not tear them down. Always pray and wait until you know what God wants you to do.

You must be led of the Spirit. If after prayer you still feel that you are to talk to someone about their behavior, be absolutely sure that you are doing it for their good and not yours. If it is what God has told you to do, you may not even want to do it, but it will be done as an act of obedience to Him. Whatever you do, do it in love.

Don't Get Burned Out

*And be constantly renewed in the spirit of your
mind [having a fresh mental and spiritual attitude].*

EPHESIANS 4:23

Expect God to show you something new
today. Some people resist change, but
God created us to need variety in our life. If we do
the same thing over and over, we get burned out on
it. God will keep our lives exciting if we seek Him
every day.

Look for new ways of doing things. If you have
been working on the same job for thirty years, driving to it the same way, at least find a new route you
can take once in a while to get there. Do something
to invite newness into your life so you can discover
God's many ways of revealing Himself to you.

Be Led by the Holy Spirit

For all who are led by the Spirit of God
are sons of God.

ROMANS 8:14

We live in a society in which people are driven to engage in many activities. We can get almost too tired to move from doing so much in a day, but busyness is not the kind of life to which God has called us.

God will not *drive* us to do things; He will *lead* us by putting in our heart what we are supposed to do. If you follow the Holy Spirit, you may have to say no to some activities that you are saying yes to right now. If what you are doing leaves you drained and worn out, you may not have God's anointing to do it. When He leads you to do something, He will also energize you to fulfill your true call.

Prune your life of things that drain you, and trust God to lead you to the works that keep you growing and healthy.

Change, Don't Complain

All things are legitimate [permissible — and
we are free to do anything we please], but not all
things are helpful (expedient, profitable, and whole-
some). All things are legitimate, but not all things
are constructive [to character] and edifying
[to spiritual life].

1 CORINTHIANS 10:23

People complain about stress, but some people would rather complain than change. It is easy to be frightened at the thought of jumping off life's high-speed treadmill, especially if you aren't sure what to give up in order to slow down your life.

God wants you to enjoy a beautiful life with simplicity, sanity, and clear direction. That only comes by spending time with Him, reading His Word, talking to Him, and listening for His response. If you are too busy to get alone with Him each day, then set some boundaries in your life. Say no to whatever is keeping you from starting your day with God.

Rest Awhile

Come to Me, all you who labor and are heavy-laden and overburdened, and I will cause you to rest. [I will ease and relieve and refresh your souls.]

MATTHEW 11:28

Getting stress out of your life takes more than prayer alone. You must take action to make changes and stop doing whatever is causing the stress. You can learn to calm down in the way you handle things.

Jesus invited us to come to Him if we are over-burdened. He promised to refresh us if we are weary, worn out, or overworked. Take time to go to Jesus anytime you feel that you are going over the edge of peace and into the pit of stress. Let His presence re-fill and refresh you.

Come Apart to Stay Together

And the effect of righteousness will be peace
[internal and external], and the result of righ-
teousness will be quietness and confident
trust forever.

ISAIAH 32:17

If you are feeling compelled to do so much that you are physically worn out, you may be driven instead of led. Remember, you have to come apart from a busy routine before you come apart yourself. You have to get away from everything before you come apart physically, mentally, and emotionally. Give yourself time to get a good night's sleep.

It is tempting to do everything that everybody else is doing, be involved in everything, know everything, hear everything, and be everywhere, but it isn't God's best for you. Be willing to separate yourself from compulsive activity before you come apart at the seams! Spend time with God, and ask Him to give order to your day.

Take a Break

Return to your rest, O my soul, for the Lord has dealt bountifully with you.

PSALM 116:7

We all need a break in the action from time to time. Resting isn't just a good idea — it is a command of God: "Six days you shall do your work, but the seventh day you shall rest and keep Sabbath, that your ox and your donkey may rest, and the son of your bondwoman, and the alien, may be refreshed" (Exodus 23:12). The Lord added that "even in plowing time and in harvest you shall rest [on the Sabbath]" (Exodus 34:21)

That means that for one day a week we are to withdraw from common labor and to rest. Don't work that day, even in the busy seasons. Dedicate that day to spending time with God, worshiping Him. Start your week off right by getting back to what is really important — honoring God.

Quality Makes the Difference

*Beloved, let us love one another, for love is
(springs) from God; and he who loves [his fellowmen]
is begotten (born) of God and is coming [progres-
sively] to know and understand God [to perceive
and recognize and get a better and clearer
knowledge of Him].*

1 JOHN 4:7

Sometimes we think that the busier we are, the more we are doing in the kingdom of God. But it is not *how much* we do, it is the *quality* of what we do that makes the difference. Most people will admit that they need to spend more of their time developing good relationships.

You can't be a good friend to somebody if you never put any time into your relationship. Ask God to bring someone to mind that He would like for you to bless today. Then follow through and let that person know that God brought them to your heart.

Rest Is God's Law

Let us therefore be zealous and exert ourselves and strive diligently to enter that rest [of God, to know and experience it for ourselves], that no one may fall or perish by the same kind of unbelief and disobedience [into which those in the wilderness fell].

HEBREWS 4:11

Don't work so hard that you miss your time with God. Rest is important for your spiritual and physical life. The need for rest can't be ignored; it is a law of God. Just like the laws concerning eating, sowing, and reaping, we cannot break the principle of rest without paying the price of disobedience.

Paul sent Epaphroditus home saying that he came near death through working for Christ (see Philippians 2:25–30), but God had mercy on him and spared his life. Find time to be still on a regular basis. It is in moments of rest that you are most likely to hear God speak to you.

Rest and Renew

So then, there is still awaiting a full and *complete*
Sabbath-rest reserved for the [true] people of God; for
he who has once entered [God's] rest also has ceased
from [the weariness and pain] of human labors, just
as God rested from those labors peculiarly His own.

HEBREWS 4:9–10

We all have gifts and talents far beyond
what we use, but many of us are so worn
out that we don't feel like doing anything. Even God
rested from all of His labors, not because He was
tired, but just to enjoy His creation (see Genesis 2:1–
3). Stop working all the time, and enjoy yourself.

Even the land needs to rest every several years
to produce good crops. If you don't rest, you are going to cut down your production and stifle your creativity. You don't have to work at God's plan for you;
He will cause it to come to pass (see Philippians 1:6).
Rest in Him.

Reenergize Yourself

*Guide me in Your truth and faithfulness and teach
me, for You are the God of my salvation; for You
[You only and altogether] do I wait [expectantly]
all the day long.*

PSALM 25:5

If you are worn out all the time, it will affect your spiritual life because you won't want to pray, study the Word, or walk in the fruit of the Spirit. If you are no longer sensitive to other people's needs, you aren't hearing from God.

If you are this tired, it is time to reenergize your life. Prune away the things that wear you out; don't try to do what you think everyone else is doing. Wait on God to lead you, and get the rest you need to enjoy your walk with Him.

Enjoy Yourself

There is nothing better for a man than that he
should eat and drink and make himself enjoy good
in his labor. Even this, I have seen, is from
the hand of God.

ECCLESIASTES 2:24

We all have things that must be done, but God wants us to enjoy our life's journey. If we are too busy, we will block the flow of what the Holy Spirit wants to do through us.

Busyness keeps us from being fruitful in the kingdom of God. God didn't put us here just to work, strive, accumulate things, and become stressed out. He wants us to enjoy Him and His creation.

Take time to enjoy what God has given you. Enjoy your family, your home, and yourself today.

Move Forward

*I do not consider, brethren, that I have captured
and made it my own [yet]; but one thing I do [it is
my one aspiration]: forgetting what lies behind and
straining forward to what lies ahead, I presss on.*

PHILIPPIANS 3:13–14

God will anoint you to do what He calls you to do. But when His anointing is gone, let it go. Get rid of the things that God's anointing was on at one time, but not anymore. Don't keep doing the same thing because people expect you to.

I encourage you to prune off activities that fill your day but don't add to your life. Sometimes we hold on to assignments that God is finished with for us. Ask God for wisdom, then walk away from tasks He no longer is asking you to do. Make room for new life to flourish through the work of your hands.

Let God Set Your Agenda

But this thing I did command them: Listen to and obey My voice, and I will be your God and you will be My people; and walk in the whole way that I command you, that it may be well with you.

JEREMIAH 7:23

Remember, you made your schedule, and you can change it. Pray about your day, your week, and your life goals to find out what God wants you to do, and what He doesn't want you to do.

If you don't do what God is telling you to do, you may let people control and manipulate you to do what they want you to do. You may end up doing things for which you are not anointed. If you do what God tells you to do, He will bless you with joy, peace, rest, and wonderful relationships.

Get Rid of Distractions

That which is desired in a man is loyalty and kindness [and his glory and delight are his giving].

PROVERBS 19:22

Sometimes you may just need to clear away the clutter so you can clearly see what is worthwhile. Here is a simple suggestion: Don't keep more than you can take care of. If you have so much junk in your home that it takes you hours to dust it, get rid of something.

Find a big carton and write "Blessing Box" on the side of it. Start putting extra things into it until cleaning is more manageable. Find someone who doesn't have much and bless them. You will be amazed at how easy it is to start your day right when you are no longer distracted by things you don't need.

Get Up and Work

And let the beauty and delightfulness and favor
of the Lord our God be upon us; confirm and establish
the work of our hands — yes, the work of our hands,
confirm and establish it.

PSALM 90:17

It is obvious we are supposed to work more than rest. Some people just lie on the couch, eating junk food and watching television all day, and then they wonder why their lives are a wreck.

Once rested, get up and work. You can't take authority over your life if you don't have authority over a sink full of dirty dishes or a messy garage. If you want to grow in ministry to others, the Word says you must get your own house in order first (see 1 Timothy 3:5). Stay home and clean if you need to; but win the battle of getting your life in order before tackling the whole world.

Ministry Is Fulfilling Work

*For you shall eat [the fruit] of the labor of your
hands; happy (blessed, fortunate, enviable) shall you
be, and it shall be well with you.*

PSALM 128:2

There is nothing more fulfilling than being rested and ready for the work that
God has called us to do. God puts the desire in us to
minister to people through whatever work we do.
But ministry is work that requires physical, emotional, and spiritual strength.

Hard work is rewarding when you follow God's
way and minister to other people through "the labor
of your hands." That is why it is so important to start
your day with God. His presence will build you up
emotionally, His words will strengthen you spiritually, and the time of rest that He calls you to enjoy
will make you physically able to handle whatever
may come your way.

Notes

Notes

Notes

Notes

Notes

Notes

Notes

_____
_____
_____
_____
_____
_____
_____
_____
_____
_____
_____
_____
_____
_____
_____
_____
_____
_____
_____
_____
_____
_____
_____
_____

Notes